GEORGE SEGAL

SAM HUNTER / DON HAWTHORNE

GEORGE SEGAL

ARTHUR A. BARTLEY
Publishers
New York & London

Endpapers:
View of the Lower Manhattan skyline, New York, seen from
the New Jersey Turnpike.

© *1988 Ediciones Polígrafa, S. A.*
Balmes, 54, 08007 BARCELONA (Spain)

I.S.B.N.: 84-343-0540-2
Dep. Legal: B. 25.889 - 1988 (Printed in Spain)

Printed in Spain by La Polígrafa, S. A.
Parets del Vallès (Barcelona)

CONTENTS

ACKNOWLEDGMENTS

The authors wish to thank George and Helen Segal for their patience and unstinting cooperation throughout this lengthy project. Sidney and Carroll Janis put the resources of their gallery and staff at our disposal, and Nicolas Brown was particularly helpful in photographic research, assisted in its later stages by Penny Walton, who also typed the manuscript. The Spears Fund of the Department of Art and Archaeology, Princeton University, generously supported the project from its inception.

DEDICATION

For Jenny Dixon

George Segal in his studio, 1982 (Photo: Arnold Newman).

HISTORY AND BIOGRAPHY;
SCULPTURE AND ENVIRONMENT

The memory is still fresh in George Segal's mind of an occasion in the late 1950s when the distinguished art historian Meyer Schapiro addressed a classroom packed with the flower of the Abstract Expressionist movement. They had come to hear him lecture on some rather recondite aspects of old master iconography, drawn by his charisma as a lecturer and known sympathies for the dominant avant-garde group. For Segal, the lesson he learned transcended Schapiro's subject matter, and the event became a methodological revelation. "Here was Meyer, talking about classical Renaissance art on five levels at once — psychological penetration, pure form, history, and philosophy, plus sensibility, plus touch. And he was the champion of Mondrian *and* Abstract Expressionist painting." The heterogeneity, the plurality of complementary perspectives that Schapiro discovered in the masterworks of Western art and reflected in his own critical discourse, represented an ideal that Segal has always sought in his own work.

In the fifties, that pluralistic model was far from universally accepted. The Bauhaus rallying cry of "truth to materials," taken to heart by America's first modernist wave, followed by the influential assertion of the flatness of the picture plane by formalist critics, and the overwhelming creative example of the first generation of Abstract Expressionists all seemed to conspire to limit the neophyte artist's options to a purist ideal.

Nonetheless, despite the attempts of dogmatists to conscript him into the service of their particular aesthetic posture and the eagerness of formalist critics to police the stragglers in the ranks of the avant-garde, Segal has remained a steadfast partisan of impurity.

It would seem only reasonable to adopt the artist's own guiding principles in a discussion of his work. Rather than attempting to pigeonhole Segal in one category or another, his work must be interrogated on its own terms. Yet this heuristic precept makes a particular demand on the vigilance of the critic, who must avoid reducing the import of a Segal painting or sculpture to a single doctrinaire aspect, whether it be spatial composition or literary allusion, environmental signs or human psychology, form or content. In the effort to encompass both the humanism and formality of the artist's oeuvre, this discussion, while eschewing mere eclecticism, will adopt a number of perspectives and a plurality of voices. It is hoped that what is lost in the cogency of a single interpretive standard will be more than redeemed by the relevance of this approach to the artist's work. An impure art requires an impurist approach on the part of the critic.

Segal's family background and his environment as a child were not the most propitious circumstances for the development of a major oeuvre in American art. Born in the Bronx in 1924 to a Jewish couple who had recently immigrated, "flat broke," from eastern Europe, Segal was never encouraged to pursue a career as an artist. "My father told me that everything was work from morning to night" — and making art, Segal remembers, was inconceivable as a worthy form of work. Still, the young Segal was strongly attracted to the arts despite parental resistance, and, in his senior year at Stuyvesant High, he edited the drawings, paintings, and photographs contributed to the high school literary magazine and was awarded the Homer St. Gaudens medal for his accomplishments.

1 George and Helen Segal, 1976 (Photo Arnold Newman).

1

But if the Segal family was not inclined to encourage their son in his career as an artist, it did provide him something that would prove at least as valuable: an inquiring intellect and an enthusiasm for what Segal calls "the life of the mind." The artist remembers many a fiery dinner table discussion in which he participated, debating everything from politics and philosophy to the fine points of the Jewish faith with parents and friends. Segal's mother and father were predisposed toward idealistic socialism and a committed Zionism, and these enthusiasms eventually led them to leave New York and their kosher butcher shop — a setting that would later be recalled in a Segal tableau — for the challenging life of the poultry farm. The Segals were among a group of similarly inclined city-dwellers, mostly Jewish, who left New York for central New Jersey in the early forties. Although they lacked expertise in farming or chickens, they prospered, at first, in the booming market created by the Second World War.

Remaining in Brooklyn with an aunt, Segal completed his high school education and, despite his parents' reservations, began formal artistic training at the Cooper Union School of Art. His studies, which included general training in drawing, painting, and carved plaster, required of an aspiring art-educator, were brought to an abrupt halt when, in 1942, he was called home to the farm to replace his brother, who had been drafted for service overseas.

For the Segals, life on the farm was anything but bucolic. The chickens required constant and scrupulous attention, and the end of the war brought a disastrous collapse in the poultry market that meant only more and harder work for the struggling Segal family. Nevertheless, Segal managed to find time to take part-time courses at Rutgers University in psychology, philosophy, literature, and, of course, painting. And, in 1946, he married the former Helen Steinberg.

In the mid-forties, Segal was far from ready to settle down to a life as a New Jersey chicken farmer. He knew he wanted to be an artist, and for a serious young man who had already tasted the atmosphere of a New York art school, the isolation of South Brunswick must have been oppressive. Accepting on faith his parents' belief that one could never earn a living as an artist, Segal enrolled in 1947 at the Pratt Institute of Design, with the intention of earning a degree in art education.

He had chosen the right moment to return to New York. A strange new style, heroic, compelling, and peculiarly American, was making its first, dramatic appearance in the lofts and galleries of lower Manhattan. Conservative in outlook and separated from the center of the new movement by the East River, Pratt did not hold Segal's interest for long. But it was in an exhibition at Pratt of student work from New York University's art program that he made his first acquaintance with Abstract Expressionism, the style that would dominate his work for the next decade. The effect on the aspiring artist was electrifying. In the summer of 1948, Segal led a rebellion of twelve students who left Pratt for New York University. Within weeks, eleven had returned to Pratt; only Segal remained in Manhattan.

He still speaks with passion of the excitement in the air in the glory days of Abstract Expressionism: "By some kind of connection with difficult, profound ideas that were learned from Europe, Americans for the first time in history could stop being provincial and deal in religious illumination. They could be anti-materialist, they could be soaring, they could put their finger on the rhythm of the universe, and it was an achievement and an accomplishment that had nothing to do with making a lot of money, becoming comfortable, or surrounding yourself with cars and objects. But it had to do with an exalted state of mind. I was instantly enormously attracted to that." Segal was enraptured by Pollock's non-figurative elegance, and de Kooning was his hero.

At New York University, Segal came into direct contact with the new art. He attended classes with Alfred Leslie and Larry Rivers, and, in Tony Smith he found a teacher who inspired and impressed him: "Tony used to walk the corridors at NYU with a small Rothko under his arm," Segal remembers, "to show students what the new painting looked like." But, beyond representing the achievements of the fledgling New York school, Smith struck a sympathetic chord in Segal's own experience: "He had a profound effect on me because, here was a guy who was always working with abstraction, and everything he referred to was a quality, a metaphor, of the visible, tangible world. Here was a guy who wasn't afraid of literary allusion, who continually worked with these spontaneous associative jumps, and still everything was rooted in the tactile.''

The single, long-term project Smith assigned his class had a profound influence on Segal, and might be considered the prototype of all his subsequent essays in environmental art. Smith presented his students with a stack of *Life* magazines and instructed them to make a room-size collage of ''the wild'' — an ''organic wilderness'' imagined as if seen from the air, and constructed with the conscious intention of breaking every rule of composition.

Segal was encouraged by Smith's exuberance for the world of the senses and his receptiveness to a plurality of styles and aesthetic strategies. But Smith's was by no means the only attitude current in the avant-garde. Indeed, Segal found to his dismay that the principles touted by most of the Abstract Expressionists and assumed dogmatically in their discussions were far different from Smith's broad-minded precepts: ''I was getting this cant and theory: keep it flat, keep it big, use five-inch house painter's brushes, if it looks figurative, wipe it out.'' Segal heard these strictures when he attended the Club, the Eighth Street gathering place of de Kooning, Kline, and the rest of the Abstract Expressionist vanguard. He heard them again when he took his next course at New York University, with William Baziotes: ''There was a great sense of triumph in the air. Baziotes was saying 'Jump on the bandwagon of the history of art with us.' He told us: throw out those little brushes, get big canvases, wipe out your minds. I froze. I couldn't understand Baziotes. I could understand Tony Smith. He was dealing with the world and abstracting from the world. I couldn't understand these other injunctions.''

Segal was initially troubled, and later deeply frustrated. His painting — ''half way between Cézanne and de Kooning'' — was, he confesses, in a state of paralysis. Feeling himself to be at a dead end, and with his degree in art education completed, Segal took the opportunity to make the first step on what he thought would be the road to financial security: he started his own chicken farm. For two years, Segal and his wife spent fourteen hours a day, seven days a week, shoveling manure, grading eggs, and tending to the care and feeding of five thousand chickens. From 1950 to 1952 Segal abandoned art completely, but not his aspiration to be an artist. With the help of a mason, he built the house in which he still lives, and the chicken coops that now serve as his studio. And, as if to consume what spare moments might remain after construction and agriculture, the Segals became the parents in 1950 of a son and, three years later, a daughter.

As early as 1964, critics were coming to the realization that Segal's sculpture owed an important debt, in its composition and frontality, to the artist's experience as a painter.[1] The observation was valid, and remains so. The problems to which Segal the sculptor addressed himself, and the various forms his work has taken since 1961, become far more intelligible if they are viewed as the outcome of his twenty-year evolution as a painter; and his painting, in turn, must be considered in the context of the second generation of the New York School, and its rebellion against the dominating father figures of the first generation of Abstract Expressionists.

When Segal returned to painting in the early fifties, he shared with many of his contemporaries a deeply ambivalent regard for the accomplishments of de Kooning, Kline, and their fellows. What had been the heretical convictions of a few pariahs in the late forties was now orthodox. On the one hand, the Abstract Expressionists had shown that America was not forever destined to be the aesthetic backwater of Europe, that it could, indeed, provide original standards of excellence for the rest of the world to emulate. On the other hand, many younger artists were profoundly disturbed by the aesthetic and philosophic creed preached by their elders, and not a little uncomfortable with the ethical and spiritual prerogatives the older artists assumed.

Segal's view of the Abstract Expressionists' existential subjectivity was shared by many: ''I don't want to report on the world as a reflection of my own blood vessels.''[2] But, unlike some of his contemporaries,

2 George Segal's studio, formerly a group of chicken coops, in South
Brunswick, New Jersey (Photo Léni Iselin).

2

3

4

Segal never shied away from the spiritual aspirations of the first generation: "I love the ambition. I love the seeking to grasp ineffable experience. I liked the idea art could be more than decoration. I objected to the aspect of it which said, do it in a particular way."[3]

Segal was particularly resentful of the dualistic dictum that linked abstraction to transcendence. Spirit, he was convinced, was not to be achieved at the expense of the body: both his Jewish heritage and sensual temperament dictated that universal emotion and psychic or sacred ideals could only be conveyed through "the reality of what I could sense, touch, and see."[4]

Segal's motives may have been unique, but his rejection of abstraction was not. Many young artists were convinced by the vastly influential teacher Hans Hofmann that there need be no conflict between abstraction and figuration, and the style they evolved combined the look of Abstract Expressionism with the presence of the figure. But for Segal, gestural realism, while allowing him to retain both literary allu-

sion and the phenomenal world, still left unresolved the fundamental conflict he perceived between the three-dimensionality of the figure and the principle, so often voiced by both Abstract Expressionists and critics, that painting must reject illusionism and assert the flatness of the picture plane. The search for a solution to that problem would eventually lead him beyond the medium of painting altogether.

Segal's own form of gestural realism went on public view in 1956 at his first one-man exhibition at the Hansa Gallery. The artist's rejection of Abstract Expressionist transcendence was immediately evident in his choice of subject matter: studio nudes and still-lifes of rubber plants, coffee pots and light bulbs. On the other hand, the influence of de Kooning was clearly visible in Segal's aggressive brushwork. In some of these early paintings, the pervasiveness of violent color and brushstroke, and the arbitrary abruptness of the composition, which tended to thrust the figure off-center and towards the picture plane, were reminiscent of German Expressionism. But more frequently, the artist showed his debt to the School of Paris, and, in particular, to the brilliant colors of Bonnard and the simplified flat color masses of Matisse. Segal has made no secret of his admiration for "the Frenchness of Modern Art: the sensuality of a Matisse painting, the raw delight in color and form, the smear of the paint, how the sun feels on you, how your eyes are dazzled by color in the water."[5] In his first one-man exhibition, this love was manifested in the strong reds, yellows, and blue-greens, and compressed space so dear to the Fauves.

Segal's promise did not go unappreciated. In 1957 he was included in "Artists of the New York School: Second Generation," an exhibition selected by Meyer Schapiro for the Jewish Museum; and in the three succeeding years he showed annually at the Hansa. The second show continued to document the artist's infatuation with Bonnard — a reviewer wrote, "One can fairly taste the palette saturation"[6] — and the large canvases were devoted exclusively to the theme of the nude in an interior. The 1957 show also saw the first appearance of pastels — small sketches from the nude reminiscent of Degas in their arbitrary interruption of the figure and glowing with the same vibrant color found in the oils.

In the succeeding shows, the earlier still-lifes and studio scenes gave way to increasingly generalized situations. Thick local impasto was replaced by thinner and broader areas of color, forming large planes in front of which figures reclined or floated. The size of the paintings also increased, to a uniform four by six feet, which made many of the figures nearly life size.

Throughout this period, Segal's painting continued to struggle toward Hofmann's ideal synthesis, combining rough, expressionistic brushwork and rich, active color with the representation of the figure. The Hansa shows received favorable reviews — one critic called him "a painter of enormous energy and convincing power"[7] — but Segal was becoming increasingly frustrated by the fundamental contradiction between the abstractionist imperative of asserting the "real" flatness of the canvas, and his own commitment to figural art which required a more illusionistic space. By way of exacerbating his aesthetic dilemma, Segal was beset by financial worries that found expression in his art. The more deeply he became committed to his craft, the more his poultry farm weighed upon him as a time-consuming and exhausting burden. The chickens required constant atten-

5

6

tion, and, as the poultry market continued to plummet, Segal found himself unable to support his family on the proceeds of the farm. He poured out his frustration in oils of dead chickens and in the repeated image of "Chicken Man" — a violently brushed figure, which, in a variation on the Ancient Mariner theme, wore a chicken around his neck.

In 1957, Segal began teaching English to supplement his income, and, in 1958, much to the joy of the entire family, the ill-fated farm was closed and the last chicken sold. Although the departure of the chickens allowed Segal considerably more time to paint, it did not solve all his financial problems: in the following years he taught art and industrial arts at a succession of public schools. Not until 1964 was he able to support himself solely on his art.

The contradiction Segal had perceived in his first paintings between illusionistic and actual space seemed so endemic to the medium that his ultimate conversion to sculpture should, in retrospect, appear inevitable. But the path from painting to sculpture was scarcely easy or obvious at the time, and the final form Segal's work has taken is as much the product of the aesthetic options that were available to him as it was a solution to his personal artistic crisis. The transition from painting to sculpture, and the decisive influences in determining the form his sculpture took, are embodied in a series of events that occurred in quick succession in the late fifties. In 1956, Segal was introduced to the Hansa Gallery. The following year, Allan Kaprow choose the Segal farm as the scene of his first Happening, and, in 1958, Segal began to experiment in sculpture. These three moments will serve as expedient benchmarks in surveying the course that leads from the early painting to the mature sculpture of the sixties.

Formed largely by former students of Hans Hofmann and named for their teacher, the Hansa Gallery was a cooperative space devoted to exhibiting the works of its members. Segal was introduced to the gallery by Kaprow, and invited to join. From 1956 until 1959, when, as acting director, he oversaw its closing, he was closely involved in the life of the gallery and showed there each year.

8

find the art form most consonant with his own personality.

In the years when Segal was a member, two trends dominated the art shown at the Hansa.[9] Jan Müller, Wolf Kahn, and Felix Pasilis pursued the gestural realism suggested by Hofmann's dictum that figuration and abstraction were wholly compatible. A second tendency, characterized by the incorporation of found materials in the work of art, discovered positive value in the detritus of the urban-industrial environment. Richard Stankiewicz, Jean Follet, and Robert Whitman were members of this second group.

Originally, Segal, like Kaprow, was attracted to the gestural realists, and, in particular, to Müller, who included explicitly literary and religious allusions in his tortured, expressionistic canvases. Populating his pictures with ghosts, corpses, witches, angels and devils, Müller drew on sources in folklore and myth, as well as Goethe, Shakespeare, Cervantes, and the Bible. While the inclusion of such obviously literary subject matter was anathema to most contemporary painters, it elicited only respect from Segal, who was to adopt the Biblical theme of Lot as the source for a major group of paintings in the late fifties.

The influence of Stankiewicz and other Assemblage artists, while less obvious than his affinity with Müller, may have been even more decisive for the evolution of Segal's art. He readily admits to the influence of Follet's three-dimensional reliefs, incorporating real objects, and Stankiewicz's ironic and whimsical figurative sculptures. Yet the works of the Assemblagists differ in obvious ways from anything Segal has produced. In a sculpture by Follet or Stankiewicz common objects are juxtaposed with no reference to their past uses or contexts, while in Segal's work, objects retain their old associations — they play themselves.

More relevant than any formal resemblance, however, is the common sensibility shared by Segal and the Assemblage artists. Assemblage was important for its legitimization as art of theretofore spurned materials and objects, and particularly of the products of what Lawrence Alloway has called "junk culture." Collage — the non-mimetic inclusion of "real" objects in painting — has traditionally been the device

More than just an exhibition space, the Hansa was a center for some of the liveliest artistic talents in New York, and Segal could not help but profit from his exchange of ideas with them. Hofmann had always demanded that his students draw from models or still lifes, and the gallery named for him showed some of the finest of the gestural realists of the second generation. Segal himself, although he never studied with Hofmann, had met him during summer expeditions to Provincetown, and remembers him as "a beaming, radiant, healthy, vigorous, optimistic teacher and painter who encompassed German inner turmoil and total encyclopedic *Weltanschauung*, French savor and gusto, and American expansiveness."[8] Segal was profoundly influenced by Hofmann's attention to the world of experience, his "search for the real," and his encouragement to each of his students to

9 Studio, 1983, with pastels of that year.
At far right, drawing of Helen; pastel study for
Street Meeting.

10 Studio, 1983, with eleven pastels made that year.

9

10

through which twentieth-century artists have questioned the relationship between art and life. As a three-dimensional form of collage, assemblage contributed to the investigation of the putative gap between the two, and this issue was to be a significant factor in Segal's adoption of a new medium.

The tendencies Segal might have found attractive in Assemblage were more fully developed and more clearly articulated by a source spiritually, and literally, closer to home. Segal still vividly remembers Allan Kaprow's first Happening, staged at his poultry farm in 1957. The occasion was a Hansa Gallery picnic. Kaprow had prepared a script of prescribed movements and, with the help of some like-minded friends and artists, began to enact the Happening in the fields near the coops. But not all the Hansa picnickers were favorably disposed to the incipient art-form: "It was a meeting of two aesthetics," says Segal. "Most of the Hansa people got drunk and began lobbing beer cans at Kaprow's sober procession. They were acting like dumb, sensual bohemians, and Kaprow was being very deadpan, very poised and restrained. We all got so angry — finally someone took a can of black enamel paint and wrote 'Yanks Go Home' on the side of my chicken coop."

The Hansa bohemians eventually returned to New York, but Kaprow's new aesthetic had come home to roost at the Segal farm. Segal believes his acquaintance with Kaprow, and the "completely different world" of ideas to which his friend introduced him were of fundamental importance in resolving the aesthetic quandary in which he found himself in the late fifties. In fact, the influence and inspiration were undoubtedly mutual.

Segal met Kaprow in 1953 through a friend at Rutgers University where Kaprow was teaching art history. Segal had been isolated from the New York scene for several years; together with Kaprow, he attended openings, classes, concerts, and other manifestations of the avant-garde. The two men showed their paintings together in a New Brunswick delicatessen. In 1956, Kaprow introduced Segal to the Hansa, and when that gallery closed four years later, they both moved on to the Reuben Gallery.

"When we met, we were both hungry for the intensity of the experience," says Segal. In the early fifties, Kaprow, like Segal, was a Müller-style gestural realist painter. And, like Segal, he was uncomfortable with many of the aesthetic attitudes inherited from the Abstract Expressionists. Kaprow's primary impulse was to question the conventional distinctions between art and life; to this instinct he added an attraction to the urban environment, and an enthusiasm for the theories of Duchamp and the revolutionary composer John Cage. With this arsenal of ideas, Kaprow and Segal set out "to invent a new aesthetic."

In the year that he staged his first Happening, Kaprow studied with Cage for several terms at the New School for Social Research. Although the nominal subject of the course was composition, Dick Higgins, a classmate of Kaprow's, recalls that few students were primarily interested in Cage's musical theory: "the best thing that happened to us in Cage's class was the sense he gave that 'anything goes,' at least potentially... the main thing was the realization of possibilities..."[10]

Cage's influence on Happenings is indisputable: the "concerted action" he performed, with the help of Merce Cunningham, David Tudor, Charles Olsen, and Robert Rauschenberg on the Black Mountain campus in 1952, is arguably the prototype for the genre. Yet it was only one side of Cage — this receptiveness to new materials and his conception of art as a prelude to the experience of life — and not his interest in indeterminacy, impersonality, chance or Zen that primarily appealed to Kaprow. Segal, who was invited by his friend to several of Cage's classes, has ranked the composer with Picasso and Duchamp as the artists "most basically responsible for the new permission in the air to incorporate non-art materials into art." When Segal speaks of Cage's impact on the contemporary art world, he could be describing the composer's influence on his own work: "His Socratic questioning of all accepted values, his incorporation of street sounds and everyday, unpretentious movement into his work have had a deep influence on New York art."[11]

Buoyed by the expansiveness of Cage's aesthetic, Kaprow was ready to pioneer a new art form. In

11 Sidney Janis, who has been Segal's dealer since 1965, converses
   with the artist in his studio, 1979 (Photo Arnold Newman).

12 The dedication at Princeton University of **In Memory of
   May 4, 1970: Kent State**; standing left to right: Sidney Janis,
   Sam Hunter, Paul Jenkins, George Segal, Augusta Newman and
   Arnold Newman. October 6, 1979 (Photo Arnold Newman).

11

12

13 Dr. Martin Weyl, Director of The Israel Museum, and the artist
    separated by **Seated Woman with Dangling Shoe**, 1982 (Photo
    Arnold Newman).

14 Helen and George Segal with their daughter Rena, 1983
    (Photo Arnold Newman).

13

14

fr. pts to environments incl. the viewer

time/space

his seminal article of 1958, "The Legacy of Jackson Pollock," Kaprow enunciated the principles of the new art. Before Pollock, modernist painting had shrunk the deep space of Renaissance perspective to the shallow space of cubist planes. By suggesting that his fields of paint extended in a continuum beyond the edges of the canvas, Pollock had invented a new sort of space "that refuses to stay on the wall or canvas, but envelops the viewer." With Pollock, paintings cease to be paintings, and become "environments".[12]

Complementing this new conception of space would be a new attitude towards materials: "Not satisfied with the *suggestion* through paint of our other senses, we shall utilize the specific substances of sight, sound, movement, people, odors, touch. Objects of every sort are materials for the new art: people, chairs, food, electric and neon lights, smoke, water, old socks, a dog, movies, and a thousand other things which will be discovered by the present generation of artists."[13]

Kaprow hastened to put these principles to work. Abandoning gestural realism, he began making assemblages out of ersatz and industrial materials, like the 1956 *Woman Out of Fire,* a plaster figure coated with roofing tar. His new conception of space — "the literal distance between all solids included in the work"[14] — found expression in environments, spaces bristling with paint, tinfoil, cellophane, lights, plastic and oilcloth among which the spectator was invited to walk. And, with Happenings, the artwork became total experience, and the spectator a participant.

Segal is quick to acknowledge his debt to Happenings and to Kaprow's environmental sensibility: "My original impulse was to make total environments that incorporated everything, movement, smells, audience participation, the old Happening ideas... As I worked, I had to reject more and more. There's my contradiction. I had to reject the movement, the smells, the audience participation in order to intensify the quality of my own experience."[15] When Segal describes his own artistic temperament, one can imagine the inventor of Happenings nodding in agreement: "What interests me is a series of shocks and encounters that a person can have moving through

space around several objects placed in a careful relationship."[16]

Although Segal scripted several "very Expressionist" Happenings, none of them was ever produced: "Temperamentally, I couldn't do a Happening. I didn't like the time sense. I didn't like the ephemerality. I prefer slow contemplation. I want to be able to walk into a space, spend as much time as I want to, and get out." Yet, in his use of real space and non-art materials, and in his blurring of the boundary between art and life, Segal demonstrates his sympathy with Kaprow's new aesthetic.

In his tableaux, Segal would envelop the spectator with the new "environmental" space Kaprow espoused. Just as Pollock's works had flouted their frames, so Segal's sculpture impinges upon the viewer's space: "My pieces often don't end at their physical boundaries," the artist has said.[17] Just as Kaprow had prophesied, space would become for Segal "a total aesthetic area which I could enter — as an intensely felt, internal experience..."[18]

"Plaster is bold and wet and clean," says Segal. "It has its own life under your fingers. It changes every second."[19] Although economic motives may have figured significantly in his choice of a medium — it could be purchased at any lumber store for eight cents a pound — Segal's use of plaster is consistent with Kaprow's Cagean insistence on the use of common, perishable, non-art materials. More generally, it reflects a desire, evident since Duchamp, to blur the boundaries between art and life. With their juxtaposition of "real," unaltered common objects with "artificial" plaster casts of people in a self-consciously artistic spatial composition, Segal's early tableaux raised this familiar issue with particular drama and urgency.

It seems safe to say that, whatever role Cage, Duchamp and Dada play in Segal's art, it is heavily dependent on Kaprow's personal interpretation of these sources, and his insistence that their importance lay in establishing new relationships between realms of the aesthetic and the real world. But it must also be remembered that the progression from canvas to the environmental space of Segal's sculpture is to a large extent the result of his experience as a

15 **Untitled.** 1959. (Cat. 324)
   Collage, 36 × 108 in.
   Collection of the artist.

16 **Nude** (Bas Relief). 1958. (Cat. 201)
   Plaster, 36 × 66 × 3 in.
   Collection of the artist.

ods would allow. Peter Agostini, while eschewing the figure for abstract forms like balls and balloons, also showed the potential of plaster as an elegantly expressive, yet durable, medium.

Segal's early sculpture may call to mind the efforts of Robert Rauschenberg and Jasper Johns to investigate the no-man's-land between art and life. Yet Segal did not meet either artist until the late fifties, and, in any event, Johns' solution to modernism's spatial dialectic was entirely different from Segal's: while Segal moved into real space, Johns — perhaps more genuinely Cagean than Segal or Kaprow — resolutely asserted the objectivity of the canvas. Rauschenberg's environmental "combine-paintings" appear to provide the better comparison to the pictorial composition of Segal's sculpture; and, in the middle fifties, Segal even created some Rauschenberg-like collages. But, unlike Rauschenberg or Johns, Segal seldom violates the narrative logic of his environmental settings for the sake of free-associative juxtaposition or surrealist effect.

Finally, some apparent parallels in contemporary art were fundamentally irrelevant to Segal's development. His early sculpture bears no relationship to the conceptual and neo-Dada works of the European New Realist movement, even though Arman and Piero Manzoni, two of its more notable representatives, made casts from life in plaster and plastic. Such comparisons can, however, prove enlightening, if only by demonstrating how Segal's work differs from that of his contemporaries. Edward Kienholz, for example, would seem to have a good deal in common with Segal. Both create environmental tableaux reminiscent of Kurt Schwitters' *Merzbau;* both populate their sculptures with objects from daily life. Kienholz exhibited *Roxy's,* his first tableau, in 1961 — one year after Segal's first combination of figures and environment — and, since the early sixties, he has cast many of his figures from life, first in fiberglass, and later in plaster. But Kienholz's work has none of Segal's formal austerity, nor does it evince his concern for spatial composition. With their generalized scenes and typical figures, Segal's tableaux often express a profound humanism and deep sympathy for their subjects; Kienholz's sculpture, on the other

15

painter; the influence of Smith's teaching, for example, cannot be ignored. Moreover, Kaprow was scarcely the only advocate of the blurring of art and life. In the late fifties, the demand for a new inclusiveness in art was general, and Segal's work can be related to the art of many of his predecessors and contemporaries.

The rough, expressionistic treatment that the human figure received at the hands of Segal's modeling technique was presaged in a number of crudely constructed, art-brut plaster figures exhibited by Larry Rivers in a 1954 show at the Stable Gallery. Segal was aware of the figures, but denies a direct influence; the relationship is better explained as an expression of a common and pervasive sensibility among members of the second generation. Lucas Samaras' *Rag Sculpture* and Claes Oldenburg's *Man's Jacket with Shirt and Tie* betray a similar impulse to return the figure to sculpture while expressing more of the energy, pathos and violence of contemporary urban life than traditional media and meth-

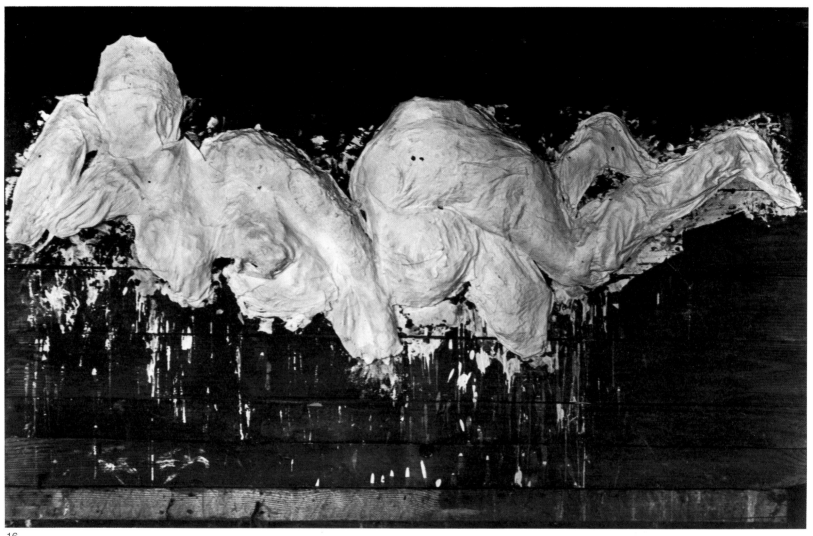

16

hand, almost invariably remains embedded in local detail and particular social or political comment and animus.

Segal's first works in sculpture were as gestural as any de Kooning canvas, and as roughly constructed as the most primitive chicken coop. In the summer of 1958, after pulling apart several department store dummies to learn how they were constructed, he modeled his first plaster figure, in the form of a reclining woman, *Bas-relief: Nude.* The plaster was expressively built up around a bedsheet that in turn rested on a framework of lumber and chicken wire. Intrigued with the third dimension, Segal soon attempted another figure — a man with crossed arms — mod-

eled on burlap and mounted on a door. The surfaces of these works, roughly swirled and pock-marked, recall not only the textured impasto of Abstract Expressionist painting, but also the monumental, eroded forms of the French sculptor Germaine Richier, whose influence Segal acknowledges.

These first sculptures look very much at home beside the figurative "new realist" improvisations of Samaras and Oldenburg, and the gritty, urban appearance of much assemblage. Segal's affinity with assemblage sculpture became even more obvious the following year, when he placed a stick figure — two-by-fours with hinges at the joints — on his old bicycle, *Man on a Bicycle I.* Although all these works pos-

17 **Man on a Bicycle I.** 1958-1959. (Cat. 3)
   Plaster, wood and chicken wire, 65 × 58 × 24 in.
   Collection of the artist.

17

his patented invention of plaster figures placed in an environment of everyday objects taken from the "real" world, Segal had found an effective and flexible means of closing the distance between the invented abstract space of a formalist generation and a new art of psychological responses, individualized associations and environmental definition. After having painted for more than a decade, he began in 1958 to move with a courageous independence towards a more literal apprehension of space, and to reconstruct in haunting plaster shells a sense of actual life and the dynamics of human interaction.

In an early *Studio International* interview, Segal declared that he did not want to "shut out any possibility."[20] He continued in this illuminating statement to describe quite precisely, if a trifle less smoothly and professionally than he later learned to reveal his artistic intentions, the spirit and ambience of a highly original vision:

I want to intensify... the sense of my own inner life. I equally want to intensify my sense of encounter with the tangible world outside of me. I can't think of divorcing the one response from the other. I differ from the Abstract Expressionists in that way, and that seemingly small point makes a big difference in the look of the work.
The first sculptures I made were traditional in the sense that I made an armature out of two-by-fours, wrapped wire around the armature and burlap dipped in plaster over them, the same way that department store mannequins used to be made before they discovered plastic. The first figures I made were very expressionistic, and I sat one on a broken real chair. The sharp edges of that real chair really sent me flying, and I began to look at real objects with their hard surfaces, different colours, as plastic objects. I could compose the air around a figure, and from the beginning it was not the figure psychologically centered, but the figure in relation to a place or a situation or a scene with the objects. Not props, but rather plastic presences powerful in their own right.
Where was the boundary? Where was my limit to the work? Nobody could answer it for me. It was only because I became more interested in this play between interior-exterior that I decided to hack out just those pieces I wanted. And when I had them all strewn around, I had to reconstruct them. The trick is not to juggle them like a school exercise, but to juggle them in a way that they shiver in a sense to a real experience.[21]

sessed unmistakable energy and promise, they were as yet rather undeveloped and experimental. Segal was groping for a new aesthetic, and his first steps were necessarily tentative.

Even before he had discovered his signatory technique of casting figures in plaster, however, Segal's primitive, freestanding sculptures were among the most important and individualistic expressions in a rather large body of work created by many New York artists that bridged the widening gap between the Abstract Expressionist vision, the abortive but influential episode of assemblage constructions and Pop Art. With his crude sculptural forms, preceding

This, of course, was the period when artists became dissatisfied with the increasingly smug rhetoric of the "Action" painters and their critical champions, and when younger artists began to drift away from free, gestural painting towards a more inclusive environmental art, which took into account the impact of popular culture and mass-produced objects. In fact, the first significant evidence of adulterations in art derived from the surrounding urban environment could even be observed in de Kooning's aggressive *Woman* series. His dominant image evolved in the late forties from a collage method that juxtaposed fragmentary commercial illustrations of lipsticked mouths with transpositions in paint of mass-culture sex idols and film stars, a sequence of brilliantly painted disturbing female forms that directly influenced Segal both in terms of their pictorial values and psychology.

It was Segal's close personal friend from Rutgers, Allan Kaprow, however, who most profoundly inspired the change in Segal's art as we have seen. Kaprow is generally credited with first announcing the interest of the new generation in the more impermanent, transitory aspects of the material environment as a source of new artistic expressive possibilities. In his article of 1958, "The Legacy of Jackson Pollock," for example, he proposed "a quite clearheaded decision to abandon craftsmanship and permanence" and advocated "the use of... perishable media such as newspaper, string, adhesive tape, growing grass, or real food" so that "no one can mistake the fact that the work will pass into dust or garbage quickly."[22] Later used as a rationale for a new kind of nonverbal, intermedia theater and performance art called "Happenings," Kaprow's statement was originally intended to bring the creative artist into more fertile interaction with the actual world around him, and to open a new dialogue with overlooked commonplace materials of the environment, and its impact on Segal was direct and profound, as it was somewhat more obliquely, and paradoxically, on the evolution of Pop Art.

In a similar spirit Rauschenberg described his method of working as a collaboration with materials, and made his oft-quoted statement, which became a slogan of the radical new realism: "Painting relates to both art and life. Neither can be made. I try to act in the gap between the two."[23]

Ideologically, the junk materials which Kaprow, Rauschenberg, and others established in a new aesthetic context could be read as a symbol of alienation from the dominant folkways of an aggressive consumer's society which extravagantly valued a gleaming, ersatz newness in its possessions. By forcing a confrontation with derelict and despicable object fragments, these artists effectively countered a culture maniacally geared to the creation of an artificial demand for new products. Their strategies cunningly posed troubling questions about the nature of the art experience and at the same time commented on the social context of urban life and mass culture which gave rise to such blatant violations of the traditional integrity of medium.

The rebellious spirit of the times was recaptured dramatically some time later by the artist Al Hansen, an originator of Happenings, when, in his book, *A Primer of Happenings and Time-Space Art,* he referred to the Reuben Gallery, where Segal had shown his early sculpture. The Reuben Gallery served as an important catalyst in the radical change in general perceptions of the art process and its new range of expanded meanings in the late fifties. "The Reuben," Hansen wrote, "became one of the most dynamic galleries ever to exist in the city on such a low budget. It became a huge thorn in the side of abstract expressionism. Once the establishment, represented at the time by a popular art magazine, referred to a big group show at the Reuben Gallery as 'more junk downtown.' The cover of this magazine had a large abstract expressionist painting. Within two or three years this 'junk' had gently placed abstract expressionism in its coffin, put the lid on, lowered it into the grave and shoveled dirt on it."

"The giant Below Zero Show," added Hansen, "was one of the most important. It involved a newspaper mountain by Allan Kaprow, Bob Rauschenberg's Coca-Cola Plan (incorporating a carved eagle and Coca-Cola bottles and blueprint) and a big plaster sculpture by George Segal of a figure on a bicycle. This was before George discovered how to mold people with bandages or rags dipped in plaster; it was an attempt at really hacking something out of

18 **Lot's Wife.** 1958. (Cat. 320)
Oil on canvas, 72 × 48 in.
Collection of the artist.

19 **Lot's Daughters.** 1958-1959. (Cat. 322)
Oil on canvas, 72 × 96 in.
Collection of the artist.

20 **Lot and His Daughters.** 1958. (Cat. 321)
Oil and charcoal on canvas, 72 × 96 in.
Collection of the artist.

18

19

rough plaster — very crude and unwieldy, always falling over and breaking."[24]

Despite his interest in the rough and primitivist new sculptural medium, Segal as yet had no intention of parting with oil and canvas. In 1958, the same year that he began to work in sculpture, he returned to painting to explore a single Biblical theme, again and again, in a series of works depicting the legend of Lot. Lot was, of course, the one pious man whom God saved from the wreck of Sodom and Gomorrah. Lot's wife, who disobeyed the divine injunction, paused in her flight to look back at the city and was transformed into a pillar of salt. But the part of the story that most fascinated Segal occurs after the destruction, when Lot's daughters, believing themselves to be the only survivors of a world-wide catastrophe, scheme to intoxicate and seduce their father. In order to perpetuate the human race, they commit incest, the unpardonable sin, and are punished by having their names forgotten by posterity.

Segal was attracted to this subject by the "impossible contradictions" it embodies — contradictions that reflected the frustration he felt in his own work. It was typical of Segal's humanistic outlook, and his unique position in the art world of the time, that he attempted simultaneously to express the emotional tensions of this literary theme in narrative and formal structure. Discussing *The Pillar of Salt,* an outstanding painting in this series, he observed: "Hans Hofmann used to talk about crashing oppositions and tensions and pulls, those things being present in every great work of art. They're in Greek tragedy, too, and this painting is an attempt on my part to clothe this powerful skeleton framework with a mythic human situation."[25]

It was through the depiction of such moral dilemmas that Segal began to work out a solution to his own aesthetic predicament. In 1959, at his last one-man Hansa show, he had exhibited several of the crude plaster figures he constructed in the past year. But what was most remarkable about this show was the juxtaposition of these sculptures with several canvases depicting the Lot story: the plaster figures seemed to have stepped out of the low-hung, life-size canvases, into the gallery space.

20

21 Legend of Lot. 1958. (Cat. 1)
    Oil on canvas, plaster, wood and chicken wire, 72 × 96 in.
    Collection of the artist.

22 **Man on a Bicycle** (Version III). 1962. (Cat. 7)
    Plaster and bicycle parts, 63 × 29 × 61 in.
    Moderna Museet, Stockholm.

23 Red Courbet. 1959. (Cat. 325)
    Oil on canvas, 72 × 96 in.
    Collection of the artist.

21

22

In retrospect, Segal realizes that these first environmental constructions were the solution he had sought: "I couldn't look at the canvas and regard it as a window on the world — an illusionist space — because that broke all the laws of twentieth-century art; from cubism on forward, space was compressed to the surface of the canvas. I couldn't use flat abstract expressionist space, because I wanted to paint the figure. Everybody was yak-yak-yakking about a pictorial space that had to obey certain rules and regulations, and I said to hell with the rules. Everybody was looking for a new way to represent reality, and the only space I could be convinced about was the physical distance between my body and the canvas — the space in which I walked."

If the plaster figure was a simulacrum of the artist regarding the canvas, it also stood on its own feet as a real, insistent presence. Segal has described how a large cinder-block chimney in his old attic studio forced its way into several of his paintings.[26] The actual presence of the chimney as a real, intrusive volume

fascinated the artist; and the plaster figures offered him the opportunity to shape the space of his compositions as forcefully as the chimney had shaped the space in his studio.

Although this development in Segal's work must have been mystifying to most viewers, critics were favorably impressed by the brute expressiveness of the figures. Writing in *Art News*, James Schuyler provided a description of the plaster figures that would become a cliché of Segal criticism: "Their effect is of swiftly improvised immediacy, with the arrested movement of a Pompeian dog."[27] Perhaps inspired by this favorable reception, Segal continued to model plaster figures on chicken wire frames. Over the next two years he made a dozen similar sculptures, and began to combine them with props like bicycles and barn doors.

In the summer of 1960, Segal's customary generosity provided him an unexpected source of inspiration. Robert Frank, the avant-garde film-maker and photographer, was looking for a location to shoot his

23

24

movie *The Sin of Jesus.* Segal invited him to use the poultry farm as the set, and even offered Frank lodging in the basement of the Segal farmhouse.

The script for *The Sin of Jesus* was based on a narrative by Isaac Bashevis Singer. Set in Moscow, it tells the story of a lusty chambermaid, who prays to Jesus to help control her insatiable, and frequently consummated, physical desires. Jesus sends the woman an angel as a husband. But, in the passion of her wedding night, the maid rolls on top of the angel and kills him. Jesus' sin, so the story goes, is to condemn the unfortunate woman to return to her former venial existence.

Frank had planned to spend six weeks on the farm. He stayed six months. The film was shot in Segal's barn, and Frank asked him to help build the sets. Segal was greatly impressed by Frank's interest in the texture of surfaces and the solidity of the Depression-era furniture, found in the barn, that was used in many of the scenes in the film. But most of all, Segal was struck by the set designer's ability to compose in space: "...setting up rooms as sets, looking at them through Frank's movie viewfinder to see how they composed... suddenly I said 'Ah hah! I can use this old furniture with my figures!' And then everything clicked together."

But if the concept of environmental construction made sense as a synthesis of Cage's and Kaprow's aesthetic notions and Segal's own spatial dialectic, it did not in itself provide the means with which to create art embodying this tangle of ideas. Segal remembers his continuing frustration: "I knew I had an idea, but I didn't know what to do with it; so I kept on painting." After supervising the closing of the Hansa in 1959, Segal moved briefly to the Reuben Gallery, a center both for Happenings and for the industrial, impermanent gutter art of Kaprow, Oldenburg, Dine and Samaras. Segal showed in group exhibitions at the Reuben in 1959 and 1960, and then left for Richard Bellamy's Green Gallery.

His 1960 one-man show at the Green featured several plaster figures with the first, minimal environments — doors and other props — but the exhibition was dominated by eight large figurative canvases. The color in these paintings was thinner than the dense impasto of a few years before, the space more ambiguous and scenery more generalized. The sketchiness which had been so evident in the *Legend of Lot* series was less pronounced, although Segal's appetite for rich primary colors was unabated, as evinced by *Red Courbet,* his improvisation on Courbet's depiction of lesbian lovers. Yet there remained an obvious tension between the necessarily illusionistic handling of the volume of the figures and the flatness of the color planes representing their environments. The conflicting tendencies of Segal's aesthetic are tellingly exposed in the 1960 painting *Red Nude and Interior,* in which an over-life-size, blurred and ephem-

25

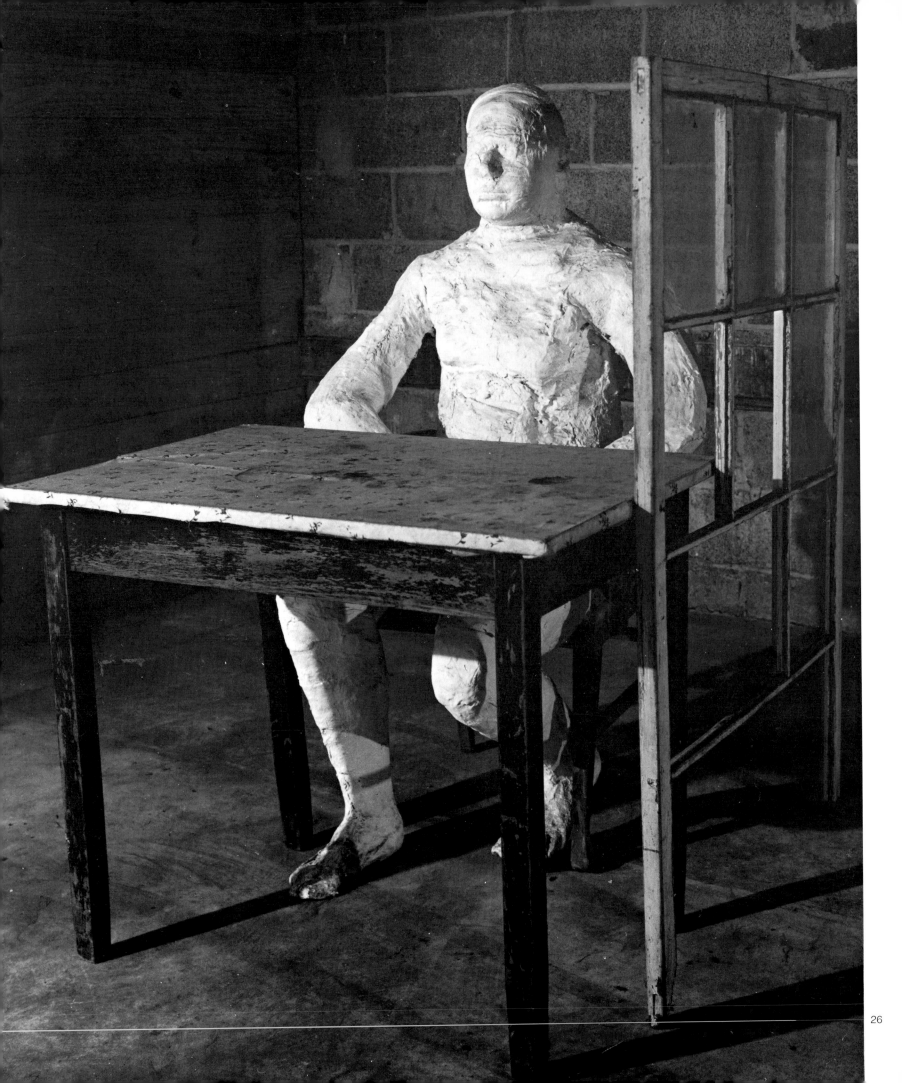

eral red nude, floating before an undefined, thinly washed off-white ground, is juxtaposed against the starkly defined contours of a solid brown chair and easel.

The Green Gallery show was not well received by critics; perhaps they dimly perceived the dilemmas that were leading Segal's painting to a crisis of frustration. Late in 1960, he expressed his anger and anxiety in a canvas self-referentially entitled *Upside Down Man:* "It was my crisis painting, it was an explosion of unresolved, contradictory extremes... I painted a guy with volume and modeling, except I turned him upside down. I painted a round table — a still-life — in abstract expressionist paint. I quoted a Goya painting on the wall and put an abstract background in it. I threw everything into the painting, all the factors that were pressuring me as truth... it was probably a turning point for me."[28] Although he painted several more pictures, and included some in his 1962 Green Gallery show, the canvas was now a closed door for him.

In the summer of 1961, Segal taught an adult painting class in New Brunswick. The class was encouraged to make use of odd and unlikely materials in assemblages, and one woman brought to class a box of surgeon's bandages. Segal took some home, with the intention of wrapping them around one of his chicken wire frameworks. Then a thought occurred to him: why not dip the cloth bandages in plaster, and apply them directly to the body? Segal sat on a chair and instructed his wife to cover him in soaked bandages. The new technique led to a few anxious moments when the plaster began to harden, heat up, and contract, and the artist lost a good portion of his body hair in the course of frantically removing the casts. With great difficulty, he was able to reassemble the pieces into a complete figure which he then placed on a chair. Next Segal provided an environment for his plaster effigy. The chair was moved up to a table, to which was nailed an old window frame. The result, entitled *Man Sitting at a Table,* marked the discovery of a new sculptural technique and a turning point in the artist's career.

Segal has never looked back. "It was such a relief to get away from the expression of making a

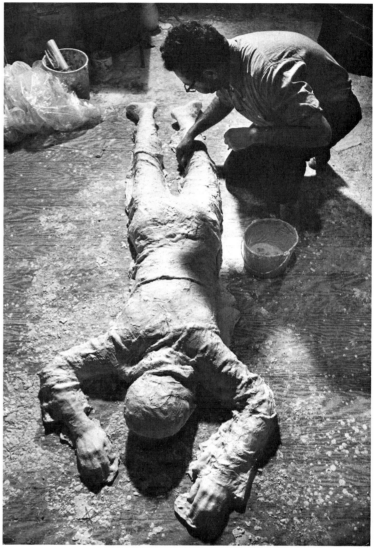

27

rough figure. It was too damn familiar. If I was looking for the hardness of the edge of a chair, it was such a relief to use a real chair with a real edge, and a real figure." By rejecting the *art brut* appearance of his earlier work, and abandoning painting altogether, Segal finally successfully concluded his struggle with Abstract Expressionist space and subjectivity. "Casting left me free to compose and to present content. I could report on my model and not on me; it was a rejection of the psychological distance of the canvas painter." When the first tableaux were exhibited in Segal's new home, the Janis Gallery, in the 1962

35

28 George and Helen Segal in his studio, 1965 (Photo Ugo Mulas).

29 George and Helen Segal in the artist's studio; the late
Alan Solomon, then director of the Jewish Museum, New York,
is seated below, 1965 (Photo Ugo Mulas).

30 **Woman in a Restaurant Booth.** 1961. (Cat. 6)
Plaster, wood, metal, vinyl and Formica
(curtain and radiator are not part of
the work), 51½ × 65 × 43¼ in.
Collection Wolfgang Hahn, Cologne.

28

29

"New Realists" show, Brian O'Doherty called them "the find of the exhibition."[29]

Segal's live casting methods and his environmental assemblages that O'Doherty admired, with their vivid backgrounds of gas stations, coffee shops, movie marquees, billboards, neon signs and traffic signs seemed to plunge him into the mainstream of the emerging Pop Art phenomenon in the early sixties. Popular culture and a variety of mass communications had just been rediscovered as a vital art source by a diverse group of young Americans influenced to some degree by the Reuben Gallery's assemblage makers, by the figural Expressionists and the Happenings' impresarios who had inventively mixed environmental flotsam with a symbolic human theater. The new generation, however, drew their imagery almost exclusively and directly from commercial and popular entertainment sources. They also differed from their immediate forbears in their aversion to personal expressiveness, and their preferences for the slick and finished advertising world surfaces. These brash new symbols of postwar material affluence swiftly superseded the derelict and nostalgic "junk" effects of the Assemblagists, with their evocative signs of age or use. The Pop artists fabricated an art based on a post-war consumer's paradise of gleaming new products, recognizable brand names, film and television icons, teen age romance or action comics, and the other standard visual fare of contemporary mass society. These artists were willing to stake their sensibilities on the vernacular of the market place rather than on traditional art sources.

Pop Art dramatically made its debut in America in 1962 across a wide spectrum of rather distinctive styles and diverse thematic preoccupations, with the exhibitions of a number of unusual artistic personalities, united in their defiance of Abstract Expressionist pictorial rhetoric, the mode of abstraction and the presumed moral superiority of the older avant-garde generation who were now viewed as sadly out of date. Ironic and populist in spirit, Pop Art soon replaced Abstract Expressionism as the major focus of serious public interest, despite a formidable pejorative campaign mounted by the defenders of high culture who were scandalized by work that flirted with *kitsch* and

1

32

33 George Segal's one-man show, Green Gallery, New York,
March 1964 (Photo Rudolph Burckhardt).

34 George Segal seated in **The Bus Riders**, 1962
(Photo Arnold Newman).

his works:
caricatures of modern society
his own work rel. to Hopper

33

trafficked with the most familiar (and heretofore despicable) images of the commercial media. Pop Art came to public notice in 1962 with the one-man shows of Roy Lichtenstein, James Rosenquist, Andy Warhol, Tom Wesselmann, and Robert Indiana. An offending shock was experienced by many artists and critics confronted by an imagery that seemed scarcely to transform its sources in the newspaper comic strip (Lichtenstein), the billboard (Rosenquist), repeating or isolated commercial brand symbols (Warhol), montage in strong relief of food products (Wesselmann). The more obviously aesthetic intention of the lettered signs and directional symbols of Robert Indiana was found only slightly more acceptable, since even he took over explicit and routine commercial or industrial imagery, road signs, and mechanical type faces.

Segal, however, immediately differentiated himself from his generally younger colleagues in the new populist idioms, isolating his art from their more commercial styles by the psychological nuances and social depth of commentary in his unique plaster forms. His environmental staging and signs of the mass media were mitigated by a taste for nostalgia-laden, derelict objects taken from the everyday world. The sense of a predigested visual experience screened by the second reality of the media was not the essential substance of his art. His subject matter remained insistently personal, taken from ordinary

daily experiences — sometimes rather private (*Woman Shaving her Leg,* or *Ruth),* and created in the voyeuristic spirit of Degas' naturalism; but his vision could also be more general and even analytical, summarizing vocational roles across a broad social spectrum (*Cinema, Dry Cleaning Store),* or even touching hedonistically on the world of entertainment (*Rock and Roll Combo).* In the sixties Segal created editorialized stereotypes of middle and lower class America, drawing his materials and subjects from the immediate environment. These sculptures were not portraits of individuals but broad caricatures, often caustic, of modern society. Despite his almost classificatory sense of human activities and quick response to social status, there was no specific social message in his work, no literary sense of anger, or the Pop ironists' implicit protest against American materialism, food habits and shallowness. The unique quality of his work was, in fact, its poetic statement, an approach in the spirit of traditional American romantic realism. His work was linked to the paintings of Edward Hopper, who was often cited in criticism as a predecessor.

The dehumanizing impact of our surroundings supports Segal's uncanny and moving plaster sculptures. His dramatic and theatrical art defies conventional distinctions between sculpture and painting, object and environment. The ghastly white humanity often seems a vulgar intrusion on a brightly lit, artificial urban landscape that has left only a marginal place for man. Segal's human replicas are pieced together, as we have seen, from castings of friends and relations who have been patient enough to leave their impressions in plaster. Immobilized in plaster and anesthetized, they exist finally as objects exist. Their most vivid identities and energies are aesthetic; since they are denied the energy and outlet of effective action, they serve the gratuitous life of the work of art, much as Claes Oldenburg's dispossessed and poetically suspended objects do. The acute and mournful sense of alienation at the heart of Segal's environmental sculpture is as much a product of his invented casting technique and apparitional medium as it is of the objects of contemporary urban life which lend his scenes their particular intensity and authenticity.

34

35 **Woman Shaving Her Leg.** 1963. (Cat. 14)
Plaster, metal, porcelain and Masonite, 63 × 65 × 30 in.
Collection Mrs. Robert B. Mayer, Chicago.

36 **Ruth in Her Kitchen** (First Version). 1964-1966. (Cat. 45)
Final version, see plate No. 160.
Plaster and wood, 50 × 72 × 60 in.
Von der Heydt Museum, Wuppertal, Germany.

37 **Cinema.** 1963. (Cat. 15)
Plaster, metal, Plexiglas and fluorescent light, 118 × 96 × 39 in.
Albright-Knox Art Gallery, Buffalo
(Gift of Seymour H. Knox).

38 **The Dry Cleaning Store.** 1964. (Cat. 25)
Plaster, wood, metal, aluminum paint
and neon tubing, 96 × 108 × 86 in.
Moderna Museet, Stockholm.

36

39 **Rock and Roll Combo.** 1964. (Cat. 26)
    Plaster, wood, tiling and musical instruments, 84 × 84 × 69 in.
    Hessisches Landesmuseum, Darmstadt, Germany
    (Collection Karl Stroher).

40 **The Gas Station.** 1963-1964. (Cat. 23)
    Plaster, metal, glass, stone and rubber, 96 × 264 × 60 in.
    The National Gallery of Canada, Ottawa.

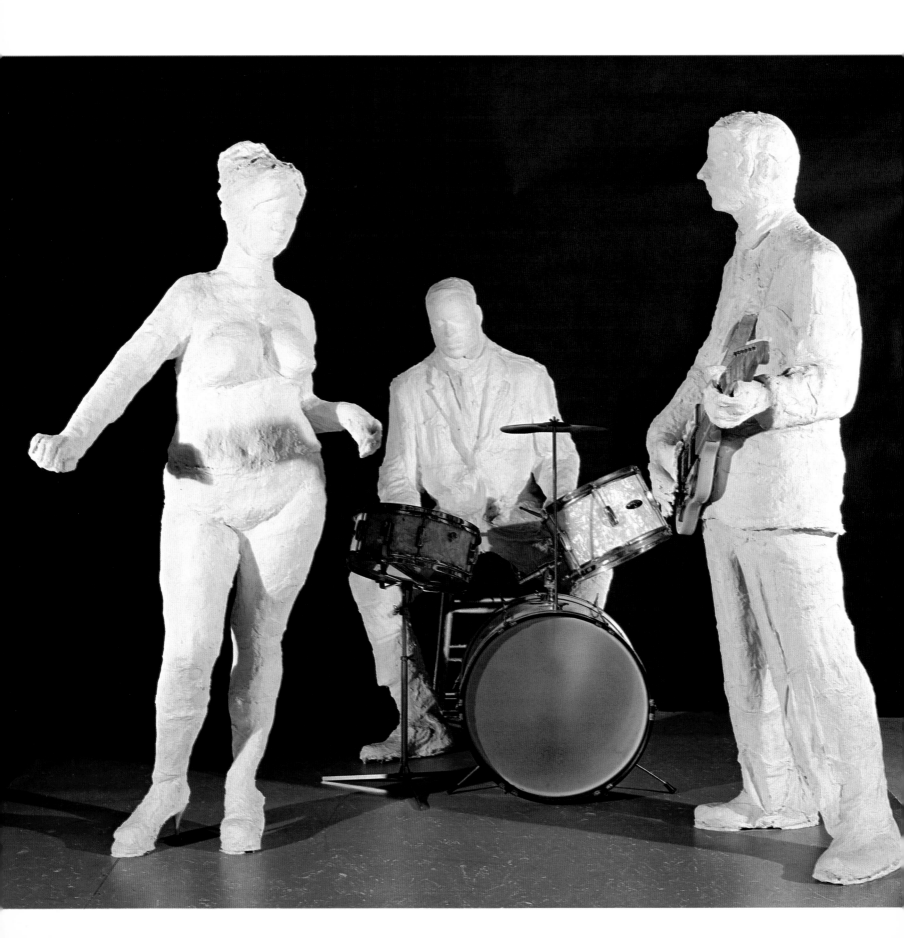

As an outstanding example of this alienating effect, and surely one of Segal's most haunting compositions, *Gas Station* epitomizes what the critic Lawrence Alloway has called the American highway subculture, with its associations of rootless wandering, personal estrangement and the loss of individual identity on the road. The dispirited and gloomy boredom of the two figures in the gas station and their immobility have encouraged the comparison to mummies. Their torpor is both intentional — an effort to symbolize human introspection — and accidental, stemming from the uncanny effects Segal discovered when he commenced building sculptural forms from plaster-soaked bandages. Like the Romans of Pompeii the gestures and routine daily movements of his actors seem arrested and fixed as if in a lava flow. Segal's stolid and immobilized figures, however, also function as an important foil and contrast to the revivified environmental appurtenances of a familiar gas station scene, which in turn takes on a kind of preternatural brilliance.

The artist told an earlier biographer that his feeling for space in this powerful work grew directly out of the personal experience of commuting by car and truck frequently between his home in South Brunswick and New York. He described his eerie sensation of driving at night when the road took on the appearance of a long and sinister corridor, broken now and then when a gas station appeared like an oasis of light and hope to relieve the tedium of night driving. To locate and define his particular *anomie* or spleen, in the Baudelairean sense, Segal has the habit of fixing his particular artistic and philosophical outlook in sharply specific personal experience. He has said in conversation:

I had one rule of thumb — if I was going to deal with an image, it had to mean something to me. The image had to stir some memory or strong feeling I had — some association I had with the object. If I didn't feel strongly about something, it really wasn't worth doing, because I spent months on each piece.

And in an interview with Henry Geldzahler in *Artforum* he described the genesis of his monumental sculpture, and revealed his dual awareness of its art historical implications even as it revealed a poignant contemporary moment:

I just finished working on a Gas Station piece. The man who posed really runs the Gas Station on the highway near my house. He's taking one step forward with an oil can in his hand. My private irony is if I took away the oil can and turned his fingers up he could be St. John the Baptist in coveralls.[30]

Works like *Gas Station* have often been compared with American Social Realism and its social commentary, or to the genre iconography of The Eight, but Segal perceives his work in more pointedly "modern" psychological terms. For him the industrial landscape yields a particular kind of alienating poetry and in the romantic discontent of his invented cast of plebeian characters he finds one of the most profound sources of his art. He has said in conversation:

An awful lot of thirties' social realism was political propaganda — people were suffering because capitalism was evil and the worker was oppressed by capital... We heard talk in the thirties that the industrial landscape was dirty and grimy, except that Léger taught me about the incredible vitality of that landscape. For years I've been driving the turnpike to New York; the refineries at Elizabeth are magnificent. They're beautiful and vigorous. At night this industrial landscape looks like pieces of jewelry, and at a certain point when I'm driving the turnpike, the refineries look like the horizontal roots of a tree feeding the trunks of the New York skyline. So I find a lot of vigor and life in industrial scenes. It's the people. They're restless, they're gloomy, they're dissatisfied. But they can't quite put their finger on their discontent. They simply know that something's wrong.

The modernism of Segal's *tableau vivant* is a combination of the extraordinary ability the sculptor has demonstrated to synthesize purely aesthetic and psychological values, so that human attitudes or states of mind can be transmitted seamlessly into the geometric structure of the work. Despite the extraordinary wax-museum veracity of his familiar roadside and urban scenes, he also conveys the sense of a terse and premeditated structure. The demarcation of his compositional spaces, the linear, frieze-like sequence of inferred movements and insistent rectilinear and repeated circular accents in *The Gas Station,* for example, help fix the scene into a grave and imposing formality. "George Segal's reality," his

41 **The Bowery.** 1970. (Cat. 96)
   Plaster, wood and metal, 96 × 96 × 72 in.
   Kunsthaus, Zurich.

42 The artist and his wife, 1970 (Photo Arnold Newman).

43 and 44. The artist in his studio, 1970 (Photo Arnold Newman).

friend Allan Kaprow has aptly said, "is a tragic one, in which the human and the artifact are alone and immobile, but as though consecrated to this state by some interior directive, to endure forever."

In *The Bowery* Segal evinced a more starkly poignant realism and a sense of social compassion, delineating a persuasively authentic scene with a drunken bum lying on the floor while another leans against a drab zinc and wood background smoking a cigarette. Typical of his best genre realism are the box-like compositions of plaster figures leaning over a sleazy red restaurant table, facing a cup and saucer and their own reveries.

On the level of a more private and intimate perception of reality, Segal's *Woman Shaving Her Leg* shows a canny intellect in his evident exploration of psychological, formal and art historical linkages even within a familiar genre study. His heavy-set female figure has a purposely gross definition to the point of caricature, in order to dispel any lingering associations with ideal beauty or seductiveness. Like Degas, Segal here assumes the role of the rapt but cold observer who sees and records, albeit in his own vivid contemporary fashion, an intensely intimate and personal world. Segal similarly enjoys the play of ironies between art and his role of the peeping-Tom, which he later, in fact, pursued in a more conscious exploitation of visual erotic stimulation.

At this point in his work, however, he is more engaged by the contrasts of his generalized, lumpy figure and a gleaming plumbing environment of chrome, porcelain and tile. As a further irony, and rather in the spirit of the contemporary construction/paintings with blatantly nude figures by Tom Wesselman, Segal manages to compose the harsh bathroom fixtures and setting in a manner that evokes the geometric power and austerity of Mondrian's grave formalism. Like all of Segal's best work this sculpture combines a rich and admiring sense of art history with an obsessive need to establish its contemporary authenticity.

The eerie presence of Segal's white plaster figures, and their often traditional art historical references to genre realism set his work off from the more immediately understood commercial signs and artifacts of conventional Pop Art. Until 1970 his plaster

42

43

44

45

46

casts were at best only approximate, taken from the exterior of the mold rather than replicated more exactly from the negative interior. His surfaces were actually impressionistic and invented rather than exactly descriptive. Most critically, this often laborious method involved a continuing, direct physical contact with the model over time, and a strong sense of his subject's personal responses to the casting process, and this in turn revealed something of the model's character. The lengthy working sessions, and their sometimes unnerving impact on the model invariably released or stirred up the model's tensions and anxieties. Segal skillfully translated these intangible psychological qualities into stance and gesture, and ultimately into his own expressive meanings.

The results were a powerful synthesis of modified portraiture and artistic self-definition, for Segal's thematic repetitions finally say something profound about every man's sense of isolation as well as his ritual patterns of behavior and his accommodation of a dominant and banal environment. Segal's environmental staging focuses on the defining limitations of his figure's actual life while the white, phantasmal plaster itself suggests an ideal reality that transcends diurnal existence and affords his morose protagonists a poetic release from their oppressively real surroundings.

While Segal kept the more blatant and familiar emblems of the Pop environment at bay, distancing them through the evocative poetic properties of his

48 **To All Gates.** 1971. (Cat. 108)
      Plaster, wood, metal, plastic and fluorescent
      light, 96 × 144 × 96 in.
      Des Moines Art Center (Coffin Fine Arts Trust Fund).

plaster effigies, he also learned to use some of these received images with finesse and in strikingly varied dispositions which attest to his compositional invention. In *Cinema* of 1963 the human figure and the fluorescent sign he is arranging attain an equivalence of emphasis. The impact of the total image essentially becomes the encounter between dissonant realities, human and mechanical, and not merely the action of placing letters on a movie marquee. Finally, the effect is that of an entirely original kind of three-dimensional collage.

Six years later, in 1969, Segal developed a series of brilliant variations around the idea of a "box" enclosure in order to frame smaller, more humanly-scaled vignettes showing partial figures in action and at rest, with sections of signs or lettering, as in *Box: Man in a Bar.* Alternately, in the same mode he alluded to a more makeshift and homely domesticity rather than to the public, shared Pop environment, in such works as *Box: Woman Looking through Window.* Then the following year he tackled a far more ambitious context in *Times Square at Night.* Two lumpish young men (the one nearest to us is a favorite model and neighbor, the sculptor George Kuehn) pose in single file, moving towards the viewer, and set off by a movie marquee in the background advertising pornographic films, overlaid with another competing neon sign for a pancake house and also showing the isolated letter Z. The illusion of the illuminated signs (which Segal elaborately reconstructed in a light box of colored gels and stick-on plastic letters) takes on a certain magic despite their sleazy references. The possible offense of the movie advertisement is absorbed by the dream-like wraiths that glide along on the darkened walk in front of the signs, their presence curiously muffling the no longer compelling erotic slogans.

Segal's realist genre themes and immobilized figures, depicted in frozen moments of profound introspection characteristic of the sixties, changed in the next decade. The young men striding into the night against the background of the blinking lights and visual excitement of Times Square already suggested a new taste for energy and movement. A variety of other urban scenes, such as *Walk, Don't Walk, The*

48

49 Walk, Don't Walk. 1976. (Cat. 143)
Plaster, cement, metal, painted wood
and electric light, 104 × 72 × 72 in.
Whitney Museum of American Art,
New York.

50 The Red Light. 1972. (Cat. 119)
Plaster and mixed media, 114 × 96 × 36 in.
Cleveland Museum of Art (Andrew R.
and Martha Holden Jennings Fund).

49   50

51

suggest through an abbreviated body language more universal values and attitudes that he had heretofore been able to articulate through rich and specific environmental and gestural detail. The new approach proved particularly effective in his wall pieces, which were divided between portraiture, lyrical figural groupings and partial individual human figures, among these most notably *Three Bathers with Birch Tree,* or the *Girl on Blanket* series. This new pastoral and hedonistic imagery was rich in visual references to themes of arcadian pleasure, reminiscent of the great classical traditions of nudes in the landscape.

Some of the boldest and most successful explorations were, perhaps not surprisingly in view of Segal's painting history and earlier candor, explicitly erotic tableaux. Speaking of his new methods after 1971 in an interview with Gerrit Henry, Segal declared:

Until recently, I've been less interested in a specific skin and bone texture. For a number of years I used the exterior of my cast, mostly to get at a sense of internal spirit, with just a few glimpses of specific qualities sticking out. Since I started the wall pieces — which are fragments of bodies — the scale is smaller and more intimate, and I've been more interested in recording wrinkles, pores, gooseflesh, against rough textures of plaster... With the new things, I'm more interested in getting subtle nuance. When I work now from the inside of the casts, I can get much more involved with sensitivity — crevices and rhythms — which can add up to very effective portraiture. The intention is not glorification — rather, it's the revelation of bodies that I like.[31]

The inside casting technique inevitably gave to his images a far more life-like surface, although they scarcely approximated the intense realism and social narratives in polyester and fiber glass, painted with oil, of the *trompe-l'oeil* illusionism of Duane Hanson and the later photorealists. Curiously, the increase in surface information and detail of the photorealists who had emerged in the late sixties eliminated the need for a relationship to a setting of actual environmental objects. Only the gallery stage was necessary, a neutral background. By contrast, the poetics and generality of Segal's humanity, and his figures' subtle tensions with their mundane surroundings created a psychic distance between the created

Red Light and *To All Gates,* and a new interest in the poetry of bodily motion and strength in a series of acrobats, dancers and circus figures all gave more emphasis to the transient and to the grace and agility of the human form rather than to the body as a symbol of physical enervation or metaphysical questioning. These changes could be ascribed at least in part to Segal's mastery of new techniques of figure construction. Beginning in 1971 he abruptly shifted from creating plaster shells, and freely modelling their surfaces, to working from a more exact and refined positive cast in hydrostone, a more durable industrial plaster, taken from the original plaster matrix formed around his models.

This method, in fact, had two contrary effects, offering the artist more freedom with more exactitude. The fuller surface detail opened the door to a more "hyper-realist" phase that re-established new relationships to classical themes and even to academic sculpture, thus transcending Segal's obsessive slice-of-life subject matter with its limited implications of a specific locale and imagery. At the same time, relieved of certain descriptive obligations, Segal could now

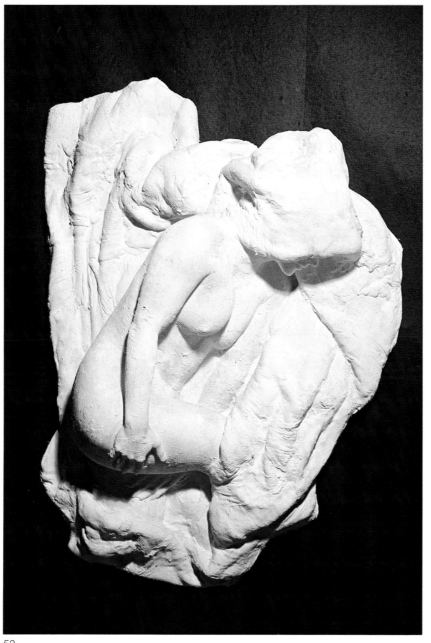

52

53

54 **Untitled.** 1963. (Cat. 333)
Pastel on construction paper, 18 × 12 in.
Courtesy Sidney Janis Gallery, New York.

55 **Untitled.** 1963. (Cat. 334)
Pastel on construction paper, 18 × 12 in.
Courtesy Sidney Janis Gallery, New York.

56 **Untitled.** 1964. (Cat. 335)
Pastel on construction paper, 18 × 12 in.
Courtesy Sidney Janis Gallery, New York.

57 **Untitled.** 1965. (Cat. 338)
Pastel on construction paper, 18 × 12 in.
Courtesy Sidney Janis Gallery, New York.

54

55

56

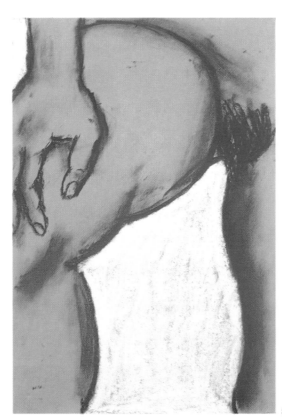

57

58 **Untitled.** 1964. (Cat. 336)
    Pastel on construction paper, 18 × 12 in.
    Courtesy Sidney Janis Gallery, New York.

59 **Untitled.** 1964. (Cat. 337)
    Pastel on construction paper, 18 × 12 in.
    Courtesy Sidney Janis Gallery, New York.

forms and their contrived, object-laden surroundings. The dual realities allowed a sense of mystery to develop, and underscored subjective values rather than social commentary, or the distracting mechanical accuracy of photographic representation in three dimensions.

Segal's portraiture generally is not designed to reveal specific persons, however, either in white plaster or in color, and the results transcend personality, even though various models, many used repeatedly, are dimly recognizable. We become far more interested in revealing elements of pose and gesture that distill and universalize certain common activities, attitudes or the human condition, through the suggestion of states of consciousness, rather than in the recognizable features or the character of a particular individual. In this sense, Segal is a modern realist working in the tradition established by Degas and Flaubert, who were interested in the whole mosaic of social circumstances that defined contemporary life rather than in the individual per se.

Like Degas in his later works, too, Segal in the seventies progressed to a freer and more expansive form of expression, paradoxically, soon after he developed the more detailed casting process by working from inside the mold. In his bas-reliefs especially, and in a powerful series of erotic tableaux, Segal emulated Degas quite consciously. Degas' late pastels of women at their toilet were intimately observed psychological encounters, and at the same time supreme plastic inventions. Segal's recent bas-reliefs often achieve a similarly exhilarating tension between realism or descriptive function, and a far more powerful feeling for the subjects themselves, which Segal began to comprehend with a new generosity of spirit, and with a force and warmth his work had never before evinced in quite the same way. He had moved in a sense from a populist reconstruction of the human situation, seen in terms of contemporary culture, and from commentary on the social scene, to a concern instead for states of feeling in a broader sense. By heightening anatomical details and fragmentary anatomical forms, Segal was able to enlarge and simplify his vision, making contact with deeper and more passionate emotions. Many of these works

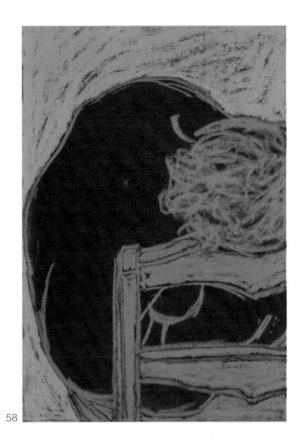

58

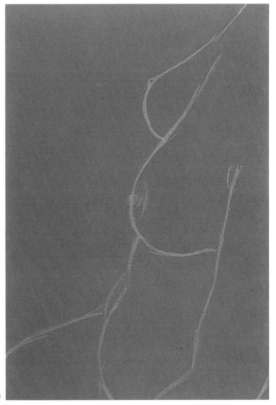

59

60 and 61   The artist's studio, 1983 (Photo Arnold Newman).
62   The artist's studio, 1970 (Photo Hans Namuth).
63   The artist's studio, 1983 (Photo Arnold Newman).

60

are in an explicitly sexual and erotic vein, and even those less charged with sensuality reveal new levels of feeling for art history. Both genres probe the artist's subjective feelings more deeply, and with an unprecedented freedom and energy.

Segal's rather moralistic sense of the artistic vocation, which took an obsessive, mythic form in his early preoccupation with the legend of Lot theme, now confronted art in a fresh way, by revealing important human truths of a Freudian character with new psychological insight and fresh formal resources. These revelations could also be linked to art history, myth and to his own vocation, with its mixed tactile and voyeuristic character, of necessity, as the observing artist worked directly from naked models whose casts he shaped by hand. As early as art school, in fact, Segal had with characteristic candor questioned the exercise of drawing from the nude, and the false pieties that confined the experience to a purely formal context, denying the presence of sexual excitement and ambiguity in the routine viewing and depicting process.

In conversation he reminisced about his first life study class, recalling his shock when he discovered that it could not honestly be purged of its sexuality:

I remember my first line drawing class. I was sixteen — a young boy, and a virgin — and here's this nude woman posing in front of me. And they told us to ignore the sexuality, and make a study in pure form and composition. I still think that's stupid. I think the primary thing about the nude woman posing was the sexual display, a certain attitude, the way this woman carried herself — all the rituals were to fend off rude sexual advances. She put her robe on during the break, she wouldn't talk to the artists. All of this ritual was to separate sex from business, but it was all there. I simply decided to face it honestly — a male artist reacting to a nude female model.

61

For Segal, as for Rodin, the first modern master of the "partial figure," fragmentary torsos and limbs came to symbolize the meeting of antique sculpture and modern feeling, with the spirit manifest even in the smallest segment of the body. Segal deeply admires Rodin, and in the French master's late works especially discovered for himself a "personal vision of life, energy and sexuality."[32] Few artists, professor Albert Elsen has pointed out in a recent article, man-

62

64 **Breast and Wicker Chair** (Fragment). 1978. (Cat. 300)
Painted plaster, 22 × 10 × 8 in.
Courtesy Sidney Janis Gallery, New York.

65 **Girl in Wicker Chair** (Fragment). 1978. (Cat. 301)
Painted plaster, 23 × 19 × 7 in.
Collection Dr. and Mrs. Earl Scott, Rydal, Pa.

66 **Hand Fragment No. 9.** 1980. (Cat. 310)
Painted plaster, 10¼ × 14 in.
Courtesy Sidney Janis Gallery, New York.

67 The artist's studio: four metal hand fragments, paper fragment
(multiple), fragment of hand and breast, head, and still life
fragment 1982.

68 **Lovers' Hands** (Bas Relief). 1976. (Cat. 265)
Plaster, 23 × 12 × 8 in.
Courtesy Sidney Janis Gallery, New York.

64

65

66

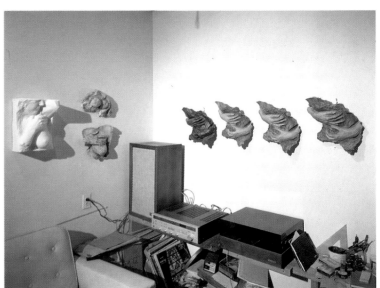

67

aged to express the feelings of tenderness in explicit physical terms between two persons as Segal has done since Rodin's time. Regarding his "Lovers" series, Segal noted that his concern with such intense personal feeling and mutuality was "inevitable... and necessary, after dealing with the hallucinatory glare and menacing voids"[33] in the earlier environmental tableaux. *Lover's Hands* is among the most daring and poignant in its exposure of Segal's erotic reliefs. The image isolates a male hand pressing on the pudenda of a female, whose hands sensitively betray her own shifting mood, as one vigorously guides the male fingers, while her other hand rests limply on his wrist, reflecting the simultaneous experience of tension and pleasure at his intrusive touch. These subtle nuances within the context of the startling physicality of the relief, with its point-blank focus on sexual exploration and response, provide an extraordinary emblem, finally, of passionate feelings of mutuality and the tenderness of touching. In a sensitively written review, Leo Rubinfein argues persuasively that even the alternation between the detailed, finished impressions of the hands and the vague matrix of plaster from which they emerge symbolize sexuality, and thus suggest the uncanny power of other themes in Segal's art as well, and his ability to transcend naturalism in order to achieve wider meanings and a deeper emotional resonance:

In their play between the explicit and the vague, the body-fragments fluctuate as consciousness itself does during sex. Where they emerge, they evoke that clarity of perception that ascends, then disappears, when, making love, one relapses into pure and silent pleasure. Where they recede, they suggest the fading of sexual memory itself, so that the whole collection of reliefs seems a display of pungent, remembered moments surrounded on all sides by an immaterial ethos.[34]

In all of Segal's recent reliefs, and especially in such female nudes as *Girl on Blanket, Full Figure* and *Red Girl in Blanket,* there are clear allusions both to classical themes and to energetic baroque composition. Mimicking classical and later traditional art forms, however, has always been an oblique aspect of Segal's work. His search for mythical associations and for a more universal subject matter in historical art suggest that his modernity required the foil of the

68

past to offset the mundane surroundings of his sculpture, with its real objects, and real, walk-through spaces. By joining his work to mainstream art history he heightened its major preoccupation in subject matter, which is the vulgar present and a commercial culture. Playing off the past and present also had other implications. His expanded awareness of art history has an ambivalence about it, as it did for most recognized artists of the Pop Art generation who often quoted the recent past, at least, in a spirit of ironist parody.

69 **Red Girl in Blanket** (Bas Relief). 1975. (Cat. 241)
Painted plaster,, 39 × 49 × 13 in.
Collection Baron H. H. von Thyssen-Bornemisza, Lugano.

70 **Picasso's Chair.** 1973. (Cat. 127)
Plaster and mixed media, 78 × 60 in.
Guggenheim Museum, New York.

69

71

When in 1973 Segal created *Picasso's Chair,* he consciously challenged an admired masterpiece of modern art in Picasso's most famous Surrealist image from the Vollard suite. It depicted an idealized classical nude staring at a monstrous anatomical/furniture construction, with allusions to male sex organs. Segal felt that the challenge was as much one of reconciling the flat pictorial space and material substance of the etching as it was of recapitulating Picasso's disturbing, brilliantly conflicted images. Avoiding the more sardonic visual responses of his contemporaries, he characteristically converted the occasion into a formal meditation on his relationship to art history, and commented:

Picasso has intimidated me all these years. He was so enormous and staggering that no artist hoped to compete. But later on, after I had started making wall reliefs and started playing with elements which projected out from a bare wall, I became intrigued with the idea of Cubism... I had the suspicion that there was a connection between classical cubist structure and Renaissance perspective structure, and I had to painfully rediscover for myself Cubism's connection with Renaissance perspective. But how do I do it? As a drawing, or a model, or a maquette? So I made Picasso's Chair, *questioning the nature of things, hunting for connections. It was liberating for me. I started putting color on to the wall reliefs and it opened up a whole new area.*[35]

Segal's nudes and bas-reliefs of anatomical fragments and figural groups reflect his nostalgia not only for art history but for the revived genres of academic art and historical painting. As early as *The Dinner Table* of 1962, a work which poses a group modelled by the artist's family and friends, seated and standing around a battered table, with a mirror on a background stage flat painted black, he for the first time used the most dismal and banal environmental objects in a concealed allusion to a famous modernist masterpiece as well. A woman attending the Sidney Janis *New Realist* show, where the sculpture was first exhibited, expressed her shock at its apparently simple factualism and asked, "What is it supposed to be?" In her mind the ensemble bore little or no relationship to revered stereotypes of high art, and seemed nothing more than a primitive replica of a banal human moment. The bewildered layman's question received a surprising answer from the sculptor, who was at hand. Segal recalls that he responded: "It is supposed to be Cézanne." He had in mind *The Card Players* in the Metropolitan Museum of Art when he designed the work, and he tried to create his own three-dimensional parallels for its monumental volumes and for Cézanne's deeply felt sense of a sober, dignified and timeless humanity.

In recent years he expressed his admiration for Cézanne even more openly, driven for various reasons to re-examine the plastic implications of the modern master's paintings, in relation to his own dilemmas about competing demands of pictorial and sculptural space. Segal's unusual applications of thin color washes on his plaster objects, in his direct Cézanne quotations, elicited a comment from the artist on the genesis of his surprising new methods of color expression:

Here I was making all these white sculptures, and I said let's see what happens if I make a sculpture darker. I wasn't even thinking in terms of color at the time, just making it darker. And then I started to put some color on the white plaster and was astounded to discover how extraordinary it was in receiving the paint. Then I used the brightest colors I could, and you start saying, well, what else can you do? Then transparent stains: extraordinary. And so every time I touched a piece of plaster with color, I was changing a whole expressive character of the piece. Astounding![36]

In the winter of 1981, perhaps seeking relief from the distractions of the unresolved and disturbing con-

troversies that had arisen around his *Kent State Memorial* and *Gay Liberation* monuments, Segal turned directly to Cézanne for renewal and spiritual nourishment. His exploration of a vivid, chromatic sculpture of an intensely private character gave him a well deserved respite from the pressures and extroversion of making commissioned public works. In this new genre of art-about-art, as it might be described, he meditated on Cézanne's familiar still life subjects in his own three-dimensional variants on a noble traditional theme, creating an enthralling series of free

copies of some of the best known Cézanne still lifes in museum collections. These he reconstructed with considerable care in sculptural form by making plaster molds of apples, oranges and onions, plates, pitchers and bottles, painting them in thin color washes and arranging them on plaster-soaked cheesecloth drapery. He even re-created in three dimensions the forward tilt of Cézanne's table surfaces, in a *tour-de-force* of translation of form from a depicted, illusionistic space into the literal physicality of sculpture. The revival of the drastically elided space of the modern-

74 **Cézanne Still Life No. 2.** 1981. (Cat. 177)
    Painted plaster, wood and metal, 32 × 40 × 18½ in.
    Courtesy Sidney Janis Gallery, New York.

75 **Cézanne Still Life No. 3.** 1981. (Cat. 178)
    Painted plaster, wood and metal, 24 × 40 × 27½ in.
    Courtesy Sidney Janis Gallery, New York.

76 **Cézanne Still Life No. 4.** 1981. (Cat. 179)
    Painted plaster, wood and metal, 57 × 48 × 24 in.
    Courtesy Sidney Janis Gallery, New York.

74

75

ist pictorial genre in terms compatible with his own poetic, realist style represented a triumphant restatement of Cézanne's elevated formal vision but without sacrificing the vitality of the vernacular idiom of Pop Art.

The delicate coloration of his sculptures during the winter of 1981 were closer to Cézanne's watercolors than to the painfully deliberated and built up color structure of his oils. These sculptures also reflected Segal's habitual pictorial concerns, dating back to his paintings of the mid-fifties, and even to more recent experiments in color and three-dimensional construction that mined the contradictions of flat pictorial illusion. His Cézanne paraphrases could be read as more than a witty stratagem for enlisting the authority of the past, in the name of admired high art, to offset an existing vernacular mode of contemporary expression. They were a challenge to traditionalism, too, in the same sense that *Picasso's Chair* represented a bold and confident assertion that even the most exalted modern invention could be grist for Segal's own sculptural invention. His Cézanne studies could also be directly related to his extensive series of figural reliefs that had engaged him since the early seventies.

In conversation at the time he said:

I had discovered that if I dealt with a fragment of the body, it was very difficult to control shapes, and if I wanted an intense, small-scale encounter, it was simpler to go into still-life elements. Cézanne had been my first influence. He found planes in nature that express how he feels the world is constructed. What I did like about Cézanne was that sense of a building block structure.

And Segal predicted, with surprising accuracy, a subsequent development in his artistic interests: "I'll probably go into still lifes, but not more Cézannes; maybe I'll do my own."

Even more recently, he has composed a new series of still lifes describing more banal studio objects, such as paint tins and other containers which were first adumbrated in pastel. The intensity of his colors in these works, colors which have progressed from transparent glazes to a heavy saturation, opacity and fluorescence, create a somewhat surreal atmosphere. They also reflect the experience of a continuing series of portrait studies, among them his brilliant half-length relief of the art historian Meyer Schapiro, with its blue saturation relieved by beige flesh tones.

Both series, animate and inanimate, deliver a new feeling of a boundless coloristic totality, reminiscent of the monochrome surfaces of Yves Klein. Segal's virulently bright colors in his reliefs and free-

77

standing figures of the seventies and eighties produce the impression of an almost intolerable vividness, in which details are lost to a dominant color sensation. There has also been a consequent heightening of the sense of irony, a downplay of sentiment, and an even more feverish sensuality in the nude studies and erotica.

He has in very recent years, since 1980, proven himself a bizarrely original colorist, acutely sensitive to the incongruity existing between his models and their banal reality, and capable of injecting into the everyday human situation a rather grand vision of the apocalyptic powers of chromatic pictorial expression. These unleashed coloristic impulses, which stem from his earlier painterly experiences but probably first emerged unequivocally in *The Costume Party*, are yet another of the many fruitful contradictions in Segal's art. They are as notable as other evident contrasts much noted by his critics, particularly the confrontations of a Suprematist severity in compositions with shabby, derelict objects. Perhaps equally dramatic are the tensions generated by his poetically vague plaster figures in white, whose disembodied ghosts seem poised between the physical and the spiritual, in the shifting contexts of the commonplace "found" objects which define their social reality.

Segal's general oeuvre and his stature as an artist have been a source of considerable debate over the years, because his visual effects open him to a rather circumscribed labeling as a limited genre realist, while his actual sculptural methods have elicited the charge of "copying." Although he has continued to cast directly from the human figure, he does so for dramatic and imaginative reasons, in a manner that serves to heighten and intensify the confrontation between his figures and their surroundings and between figures and the spectator. Despite his constant reference in conversation and published statements to formal and abstract considerations in his compositions, their real force lies in his control of dramatic situations. These he has manipulated, and mastered with consummate skill and a controlled emotive power for more than two decades.

In an early statement Segal emphasized the importance of personal associations, familiarity and emotion in the choices of subjects and in the evolution of his work. His personal involvement as creator and witness to the scene at hand remains intense; and his close relationship with familiar models permeates all his work, sustained by the remarkable intimacy of the discovery process necessarily involved in the act of casting from living models. His methods provide him with an otherwise inaccessible mode of knowing, touching, probing and mentally infiltrating the bodies and psyches of his subjects in a way few artists have either wished, or been able, to realize historically. Segal has noted the importance of his relationship to the sources of his sculptural inventions:

I usually make sculptures of people I know very well in situations that I've known them in. And if that involves a luncheonette counter, places in the house or other places where I go: gas stations, bus stations, streets, farm buildings, this must all have to do with my experience. I live in this environment... It is a huge heap of art material for me... I remember my life with the objects and I also look at these objects "plastically," for what these shapes are. And how people relate to these shapes and how they don't relate in a human way, intrigues me... As long as there has been a very alive emotional experience between me and the person, or between me and the object, or both, only then do I incorporate it into my own work.[37]

Given his working methods and philosophical attitudes Segal's otherwise remote and withdrawn plaster figures become emblems, or objective correlatives, for distilled emotion itself.

78

80 **The Farm Worker.** 1963. (Cat. 20)
Plaster, wood, glass and imitation brick, 96 × 96 × 42 in.
Galerie Onnasch, Cologne.

80

As early as 1968 the critic John Perreault boldly raised the question of Segal's stature when he declared that his most recent exhibition "will do much to establish his position as, surprisingly enough, a major artist who, along with three or four of the other Pop Popes, proves his art artful enough to survive the labels that served as handy introductions but not as adequate definitions."[38] After Pop Art lost its momentum as a group style in the late sixties Segal, a figure never very comfortable within it, in any case, transcended the expressive limitations of the movement and has continued to develop as a major innovator in American art. He has since proven himself far more persuasively linked with a familiar and enduring historical tradition of realism, for his work makes both a powerfully human as well as a clear aesthetic statement, with the kind of gravity associated with highly formal styles of realism, from Vermeer to Hopper. While there have been significant technical modifications in his sculpture since the early sixties, when he first achieved a whole vision in an original style, and he managed to create an expanding range of iconography and formal invention, in essence, Segal has remained surprisingly faithful to his original formula. He has also given mythic dimensions to humble subjects and to his own personal experience within a more populist, accessible scheme of public sculptural meanings over the succeeding two decades in an astonishingly productive, unbroken round of creative activity.

When Henry Geldzahler posed for *The Farm Worker*, he aptly described it as "realistic and natural in its bounds and its setting — removed and mysterious at its center and in its meaning."[39] The mysterious center of Segal's work is not simply the literal scene evoked, or the psychic tensions beneath the plaster shells of his phantomic figures in white, or in color, although both the narrative situation and human psychology are essential to his vision. It is finally the entire panoply and mystery of his stagecraft that stir the deepest responses in the viewer to his haunting art. Fact plays off fiction, and an ironic Pirandellian sense is conveyed of the analogy between his artistic concerns and the characters peopling his stage. They thus transcend their everyday plausibility and familiar contexts, and we come to realize that they can only exist through the miracle of artistic imagination, and through the medium of Segal's psychologically astute perceptions and generous human spirit.

NOTES

1. Ellen H. Johnson, "The Sculpture of George Segal," *Art International,* Vol. VIII, No. 2 (March 20, 1964), p. 51.

2. William C. Lipke, "The Sense of 'Why not?': George Segal on his art," *Studio International,* Vol. CLXXIV, No. 893 (October 1967), p. 149.

3. Phyllis Tuchman, "Pop," *Art News,* Vol. LXXIII, No. 5 (May 1974), p. 25.

4. George Segal, *Sculptures, Paintings Pastels: A Discussion of My Recent Work,* Master of Fine Arts Thesis, Rutgers University (May 1963) p. 11.

5. Ibid, p. 4.

6. P(arker) T(yler), review, *Art News* (May 1957).

7. R(obert) W. D(ash), review, *Arts* (February 1958).

8. Segal, MFA Thesis, pp. 2, 3.

9. Irving Sandler, *The New York School: The Painters and Sculptors of the Fifties,* New York City, Harper & Row, 1978, p. 36.

10. Cited in *John Cage,* ed. Richard Kostelanetz (New York: Praeger Publishers, 1970).

11. Segal, MFA Thesis, pp. 3, 4.

12. Allan Kaprow, "The Legacy of Jackson Pollock," *Art News,* Vol. LVII, No. 6 (October 1958), p. 56.

13. Ibid, p. 57.

14. Kaprow, *Assemblage, Environments, and Happenings* (New York: Harry N. Abrams, Inc., Publishers, 1966), p. 160.

15. Tuchman, p. 25.

16. Henry Geldzahler, "An Interview with George Segal," *Artforum* (November 1964), p. 27.

17. Ibid, p. 29.

18. Cited in Barbara Gold, "George Segal's 'Portraits in Plaster,'" Baltimore *Sun* (November 5, 1967).

19. Cited in George McCue, "The Frozen Images of George Segal," Saint Louis *Post-Dispatch* (December 13, 1970).

20. Lipke, "The Sense of 'Why not?': George Segal on his art," p. 147.

21. Ibid, p. 147.

22. Kaprow, "The Legacy of Jackson Pollock," p. 56.

23. Cited in *16 Americans* (New York: The Museum of Modern Art, 1959).

24. Al Hansen, *A Primer of Happenings and Time-Space Art.*

25. Segal, MFA Thesis, p. 15.

26. George Segal and Sidney Tillim, "Pop Art: A Dialogue," *Eastern Arts Quarterly,* Vol. II, No. 1 (September-October 1963), p. 15.

27. J(ames) S(chuyler), review, *Art News* (February 1959).

28. Cited in Graham W. J. Beal, "Realism at a Distance," in *George Segal: Sculptures,* catalogue (Minneapolis: Walker Art Center, 1978), p. 60.

29. Brian O'Doherty, "Art: Avant-Garde Revolt," *New York Times* (October 31, 1962).

30. Henry Geldzahler, "An Interview with George Segal," *Artforum* (November 1964) p. 27.

31. Gerrit Henry, "Ten Portraits: Interviews/Statements," *Art in America* (January/February 1975) p. 36.

32. Albert A. Elsen. "Mind Bending with George Segal," *Art News* (February 1977).

33. Ibid, p. 34.

34. Leo Rubinfein, "On George Segal's Reliefs," *Artforum* (May 1977) p. 44.

35. Martin Friedman and Graham W. J. Beal, *George Segal: Sculptures,* Walker Art Center, Minneapolis, Minn., 1978, p. 49.

36. Malcom N. Carter, "George Segal," *Saturday Review* (May 1981) p. 29.

37. Jean Dypreau, "Métamorphoses: L'école de New York," *Quadrum* XVIII, 1965, p. 54.

38. John Perreault, "Plaster Caste," *Art News* (November 1968) p. 54.

39. Jan van der Marck, *George Segal* (New York 1979) revised edition, p. 76.

THE CASTING PROCESS:
IN SEGAL'S STUDIO

Portrait sculpture has always promised a kind of immortality to its subject that is equally alluring and mysterious. When primitive artists depicted their rulers or embodied supernatural powers in sculptural form, they were moved as much by superstition as by the aim of realistic representation. An effigy that physically assumes the space and persona of the individual portrayed is more than a simple depiction; the sculpture that immortalizes threatens also to displace the subject, to assume a magical life of its own. Religion, myth and literature are full of the antics of such ghostly *Doppelgänger*, but it is the creation of these effigies that is most highly charged with the air of magic and the mystery of communion between the human, the inanimate and the supernatural.

The indescribable and insistent presence of Segal's plaster figures may perhaps be understood in the light of this ancient tradition of myth and ritual. Watching Segal cast a model, one sees a modern-day shaman, mystically constituting particular forms of animation and universal meanings in an inanimate effigy.

The time limitations prescribed by Segal's quick-drying materials, and the consequent need for quick, gestural modeling, set his sculptural process apart from more familiar techniques of modeling or casting from life. The rhythm of Segal's movements, his alternation between contemplation and expressive action, and the constant pressure for immediate decision-making surprisingly recall the combination of gesture, temporal sense, and improvisational choreography recorded in Hans Namuth's celebrated photographs of Pollock's graceful, rapt athleticism in the act of painting his large, open "drip" canvases. The critics who have called Segal's tableaux "frozen happenings" are not very wide of the mark: every cast is the record of a theatrical confrontation, staged in the environment of Segal's studio-chicken coop and supplementing a ritualistic plot line with improvisation and chance. The artist's creative process cannot be understood apart from the urgency and logic of its temporal sequence, which is documented below for *Seated Woman Dangling Her Shoe*, 1982.

1:15 pm, February 20, 1982

The scene is Segal's New Jersey studio, a cavernous chain of former chicken coops linked by low doorways. Eight feet high and over three hundred feet long, the structure has an atmosphere at once mysterious and strangely evocative; it has not gone unnoticed that the dimensions of this space leave their mark on the spatial dynamics of much of Segal's work.[1] Norris Mailer, an artist, the novelist's wife and a veteran of several casting sessions, is sitting cross-legged on a park bench. A local rock station plays softly over a stereo as photographer Arnold Newman rigs lighting and checks cameras. Segal circles Mailer, studying the angle of her head and the rhythms of dress and hair. Constantly talking to the model, asking if she is comfortable, sometimes adjusting the placement of an arm or a fold of her dress, Segal finally seems to be satisfied with the form he will cast. Then he pauses: the sweeping diagonal formed by the left arm and hand, which will dominate the composition, is not quite right; he makes a half-dozen small adjustments before he is content.

While he makes some final preparations, Segal encourages the model to relax and walk around the

81 to 89   The artist studies his model, Norris Mailer, before casting her figure
for a sculpture whose progress the photographer, Arnold Newman,
documented on the afternoon of February 20, 1982.

81

studio; her pose has been recorded by blue chalk tracings on the bench and floor. The casting materials are marshalled around the park bench: buckets of hot water, Nivea cream — to protect the model's skin and hair — and piles of Johnson and Johnson "extra-fast setting plaster bandages." The swatches of plaster-impregnated cloth were designed for use in setting broken bones; they have the advantage of hardening in less than five minutes into a firm, flexible cast that can be removed without disintegrating or cracking. The Johnson and Johnson bandages represent an improvement over Segal's old method of dipping cloth in plaster, which required the model to hold his pose for forty-five minutes while the cloth stiffened. When Segal learned of the bandages, he abandoned his old technique: "I just decided to be less sadistic," says the artist.

Segal's wife, Helen, will not participate in the casting today. Usually she is George's unflagging assistant, providing advice and an extra pair of hands. Today, her only contribution has been a suggestion to Mailer that she help Segal choose the clothes she will wear for the casting. And, when the artist and model traveled to a local department store this morning, it was Mailer who picked out a pair of sandals and a sundress with detailed stitching and rick-rack, which she thought would provide an interesting surface for the sculpture. Segal says that the choice of clothing is not important to the finished piece, but his reliance on the model's taste and judgment also has the positive effect of contributing to the revelation of personality and attitude in the finished work.

1:30 pm

"Just consider the plaster a beauty treatment," Segal jokes, as the model resumes her pose on the bench. Mailer's legs receive a coat of Nivea moisturizing cream and then, dipping four bandages in a bucket of warm water, Segal begins molding damp plaster around her feet. The sculptor works up the right leg to the kneecap, then down from the left knee to the foot, where he pays careful attention to the detail of a sandal. The speed with which the bandages harden paces the artist and determines his technique: he applies several bandages at once, then works them

around the surface with his fingers and knuckles. Smoothing the cloth out with the heel and the side of his hand, he snatches more bandages, dampens and applies them, all in a quick rhythm punctuated by the clicks of Newman's cameras. A telephone rings in the studio, but Segal ignores it. In order to fashion a continuous plaster surface, he must be able to join and smooth overlapping bandages, and hence an entire section of the body must be completed at once.

1:44 pm

The model's legs are encased in plaster to the knee. Segal now begins to work on the lap and thighs. He has some difficulty in making the plaster bandages stick inside the hem of the dress, and devotes several minutes to shaping the delicate folds along the hem. But, turning to the swath of cloth across the model's lap, his hand moves in broader, more expressive strokes, as if sketching in plaster.

Moments of silence are interspersed with Segal's comments. He mentions his source of inspiration in the formal purity of classical Greek sculpture, and talks to Mailer about the composition he is trying to record: "Form is more important than fabric. Everybody forgets the real purpose of fashion. You'll think I'm a chauvinist, but it's to make women beautiful." The artist refills a water bucket and works the bandages up to the model's waist.

1:54 pm

Satisfied that the bandages have already dried, Segal begins the painstaking process of removing them. First he opens a seam on the back of the right leg, prying it with his fingers, and splits the cast up to Mailer's waist. The right leg is freed, and the cast loosened at the waist. Working his hands between dress and plaster, Segal extricates the lap and thighs. Finally the lower section comes off in three parts; the artist marks each seam with a pencil before removing the cast, so the sections can be easily re-aligned.

2:06 pm

After a few minutes of walking around the studio, the model is ready for the next step in the casting. She resumes her pose and Segal spreads Nivea

82

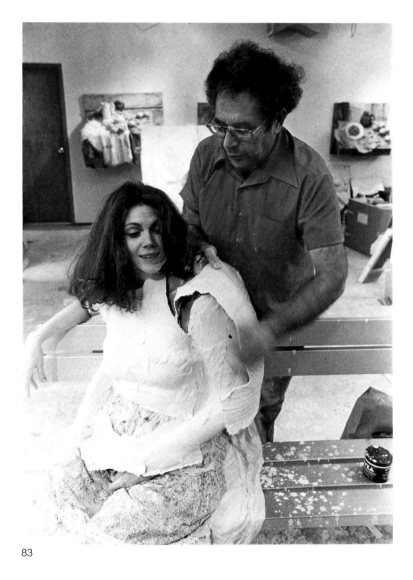

83

cream over her arms and shoulders. "Lucky I'm not ticklish," Mailer jokes, as Segal rubs the cream under the spaghetti straps of her sundress. In a moment, her back is coated with plaster bandages, which Segal smooths with his fingertips. When he reaches the shoulder, the pace slows: the line from the left shoulder to the left hand will be the focus of the composition, and the sculptor spends a good deal of time defining and emphasizing its curvilinear rhythm, working the plaster with his thumbs and the heel of his hand. The goal is not merely formal resonance. Segal also seeks to communicate the erotic energy of the female

form: "There's nothing more sensual than an armpit," he observes, as his fingers work the plaster around Mailer's left shoulder.

As the work progresses, the atmosphere becomes hushed. Even Segal's comments, directed exclusively now to the model, are murmured sotto voce. Somehow this steady stream of talk — asking if Mailer is relaxed, explaining what forms he is trying to emphasize, discussing his arthistorical enthusiasms — seems to establish a peculiar rapport, an exchange both intellectual and emotional between artist and model, the correlative of the direct

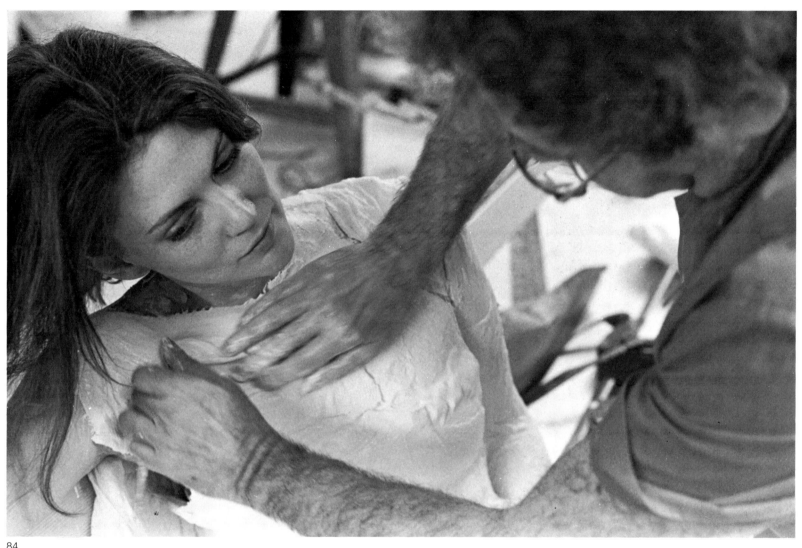

84

physical relation between them. Mailer, a practiced model, says that no other experience in her career can approach the intensity of a modelling session with Segal.

For his part, the artist has always admitted the importance of the model in determining the shape his sculpture takes: "The look of these figures is both accidental and planned. I usually know generally what emotional stance I'd like to have in the finished figure and I ask the model to stand or sit in a certain way. That model though is a human being with a great deal of mystery and totality locked up in the figure. Certain

truths of bone structure are revealed and so are long time basic attitudes of response on the part of the model. If you have to sit still for an hour you fall into yourself, and it is impossible to hide, no matter the stance."[2]

2:28 pm

The plaster has dried from waist to neck, and Segal begins to remove the shell. He splits the left arm off, then loosens the plaster cast from Mailer's back and removes the torso section in two halves. The seams are marked with a pencil, and the model

85

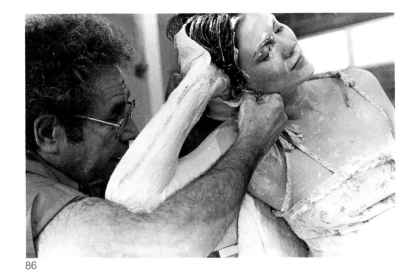

86

87

relaxes as Segal prepares for the final, and most difficult, section: the head and right arm.

2:24 pm

Mailer resumes her pose and Segal applies Nivea — "that greasy kid stuff" — to her arm and face. Eyebrows and lids receive special attention, the lips and chin are thoroughly covered, and Segal smooths handfuls of the cream into Mailer's hair. Finally he is ready to begin, and quickly swathes the right arm in bandages. The right hand, on which Mailer rests her head, gives Segal some trouble, for the plaster will not conform as closely as he wishes to the shape of the ear and fingers. Eventually, the cloth stays in place and, after a last-minute decision to re-arrange

the fall of Mailer's hair, he encircles her neck with the bandages.

2:56 pm

The face is easily covered: three strips, placed laterally across the eyes and forehead, the bridge of the nose, and the mouth. But the moment when the face is encased in plaster makes the greatest demands on artist and model. Minutes before submitting to this mummification, Mailer remarks: "George is very good about explaining the process as you go along, so you don't get nervous. And he says you'll always be able to break out of the cast, so there's no reason to panic."

Mailer remembers that even her first session with

89

Segal was not in the least frightening. A high school art teacher, she had taught her class to make "Segal-casts" as one of their course assignments, so the experience was familiar the first time she walked into Segal's studio. But even if the model is not inclined to panic, the moment when eyes, ears, and mouth are sealed in plaster is necessarily a unique and compelling adventure, occasioning flights of free-association and disembodied reverie.

The modeling of the head also challenges Segal's dexterity. Working the bandages over the chin and neck, he brings out detail by tracing the lips with his fingertips. Thin strips of bandage are cut and placed between and directly under the nostrils, and more strips are applied to build up the bridge and sides of the nose. Segal smooths the bandages over the top of the head, repeatedly running his hands over the surface to emphasize the contours of the underlying bone: "Nobody pays any attention to the fact that you have a shape to your skull, just like you have a shape to your hips."

3:10 pm

Opening a seam up to each ear, Segal removes the cast from behind and then leads the model to a sink to wash the cream from her eyes and the plaster from her hair: the cast is complete. Mailer heads for a shower in the studio to remove the plaster more thoroughly — "It stays in your hair for days," she says — and exchange the soggy sundress for street clothes. Like an Apache in his warpaint, sporting plaster smudges on his nose and forehead, Segal examines his handiwork: the cast, he says, is excellent.

Ahead lies the difficult process of reassembling the sections. Each seam must be dampened and adjacent sections rejoined — a constant battle with gravity in which the cast threatens to dissolve into an amorphous mound of damp plaster. Finally, in a process similar to the traditional lost-wax casting technique, the mold will be filled with hydrostone — a quick-drying industrial material, more durable than ordinary plaster. When the hydrostone hardens, the plaster mold is removed and the complete figure will be ready to take its place on another park bench, perhaps as a part of a larger tableau. But for now, the casts lie in wait on the cluttered floor of Segal's studio, only one among the dozens of sculptures abiding in the tangle of hollow torsos and plaster limbs.

NOTES

1. Jan Van Der Marck, *George Segal* (New York: Harry N. Abrams, Inc., 1979), p. 30.

2. "An Interview with George Segal," with Henry Geldzahler, *Artforum* (November 1964), p. 27.

PUBLIC SCULPTURE: POLEMICS, ISSUES, THE WORK

The day is long past when a sculptor could depict a Civil War general on a rearing mount with the satisfaction of knowing that he had created an image that at once communicated with its audience and succeeded by the standards of his fellow artists and critics. In the years before the First World War, sculptors, confident that aesthetic quality and accessibility were not incompatible, peopled the municipal landscape with slightly pompous Neo-Roman and Baroque *Beaux-Arts* monuments to great deeds and fallen heroes. Although the vast majority of these works are decidedly undistinguished from a critical standpoint, and appear bombastic and frivolous to the contemporary eye, their initial success in speaking to a wide audience remains undeniable. The academic sculptors in the *Beaux-Arts* monumental tradition could assume that a large portion of the general public had mastered a certain vocabulary of allegorical imagery, and that this public also shared a set of ethical, spiritual, and political expectations that guaranteed similar responses to the same allegorically encoded message.

That ideal, esthetically conservative, audience has been a casualty of the twentieth century. The First World War can serve as an exemplary moment from which to date the dissolution of the ethical consensus that had insured broad agreement on the value of any maxim or precept communicated by public art. Abstraction, and the increasing sophistication of aesthetic strategies, has since cast in doubt the ability of art to communicate to the general public at all.

Yet without theoretical sanction or even the assurance of an audience, public art has, in the last two decades, returned to the American scene. The physi-cal size of Abstract Expressionist painting, the spatial presence of minimal sculpture, and the environmental sensibility of earth art all contributed to the demand for a new monumental art. Encouraged by the formidable example of David Smith's Cubi series, such sculptors as Tony Smith, Robert Morris, Ronald Bladen, and Mark di Suvero began to produce sculpture on a grand scale for display in parks, along city streets and on corporate plazas. Inspired by both utopian conceptions of the social role of the artist, and the growing awareness of America's unique cultural destiny, the sixties and the seventies witnessed an unprecedented proliferation of public art, much of it funded by federal, state, and local governments and intended for the appreciation of the man in the street.

Despite the visible success of modern art and artists in adorning the urban landscape with monumental abstract forms, the cultural mission of the public monument in contemporary society has nonetheless remained unresolved. The abstruse formal vocabulary of contemporary abstraction remained a forbidding barrier to those members of the public potentially receptive to public art. Less charitable critics have branded government support of public art a conspicuous waste of tax dollars, and loudly demanded an end to public funding and the removal of offensive works. But, even for those members of the public for whom abstract sculptures are not unintelligible, slightly menacing agglomerations of steel and bronze, the problem of the social function of public art remains unresolved. Obviously, a return to the merely commemorative function of the *Beaux-Arts* monument is unlikely in view of the diversity of the public's beliefs and attitudes, and probably undesirable. An alternative social role for the monument, however, has yet to present itself. Perhaps the public monument can appeal to more general civic values or spiritual aspirations shared by the majority of those who view it. Perhaps the abstract construction of metal or glass encountered in the streets of our cities performs its most socially profitable and personally rewarding function in reinvigorating perceptions and challenging expectations, rather than delivering patriotic rhetoric. In any event, the proponents of public sculpture have yet to mount a unified and theoretically convincing defense of the presence of public art that seems entirely persuasive to the man in the street, innocent of artistic values and not conversant with contemporary styles.

Compounding the problem are a number of aesthetic difficulties that the artist encounters when he enters the public arena. In the nineteenth century urban planners favored broad vistas and open plazas that provided natural, and often dramatic, locations for the heroic monument on a pedestal. Far from focussing attention on monumental art, the contemporary city raises such a cacophony of architectural voices and centers of activity clamorously competing for the attention of the passerby as to detract from even the most theatrical monument. The advent of the modern skyscraper has provided a further challenge, for no sculptor can expect his work to hold scale against such an overwhelming architectural backdrop. Too often the economics of construction and the indifference of architects induces planners and designers to consider public sculptures as little more than fancy, relatively interchangeable baubles, decorating pre-conceived spaces. Artists very rarely have the opportunity to cooperate with architects in the planning of a space that will include public art; often, public sculpture is designed without any specific relation to the site it will occupy.

In the eighties, it appears that public art will encounter only greater challenges, and more vociferous critics. A troubled economy and conservative retrenchment in government expenditures for the arts and humanities threaten to reverse or at least decelerate the trend of two decades towards continuing support of public art. Even some members of the art community have become pessimistic about the future of public art in America. Critics and historians have wondered whether an "elitist" art representing even a broad and diversified spectrum of vanguard tastes has any future in a democratic society, and some artists are doubtless troubled by the apparent contradiction in an avant-garde public monument: is the artist tweaking the nose of the bourgeoisie, or celebrating its cultural hegemony? Are the only alternatives a popularized, emasculated culture, and an elitist, unintelligible art for the mass public?

Since the mid-seventies, Segal has been providing his own answers to these dilemmas in sculptures that seem particularly appropriate to the arguments of the proponents and critics of public art. Segal's figural art is far more accessible than the work of abstract sculptors, and yet depends for its effect on the compositional, spatial and coloristic principles characteristic of the most non-objective of contemporary artworks. The subjects of many of his public sculptures have been investigated repeatedly in the course of his artistic development, and cannot be fully understood without some acquaintance with the formal and allusive interests that he has pursued throughout his career. Can such a private, introspective, and contemplative art survive the transition from the gallery to the street? Can outdoor works, deprived of the controlled space and light of the gallery, succeed aesthetically, at the level of the best indoor pieces, and connect with an untrained, often unsympathetic audience as well? *The Restaurant,* Segal's first venture into the public arena, is remarkable in the extent to which it answered these questions with a resounding affirmative.

The commission for *The Restaurant* had its origin in some opportune criticisms of the efforts of contemporary public sculptors: "I've liked some of the outdoor abstract sculptures I've seen, disliked many, many others," Segal once said. "I thought they were too large, too rhetorical, too pretentious, and tried to challenge the architecture without being that much more interesting in their own forms... I remember giving these criticisms and reservations to some people I knew in Washington who grinned at me. They called my bluff when they asked me to make a public, outdoor sculpture."[1] Segal's Washington acquaintances

91 **The Restaurant.** 1976. (Cat. 144)
Bronze, brick, cement, steel, aluminum, tempered glass and
fluorescent light, 120 × 192 × 96 in.
Federal Office Building, Buffalo.

91

were officials of the General Services Administration, the government body responsible for constructing and maintaining the thousands of federal buildings across the country, and one of the most generous federal patrons of the arts. In 1974 a panel appointed by the National Endowment for the Arts selected Segal to execute a major sculpture that would adorn the new Federal Building in Buffalo, New York, and, the following year, the artist was offered a contract.

Segal hesitated before laying his cards on the table: "I'm accustomed to keeping myself independent of the opinions of people who don't care about art... I have a... history of insisting on the privacy of my work... working independently and not to satisfy any public taste... I had all kinds of hesitations — reservations about what was public art... I didn't want to lose the intensity of personal experience and response. I thought a long time — almost turned it down until I could figure out how to make something big enough that I could walk into, that would be intense enough and personal enough so that I would feel comfortable with the statement."[2]

Despite his reservations, Segal accepted the contract and traveled to Buffalo to inspect the site — a broad plaza and pedestrian walkway at the main entrance to the Federal Building. But the artist was interested in more than the immediate surroundings of the sculpture: "Previously, I had only gone to the Albright-Knox to an 'opening' and seen that extravagant, highly selective display. I hadn't seen much of the town... I began to see the range of the city. I was walking back streets. It seemed to be a place where a lot of people lived in ordinary homes and the kind of life I'm super familiar with."[3] The streets and storefronts of Buffalo left a deep impression; Segal was determined that something of their character, spatial and spiritual, would be embodied in his sculpture: "What struck me about Buffalo, as it does about many Northeastern cities, is the severe, Puritan architecture. It's a tough life; it's a tough winter, and these people work hard. There's none of this tropical sunshine nonsense, palm trees and blue surf. Somehow the streets, the architecture, the way people dress, the way people look, the way they hold themselves reflect the inside and outside of their lives. I wanted the sculpture to have something to do with what I think is the inner life of someone who lives in Buffalo."[4]

The image he finally selected expresses the inner life of an artist as well as a city. The choice of a restaurant as the locale of the Buffalo tableau was inspired by the immediate landscape: there are dozens of one-story, store-front coffee shops and lunch counters in the neighborhood of the office building. There are also some half-dozen variations on the same theme in Segal's earlier sculpture. The restaurant and its customers are one of several motifs that Segal has obsessively explored: "I have certain themes I have ideas about that I find hard to exhaust in one sculpture," he says. "Instead of packing the sculpture to the point of unreadability — which is the same kind of delight and aggravation I have with Duchamp's work, and the kind of delight and aggravation I have with James Joyce — I always have to fight my own tendency to pile up one kind of complication on another. It's like a hunt for simplicity, clarity, and essence."[5]

The Diner (1966), The Bar (1971), and the three versions of The Restaurant Window (1967-1971) all depict the archetypal American scene encountered in The Restaurant. The second version of The Restaurant Window is, however, the work most closely related to the Buffalo Restaurant. In The Restaurant Window II, a woman sits at a table behind a large, double-paned plate glass window mounted in a rectangular façade of black wood. Her table is framed by the left pane of glass. From the right a man walks past the fluted false columns of the façade, which emphasize, in their funereal severity, the psychological distance between the illuminated interior and the implied sidewalk outside. The figures are seen in rigid profile. Their eyes define parallel rays, directed right and left, that pass without a flicker of acknowledgement.

The Restaurant adds to this scene a third figure — a young girl, leaning against the left side of the façade. The plate glass is now divided into three panes by an additional mullion, the store front is reproduced in steel and cinderblock faced with brick, and the fig-

92 **The Diner.** 1964-1966. (Cat. 47)
Plaster, wood, metal, Formica, Masonite and fluorescent
light, 102 × 108 × 87 in.
Walker Art Center, Minneapolis.
(Note: The relationship of the two figures has been
changed from the original.)

93 **The Bar.** 1971. (Cat. 113)
Plaster, wood, metal, glass, plastic, neon light and television,
96 × 102 × 36 in.
Collection Martin Z. Margulies, Grove Isle, Florida.

92

93

ures are cast, of course, in bronze, with a pale-green Statue of Liberty patina. Some of these changes were influenced, if not dictated, by *Restaurant*'s outdoor, architectural setting. Segal was not interested in relating the scale of his work to the size of the building: "I... turned the conception upside down, the conception of most public monuments. Many sculptors want to rival the architecture — make forms that are almost as big as the building. So much the better, I think. I consciously turned my back on rivaling the building."[6] Rather than attempting hopelessly to hold scale against the federal building, Segal's work stands independently, relating to the scale of its own stage-set façade and to the physical dimensions of passersby — his unique solution to a perennial problem of figural monuments. But *The Restaurant* does not ignore its imposing architectural backdrop: "I'd seen the façade of the building, which is a serial grid," remembers Segal. "I wanted the sculpture to echo that kind of vertical repetition." The integration of building and sculpture is coloristic as well as formal: the green of the figures rhymes with the dark tinted glass of the windows in the office building, while the severe black steel framing the restaurant oxymoronically opposes the building's white marble facing.

The Restaurant's variations on the theme of *Restaurant Window II* also redouble and deepen the implicit psychological drama: "The thickness of a pane of glass is deceptively transparent," Segal says. "You can see through it, but it is like a ton of lead separating worlds. So the guy outside — walking outside on the street — is missing making contact with the girl inside. Like they're self-absorbed, looking in different directions, and the transparent window, where they could easily have turned their heads and glanced and locked glances — they're not, it's not happening. Then the girl leaning against the brick column — well, we don't know if she's going to connect with the guy or not, but she's a teenager. The guy is middle-aged and the girl inside is thirtyish. The ages were important to me."[7]

Beyond these suggestions, Segal is reluctant to specify the details of the confrontation between the figures: "I like to let people invent their own stories," he says. One can be certain, however, that the spa-

94

95

tial composition of a Segal work is never merely a formal exercise. When Segal's foundrymen were casting *Restaurant,* he asked them to delay welding the anchors on the bottom of the figures' feet. The casts arrived unattached, and Segal spent an afternoon standing them up and trying one position after another until he found the configuration he wanted: "I can start with an idea in my head," he says, "but then the physical reality of my encounter with all the objects forces me to jiggle them around. Any move I make, where I place something, where a weight is, where an empty void is, has to be psychologically felt."[8]

The voids and distances between figures and environment in *The Restaurant* are many; Segal has purposely arranged the piece so that new configurations, new connections and disjunctions, will be constantly revealed to the ambling eye. This technique of figural sculpture composition has few precedents in art history. In *The Burghers of Calais,* Rodin began to explore the possibilities in a looser, more de-centered composition than his academic predecessors had tolerated, and one lacking the conventional plinth separating sculpture and public. Half a century later, Giacometti mounted his lonely, dematerialized figures on stark bases which, in their severely geometric style and environmental control, anticipate the compositions of Segal's public sculptures. But Segal stands alone in contemporary art for his combination of these essentially abstract principles of composition with the sympathetic and psychologically revealing depiction of the human figure.

The spatial deployment of figure and environment in *The Restaurant* is heavily indebted to Segal's experience as a painter. The perimeter of the window, and the façade as a whole, resemble concentric picture frames, while the frontality of the composition and the positioning of figures along horizontal and vertical axes strongly suggest the two-dimensional canvas surface. To be sure, the real depth of the sculpture allows the composition to change with the spectator's perspective. Yet the formal and psychological focus of the composition — the void created by the middle window, which divides the man from the women, and sends each spinning off on his own trajectory — far from representing the window on the

96

97

world of illusionistic space, dramatically manifests the flatness of the picture plane.

Of course, the media employed in *The Restaurant* was somewhat more substantial than pigment and canvas. The Buffalo sculpture was Segal's first encounter with bronze, and the unique qualities of this metal, and of the other durable materials required by his federal patrons, made a deep impression on him. "I have to admit," he says, "when I first got the commission I was laughing at what I thought was the conceit and folly of the government's insistence on eternity... Next, I got lost in the beauty of those materials. I had my own pleasure in looking at the bronze and the brick and sensing their weight..." As Segal contemplated his media, his plans for the sculpture gradually changed. "I think the piece got increasingly so-

ber... I wanted it to look like an Egyptian Rite of Passage, as if this sculpture had been extracted from a passage in the labyrinth of an Egyptian pyramid. I wanted it to feel that way but look like an ordinary American restaurant."[9]

For its part, the GSA, aside from its insistence on permanence, was relatively unintrusive. Testifying before a Senate sub-committee three years after executing *Restaurant,* Segal remembered that he was "astounded about their enlightened stance" and willingness to "respect the particular judgment and free-thinking of the artist."[10] Unfortunately, not everyone in the GSA seems to have respected Segal's tableau: after commissioning and paying for the work, the agency decided not to dedicate it and forbade its employees to attend the alternative dedication ceremony organized by the Albright-Knox Art Gallery. High officials in the GSA complained, improbably, that the work was "pornographic," although controversy surrounding other agency commissions might also explain their unwillingness to acknowledge their commissioned work, which Segal found annoying and cowardly.

Apart from the reservations of a few misguided federal bureaucrats, however, Restaurant was a popular and critical success. Buffalo newspapers wrote favorably of the sculpture, and one local critic said that it "points up the infinite importance of public artworks that touch the human spirit."[11] Segal would not be put off by the rhetoric of that phrase; his work has always aspired, without irony, to spiritual significance and universal meaning. On the other hand, he is as conscious as any artist of the dangers of having his work dismissed as unintelligible or, in a glance that appears sympathetic, but is little better than a philistine rejection, facilely accepted and only superficially understood. Since his work is figurative and looks "easy," it is more subject than most contemporary sculpture to the latter peril: his tableaux have appeared everywhere from advertising campaigns to the covers of trade magazines, usually in hackneyed reference to the alienation, isolation, and despondency of modern life. But the artist is willing to confront the challenge of embodying more sophisticated content in a form that will remain meaningful to the general public.

"The nature of the art has changed," Segal says. "When I was a student, I grew up with an intense, personal, private art — all in a private club or a couple of restaurants, shut away from the world. Nobody was paying for it, it was intense, and it belonged only to an elite. Now the question is, can you maintain your eliteness, the density of your subject matter, a high level of thinking, multiple levels in the work, and still be accessible to a lot of people?"

Segal would not hesitate to answer that question. But accessibility must not be incompatible with intensely personal meanings: "The pieces I do are about my inner state, about myself ruminating, dreaming, thinking... I work for myself, my own standards, and if I can touch upon my own feelings, then somehow I

am connected to everyone... Public art should be a personal experience."[12] Perhaps the ability of many of Segal's works to communicate serious and sophisticated intent to a wide audience can be explained by his sympathy with that audience, with common people's emotions, attitudes, and aspirations. As Segal once said in explanation of the evocative power of The Restaurant, "The look of Buffalo and the look of my own mental interior are very close."[13] The success of that work suggests one solution to the problem of accessibility: when sophisticated formal devices are employed with the object of emphasizing a psychological encounter in a realistic environment, the audience for avant-garde art may be as large as mainstreet.

Segal cast his second public sculpture, Girl Standing in Nature, a few months after completing The Restaurant. Nothing could be better proof of the variety of his aims and attitudes than the differences between the two. The Restaurant, very much a reflection of its urban environment, is extroverted, assertive, and compositionally complex; the Girl, a naiad of the woods, is introspective, retiring, and private. The Restaurant brings its environment with it; the Girl depends on the surrounding curtain of rocks and trees, and the imagination of the spectator for its narrative, spatial, and psychological contexts. Segal's success in both works is a testament to the continual novelty and invention in a body of work that may appear repetitive to the superficial glance or the unsympathetic eye.

The beauty of the solitary female nude is, of course, one of Segal's continuing preoccupations. Yet the majority of his early nudes are self-absorbed, engaged in the familiar round of domestic activities and motions. Girl Standing in Nature is on her own in a wilderness, unprotected by the rituals of domesticity, and all the more vulnerable for it. The prototype for Girl, a studio piece entitled The Rock, was cast in plaster in 1974. The massive boulder that overhangs the slightly sullen nude in that work was cast from a latex rubber mold of a natural rock formation the artist found outside Jerusalem.

The outdoor sculpture shares with The Rock similarities of mood and attitude, but in its treatment of

99 **The Rock.** 1974. (Cat. 135)
Plaster, 114 × 120 × 36 in.
Courtesy Sidney Janis Gallery, New York.

99

in Nature in reaction to giant overscale abstractions in front of giant overscale corporate headquarters, where one is as impersonal as the other." Segal believes that his work expresses something else: "*Girl Standing in Nature* shrinks from public display. She's shy, trembling, on the edge of motion, in a hidden glade in front of a massive chunk of rock. Intensity of private encounter can be public, I think."[15]

Although he once admitted to being intimidated by the thought of working in metal, Segal has taken enthusiastically to bronze and, since *The Restaurant*, has methodically explored the possibilities inherent in the new medium. From the technical standpoint, the move to bronze was a logical step after Segal's adoption, in the late sixties, of the inside casting process, which produces the finished plaster figure from the inner surface of the cast Segal makes of his model. Still, he needs the help of skilled foundry workers to convert a completed plaster cast into a finished bronze. Segal casts first a hydrostone figure himself, from the inside of his plaster cast. The work is then taken to a foundry, where craftsmen pull a precise rubber mold from the original hydrostone. The rest of the procedure is essentially no different from the lost-wax casting process familiar to the ancient Romans. A positive is cast in wax from the inside of the rubber mold. The positive is filled with a core of refractory material, and another refractory layer is molded around it. The wax is then melted, leaving a cavity between the refractories into which molten metal is poured. When the metal hardens, the external refractory and the core are removed. Segal has worked with a number of foundries in the course of refining his use of the lost-wax technique; he is now considering casting in metals other than bronze.

The first outdoor sculptures, however, presented Segal with the challenge of mastering both a new technique and the politics of presenting artworks outside the sheltered gallery system. Segal remembers that neither hurdle was easily overcome: "Everything was completely brand new to me. Usually, after I finish making a plaster figure and the environment, I'm all done. It's simple. Now when I first started doing the outdoor pieces, I had to deal with committees, with architects, with grounds managers. And every-

space and color, it is clearly superior to the earlier work. The *Girl's* dull green patina emphasizes the organic continuity between the nude and her surroundings of rock and foliage. She stands on her own feet, alone in an outdoor space, with no pedestal to set her apart from her environment. Yet, through his masterful placement, Segal has succeeded in harmonizing the figure's gesture and stance with the hang and pitch of the surrounding boulders; rather than abandoning his sculpture to nature, he has transfigured a natural environment into art space, or, as the artist puts it, "a magic place."[14]

Girl was first shown as part of a bicentennial group exhibition of outdoor sculpture sponsored by the Greenwich Arts Council. With perhaps a sidelong glance at the monumental abstract sculptures submitted by other participants in the exhibition, Segal recalls: "I was being perverse. I made *Girl Standing*

one, in his own area, is king or boss. Much more complicated. So I had to decide — could I handle those complications? But I've been lucky — I've found good craftsmen and foundries. You've got to find a craftsman who is selfless; he has to be devoted to exactly duplicating my marks, and taking pride in that. I'm still a baby at it. I need their skills.''

If bronze provided new challenges, it also brought with it new possibilities, far different from the options available in the white plaster of indoor works. ''The pressure on me is to go from ersatz, salvaged junk to the most permanent material,'' Segal says. ''And the problems change, the expressive radiations change. Look, when you have a bronze figure next to a real, squat, heavy brick column, it says something totally different from a plaster environment. It's interesting to watch what happens. I like it because it's unknown territory.'' Although he has never thought of giving up plaster, Segal is strongly attracted to the new medium: ''Bronze is incredible — it's got its own characteristics. It has a color that comes from a very thick, dense, implacable, relentless metal. It looks like itself, and I respect it. I'm just trying to figure out how to use its nature to express the things I'm trying to say — how to dance with it, instead of mastering it.'' In 1979, Segal cast a black bronze, and, the following year, he made two casts of *Girl Standing in Nature* finished with a white chemical patina, which has become a favorite for outdoor works. ''It's totally unlike plaster,'' says Segal. ''There's a sense of the bronze underneath.''

After the *Girl,* Segal executed no outdoor commissions for several years. But when he returned to public art in 1979, he quickly attracted more popular attention, and more controversy, than he had enjoyed in two decades as a sculptor. Both *Kent State: Abraham and Isaac* and *Gay Liberation* are monuments in the traditional sense: the first commemorates an historic event; the second, the struggle for recognition of a persecuted minority. Furthermore, both works clearly succeeded in communicating their commemorative intention to the public, largely because of their figural realism. But this does not mean that *Gay Liberation* or *Abraham and Isaac* resolved all the dilemmas of the contemporary monument. In each

case, when a work was debated in a public forum, discussion inevitably ignored its value as an art object, and concentrated instead on the merits of the issues it memorializes; Helen Segal remembers that more than nine-tenths of the letters she received discussing *Kent State* and *Gay Liberation* did not even mention the artworks, but proceeded to debate the issues of homosexuality and campus unrest. Undeniably, the power of Segal's works was reflected in the urgency with which observors felt called upon to defend their views. Nonetheless, these monuments too often had no more effect on their viewers than to remind them of a topic about which they already held strong, and often very different, beliefs — a phenomenon that has less to do with any peculiar quality of Segal's work than with the typical disregard of allegory for the fine points of its vehicle.

In early September, 1978, officials of Kent State University announced that Segal's sculpture, commemorating the killing of four university students on May 4, 1970, by National Guardsmen, was unacceptable for exhibition on the campus. It had been eight years since the students had been shot to death in an antiwar demonstration that had gained national prominence and symbolic value for propagandists of the left and right. But eight years was not long enough. In a statement explaining why the university was rejecting the gift of the Cleveland-based Mildred Andrews Fund, which had commissioned the work, Robert McCoy, the executive assistant to the president, said, ''An act of violence about to be committed is inappropriate to commemorate an act of violence.'' He added, ''We were afraid it would upset the delicate balance we have here now at the university. We simply could not afford this type of art — even if someone was giving it to us.''[16]

Segal was shocked, and for a variety of reasons. Only months before, the university had agreed to accept the work, if Segal would etch on its base the fourteen lines from Gènesis explaining that the father spares the son. Apparently reneging on this proposal, the university then rejected the work completely, and suggested that Segal instead depict a young, nude woman employing her feminine wiles to entice a soldier to put down his gun and leave the battlefield.

100 **In Memory of May 4, 1970: Kent State - Abraham and Isaac.**
1978. (Cat. 157)
Bronze, 84 × 120 × 50 in.
John B. Putnam, Jr. Memorial Collection, Princeton University.

101 **In Memory of May 4, 1970: Kent State - Abraham and Isaac.**
1978. (Cat. 158)
Plaster, rope and metal, 84 × 120 × 50 in.
Collection of the artist.

100

101

"She could be nude or seminude to suggest innocence and perhaps vulnerability," [17] McCoy proposed.

But most disturbing to the artist was the unwillingness of the university's administration to discuss, or understand, the ethical and aesthetic positions actually represented in the work, and in the parable of a man whose faith is tested by his readiness to sacrifice his own son. "Everyone that spoke to me about the Kent State piece was talking about politics, either radical right or radical left politics," Segal said. "What I think was missing was more of a sense of ethics, of moral values. A father does have life or death power over his son. Doesn't a father have to stop and think about declaring war and sending his son out to be killed? I don't think I was presuming to answer the problem. I was raising the question."

Understandably unsympathetic to Kent State's alternative proposal, Segal refused to alter his work. "The people in power there seem to be extremely right-wing," he observed. "They were still furious at the radical-hippie disregard for patriotism. Those people were behaving as if the Vietnam War hadn't ended, as if Nixon and Agnew had never been chastised for Watergate and everything else. I was apparently interfering with the real exercise of power on the campus. Why I was considered a threat, I don't know... I refused to modify my work to make it acceptable to their standards, because I don't believe in them." [18]

Although Segal received support from many quarters, including the faculty and student body, the university stood firm and the Mildred Andrews Fund withdrew its gift, which was eventually transferred to Princeton University. When the work was finally dedicated at Princeton, on October 5, 1979, six of the students wounded in the Kent State shootings, and the parents of three of the four who were killed, were present. Fred Licht, the director of the University Art Museum, said that the work represented a return to "the monumental origins of sculpture, the possibility it gives us to express our culture and our society. We have a good deal of first-rate twentieth century sculpture on our campus, but none has a specific relationship to the crises that contemporary students and contemporary teachers have lived with. This

sculpture has a living presence that goes beyond the appeal of our other works and has a direct meaning which can hold the attention of all our students, even those who are not interested in art as such." [19]

Segal chose a site on the Princeton campus between the library and the university chapel — a location appealing to him for its symbolic juxtaposition of historical knowledge with religious and ethical values. He now admits that he would prefer to display the work in a more open area, with more sunlight. In any event, the strong horizontal and vertical human geometry of Abraham and Isaac succeeds in its present location in echoing the severe verticality of the chapel without attempting to compete with it. The figure group, almost oppressive in its sable finish, reveals an expressive, controlled energy reminiscent of Rodin, and compares favorably with Segal's earlier forays into social and political commentary, like his 1967 plaster tableau, The Execution.

Reflecting on Kent State, Segal once said: "I found that sculpture interesting to do because I could deal with a literary metaphor. I could deal with poetry. I could deal with very complex layers of interpretation of what seemed a loud, blunt, clear political event that I thought was far more complicated than it appeared on the surface." [20] A complex monument commemorating a complex event, Kent State is the embodiment of a number of Segal's deepest preoccupations. It is a reflection of his longstanding appreciation of literary and Biblical allusion. It is the direct thematic descendant of his 1973 plaster tableau Abraham's Sacrifice of Isaac, which was inspired by Segal's introduction to the extremes and contradictions of life in an embattled Israel. It is a manifestation of the artist's unshakeable conviction that spirit must be revealed through the body. Finally, it is an attempt to memorialize past events for future reference — to "help us to connect our history lessons," as Segal would say — that does not openly declare itself for one interpretation of that event over another.

Segal is well aware of the difficulty of the role assumed by the engagé artist. Reflecting on his work of the sixties, he once said: "There I was in a tribal society, fighting like hell to keep my independence. Yet everything is all tangled together. Everybody's got

102 **Abraham's Sacrifice of Isaac.** 1973. (Cat. 128)
Plaster, 7 × 9 × 8½ in.
Donated by Tel Aviv Foundation for Literature and Art to the
city of Tel Aviv-Yato.

102

this responsibility for society. Is there a value or a place for free play of the mind in art? How useful do you want to be? Or are you useful letting your minds and hands go? It's not settled yet."[21] In *Kent State,* Segal offered a provisional answer: by remaining sensitive to the ambiguities and ambivalence of an historical event, he created a work that captures the human dimension of a politically charged situation, without sacrificing the artist's independence to any political orthodoxy. The unattractiveness of this solution to extremists of any stripe suggests one of the greatest obstacles to a contemporary public art: our society lacks the ethical and political consensus that would guarantee *any* treatment of the incident at Kent State a favorable reception.

For all the controversy surrounding it, *Kent State* has finally found a calm and relatively sympathetic home in Princeton; the story of *Gay Liberation* has thus far no such happy ending. In 1979, Segal was asked by Peter Putnam, the administrator of the Mildred Andrews Fund, if he would be interested in executing a sculpture honoring the gay-rights movement. According to Bruce Voeller, the founder of the Mariposa Foundation, which originated the idea for the work and acted as Putnam's agent, the commission specified only that the work "had to be loving and caring, and show the affection that is the hallmark of gay people — it couldn't be ambiguous about that... And it had to have equal representation of men and women."[22]

At first Segal was reluctant to accept the project. "I'm an unregenerate heterosexual," he said, "and my first reaction was that a gay artist should do it. But I've lived in the art world for many years and I'm extremely sympathetic to the problems that gay people have. They're human beings first. I couldn't refuse to do it."[23] Following his usual procedure, Segal toured the Greenwich Village site with his wife; after viewing the proposed location at Christopher Park in Sheridan Square, he was determined to approach the subject in a manner appropriate for a neighborhood where he saw "young mothers pushing strollers." Segal has lyrically and passionately celebrated the theme of physical love throughout his career. *Gay Liberation* is the logical successor to such works as

Lovers in Bed (1962), and *The Girl Friends* (1969), which depicts lesbian lovers in an understated demonstration of affection. The public location of *Gay Liberation* would not permit Segal the frank celebration of sexuality and eroticism typifying many of his gallery works. Instead, he depicted two couples, one male, one female, each absorbed in a gentle, affectionate exchange that loses nothing in emotion or sensuality for all its restraint. The men are standing, one resting his hand on his partner's shoulder. The women are seated on a park bench; one tentatively holds a finger to her mouth, while the other rests a hand on her knee. Segal said: "The sculpture concentrates on tenderness, gentleness and sensitivity as expressed in gesture. It makes the delicate point that gay people are as feeling as anyone else."[24]

But *Gay Liberation* is not only a sensitive and perceptive social statement; it is a masterful composition in space. The two park benches in the work barely adumbrate an environmental setting, yet provide a strong horizontal that the figure groups accent like grace notes. Both couples contain strong diagonal rhythms, which balance each other and play off the intersections in the black steel of the park bench. Finally, the bench invites the spectator to join the scene, at once adapting the sculpture to its environment and domesticating a potentially threatening subject — as one observer commented, Segal's piece is a "trompe-le-derrière."[25]

Although the work was offered as a gift to the city, it required the approval of a gauntlet of city organizations and community groups. Despite the endorsement of Greenwich Village political leaders, including Representatives Theodore Weiss and Bella Abzug, the Village Independent Democrats, and the city's Director of Historic Parks, as well as the editorial support of the *Voice, Gay Liberation* encountered vocal opposition at three separate public meetings in the summer and fall of 1980. Debate at the meetings, from which Segal was absent, was theatrical and bitter. At one hearing, Vera Schneider, a leader of "The Friends of Christopher Park," produced a list of 546 signatures, some of which were called fraudulent by her critics,

103 **Lovers on a Bed I.** 1962. (Cat. 13)
Plaster, wood, metal, mattress and cloth, 48 × 54 × 70 in.
Collection Mrs. Robert B. Mayer, Chicago.

104 **The Girl Friends.** 1969. (Cat. 85)
Plaster, 41 × 72 × 42 in.
Sidney Janis Gallery, New York.

105 **Gay Liberation.** 1980. (Cat. 165)
Plaster and metal, 71 × 192 × 80 in.
The Museum of Modern Art, Seibu Takanawa, Karuizawa, Japan.

103

104

opposing Segal's work. At the next hearing, Voeller unrolled a pink scroll bearing 3,438 names of individuals in favour of the sculpture. Robert Rygor, a gay politician, complained that the figures were "cruising clones" and "grotesque stereotypes." The men and women who had posed for the statue, understandably upset at Rygor's words, returned to the next meeting and assumed their poses on stage in sweat shirts bearing the inscription, "Grotesque Stereotype."[26]

Critics of the proposed monument divided into two camps. Community members like Schneider complained that the sculpture was too big for the park, that it was "wildly inappropriate to the architecture of the neighborhood," and that it would attract an influx of crowds and tour buses, threatening to "ghettoize" the district.[27] Some objectors spoke openly of the undesirability of a monument honoring what they considered an ethically repugnant practice. On the other hand, a number of gays also opposed the monument, which gained a particular importance in their eyes from its placement near the Stonewall Inn, the site of the 1969 riots against police harassment, which many consider the symbolic advent of the gay rights movement. For Voeller, this was an argument in favor of accepting the statue:

"The blacks have their Selma, the Jews their wailing wall, the Arabs their Mecca or Medina," he said. "For millions and millions of gay people throughout the world Christopher Park on Christopher Street opposite the Stonewall Inn is the logical place to put a sculpture commemorating the contributions and lives of gay people."[28]

Not everyone agreed. Some gays protested that the sculptor ought to have been a homosexual selected by the gay community, and that the work was not properly representative of the diversity of homosexuals. Voeller replied that Segal had only been considered after gay artists of comparable stature had been approached, and that any public consultation on the subject matter or choice of a sculptor would have ended in a hopeless, and divisive, deadlock. As for the latter objection, one critic observed that the representative approach to subject matter would result in "a sculpture requiring 8,763 separate figures in order to scrupulously reflect all our statistical elements, right down to a single black lesbian grandmother in a wheelchair."[29]

Although *Gay Liberation* has passed reviews by the Fine Arts Commission, Community Board Two, and the Landmarks Commission, the city has never allocated the funding to install the work and provide

additional landscape architecture for the park — a rider that was added in a compromise with the work's critics. Putnam's fund sponsored a second bronze for a public site in Los Angeles, but *Gay Liberation* met much the same fate in California as it had in Greenwich Village. The local government has refused to accept the work on public land; and Putnam has insisted that it be installed nowhere else.

Today both bronzes remain in Segal's studio, the issues they addressed still unresolved. Despite the noisy and generally irrelevant objections of a few detractors, it seems clear that a majority of the parties to the dispute over *Gay Liberation* — including over one hundred leaders in the gay community who endorsed the work — approved of the sculpture and wished to see it in Christopher Square.[30] Although much of the debate in the community meetings concerned the aesthetic virtues, or alleged faults, of the piece, the inability of the disputants to agree on any quality of the sculpture suggests both that emotional reactions to the subject matter, and not the art, determined the response of many, and that such public hearings may not provide the best forum for considering the merits of works of art. In *Gay Liberation,* Segal had once again found a subject that revealed the divisiveness of our society, and not its common sense of purpose. But the controversy surrounding the work demonstrates a more fundamental limitation in the audience for the contemporary commemorative monument. Rather than identifying themselves with the representative individuals depicted in the sculpture, critics of *Gay Liberation* dwelt on their differences, as if to suggest that monuments can only recognize one group, or celebrate its successes, at the expense of another. Few people seemed willing to cede Christopher Square to a ''special interest.'' Fewer still were ready to admit their share in a universal debt to the achievements of such special interests and unique individuals.

In the same year that he executed the bronze version of *Gay Liberation* and consigned it to the depths of his studio, Segal embarked on another public sculpture in Youngstown. In welcome contrast to his experience in Greenwich Village, Segal's second Ohio project provided abundant evidence that public sculpture can still play its old role as a rallying point for civic pride, and elicit a sincere and idealistic communal response.

In 1977, the Youngstown Area Arts Council offered Segal a commission for executing a sculpture for the new Federal Plaza pedestrian mall. The site was forbidding. Located in a rather dilapidated section of town, the mall was framed by heavily traveled roads, an unattractive, over-sized kiosk, and a motley of façades and marquees. The Council hoped that a new public sculpture would help revitalize the neighborhood, and Segal responded enthusiastically. Arriving in Youngstown a week after he received the council's invitation, he began, as usual, by walking the streets, immersing himself in the life of the city. Segal was particularly struck by the steel mills, the heart of Youngstown's economy, and, after some deliberation, he decided upon the theme of steelworkers tending an open hearth furnace.

The Arts Council had originally received a grant from the National Endowment for the Arts in support of the commission, but the council's efforts to raise matching funds in the community were threatened by a dramatic turn of economic events. In 1978, Youngstown Sheet and Tube closed its Campbell Works mill, and five thousand steelworkers lost their jobs. In the following months, U. S. Steel's Ohio works, the McDonald rolling mill, and the Brier Hill mill all shut down; five thousand more employees were on the unemployment rolls. An attempt by a coalition of workers to purchase and run one of the defunct mills failed, and the only thing less promising than Youngstown's economic future was the prospect of financing a public sculpture.

Miraculously, funds began to pour in. Segal's work had been adopted as an emblem of civic pride, and donations from banks, local businesses and foundations followed. But when Segal announced the subject of *The Steelmakers,* contributions began to appear from completely unexpected sources. In what must be one of the few instances of true grassroots support of avant-garde art, the Building Trades Union pledged in-kind assistance in fabricating and installing the sculpture. ''The unions lent credence to the project,'' said the Arts Council official who organized

106 **The Steelmakers.** 1980. (Cat. 166)
Plaster, wood, plastic and metal, 120 × 120 × 60 in.
Courtesy Sidney Janis Gallery, New York.

107 **The Steelmakers.** 1980. (Cat. 167)
Bronze, painted plastic and steel, 216 × 240 × 180 in.
Commission Youngstown Area Arts Council, Youngstown, Ohio.

107

the fund drive. "People who felt kindly about the mills began to give, including those who had family in the steel industry."[31] The Jones and Laughlin Steel Corporation donated an open hearth furnace from its idle Brier Hill mill; local arts groups sponsored parties, auctions, and art sales to benefit the sculpture. Despite, or, perhaps, because of, the city's economic crisis, the project prospered.

Segal was delighted with the gift of the furnace — "a twenty-foot section, like the tomb of Mohammed — a giant black box," as the artist described it. He was determined to recreate faithfully the experience of the men in the mills: "It had to be real — nothing fake. The motion, the position, the feeling, all had to be right."[32] He wanted to depict two men testing the carbon content of the steel in the furnace; but he was concerned about finding the right models. No one who had not labored in the mills could satisfy Segal's desire to portray "how you hold yourself after years of facing a certain set of problems."[33] Accordingly, he packed his plaster and bandages and set up a makeshift studio in a classroom at Youngstown State University. The choice of models was left to the union, and Segal was delighted with their selections: "They couldn't have chosen better — a black man and a white man, one younger, one older."[34] Segal cast them in work helmets, goggles, and gloves, and returned to New Jersey to assemble the plaster sections.

The final appearance of *The Steelmakers* was the result of a good deal of improvisation. Segal originally had the figures cast in an amber-colored patina. He had planned to paint the furnace flat black and apply a turquoise patina to the workers, but he was so struck by the appearance of the huge, rusting cast iron furnace — "enough to make Richard Serra weep with envy" — that he decided to leave it untouched. When the furnace was moved to the pedestrian mall, Segal once again revised his plans. The furnace was no longer overpowering in the company of the nearby buildings, streets, and storefronts. Its character had somehow changed, and Segal decided to eliminate the fire brick that normally encases a blast furnace in operation. The effect was to exchange the monolithic bulk of the enclosed furnace for a lighter,

airier structure, punctured by gaps that allow the viewer to see through to the sculpture's environment. The bared metal reveals a baroque polyphony of masses and voids, gears, wheels and chains that recall the dense fabric of Piranesi's dream prisons. The figures, standing on the sidewalk pavement, provide an index of human scale that preserves much of the overwhelming power of the massive furnace, without forcing it to compete with the surrounding buildings.

After the figures had been mounted in concrete, Segal made a further, unprecedented modification. For the first time since he began casting in metal, he decided to work the surface of the figures directly, with torch and chemicals. Stroking the patina with the torch, altering colors and scumbling the surface, he achieved seductive coloristic effects betraying the process of their fabrication that evince his continuing infatuation with abstract expressionist brushwork.[35] As a final coloristic flourish that at once brought a charge of contemporary life and the downtown street into the classical medium of bronze, Segal painted the workers' helmets with a bright, industrial orange enamel, which harmonized effectively with the deep, burnt-orange tones of the rusting hearth.

The Steelmakers is not Segal's first depiction of men at work: in 1966, he cast a figure painting a billboard amid the ropes and pulleys of a scaffold; and *The Billboard* was soon followed by *Man on a Scaffold* (1970), *Man on a Ladder* (1970), and *Man on a Printing Press* (1971). Yet *The Steelmakers* clearly has a different character from all these earlier variations on the theme of labor, and what sets it apart, aside from obvious differences of scale and medium, is the unique quality of Youngstown's streets and storefronts, embodied in the stance of the workers and the configuration of their environment.

The architecture of downtown Youngstown fascinates Segal: "Like New Brunswick, it looks sort of seedy and run down. But take a look at the second stories: there are arches, ceramic details... The city was modernized in the 1920's, and in 1940, and then again in 1960, so the whole thing has got a collage layer of architectural styles, and the styles vary within themselves. I think the mainstreet is beautiful, and no one has tuned in to its collage surface, and its time

109

110

sense. It gets pretty exciting when you start dealing with a street that has its own life. When you put the furnace — a pile of incredibly massive chains and steel girders and doors — against Neoclassical architecture and 1940's signs, you get a whole, varied play of three-dimensional elements. So the sculpture becomes part of the whole composition.''

Of course, *The Steelmakers* is more than a composition. It is an unidealized celebration of labor, an evocation of working-class experience that unquestionably entitles Segal to the suggestive epithet coined by Martin Friedman of the Walker Art Center, ''proletarian mythmaker.'' Unlike the grandiose portrayals of social realism, *The Steelmakers* remains at the level of individual experience, conveying the drudgery, the drama and nobility of work in the mills. The muscles of the union men in the tableau had been educated by twenty years of routine strain and stance. Creating a monument to them, Segal drew on both his own first-hand acquaintance with heavy labor, and the imaginative identification with the factory workers that he expressed in his account of his first trip to the mills: ''The open hearth scenes were spectacular — gloomy darkness, hissing steam and smoke, urgent foghorns, giant trucks, cranes, railway cars moving fluidly in different directions — the awesome pour, light you can't look into, heat, sparks hugely bigger than we are, and dangerous unless you move exactly right. This reality is more fantastic than the most fevered imaginings. I thought we were all Jacks who had climbed the beanstalk and magically learned how to move all the pots in the giant's direction — then watching the slow deliberation of tiny men

113

effortlessly moving a control hand to send an immense surrogate for a male genital ramming a potent load into a fury ravenous female furnace, the whole process splashing fire and molten slag. No wonder these men love it. They spend their lives re-enacting some profound mystic ritual..."[36]

Art critics and the popular press joined in their acclaim for *The Steelmakers,* and Segal was understandably elated: "It's real. Steelworkers stop to look at it, and they say. 'You got to watch out, because that door blows off when it gets too hot.' Privately, I was knocked out by the fact that these steel members look like classical ruins translated to modern rust. I'm doing my private thing and the town loves it, and it's full of macho strength and it's romantic and oh, boy, terrific, a great success, no scandals."[37]

It is not easy to say what accounted for the very different receptions accorded the Youngstown work and the earlier public sculptures. In part, the Youngstown success was the result of circumstances that had little to do with the sculpture. The support of the union, for example, may have been responsible for legitimizing the artwork in the eyes of the working people of Youngstown, but it was scarcely the result of a critical evaluation of the work's aesthetic merits. Of course, the sculpture benefited enormously from presenting a recognizable image, and thereby stirring emotional associations in a way no abstract image could. The theme of the work was well chosen, and the resurgence of local pride under economic pressure did nothing to lessen its appeal. Yet the sculpture's strength as a symbol finally depended on its emotional resonance and the power with which it presented a familiar scene, intensified through masterful composition and a command of the formal vocabulary of abstract art.

When a sculptor moves from the studio to the street, he inevitably loses a certain amount of control over the spatial composition of a work; the aesthetic success of *The Steelmakers* is all the more remarkable for its placement on a busy urban thoroughfare. Artists have traditionally tried to overcome the challenge of outdoor public sites by sculpting on a monumental scale, so that their work might define a space

111

in relation to the streets, buildings, and plazas surrounding it. Yet today, only the most massive outdoor sculptures can hope to hold scale against the skyscrapers and endless concrete vistas of the modern city. The problem is particularly urgent for Segal, whose casting process produces only life-size sculpture. "I'm told there's a very simple method — a pointing machine invented in the Renaissance — with which I can make my figures any height I want," says Segal. "So far, I've resisted that. I don't want to lose the intimacy. I don't want to be 'heroic' — no Mussolini modern. In the twentieth century, we've been clobbered so much with totalitarian dictators that I'm skittish about that grandiosity — we've all been burned." Segal is concerned that his work remain democratic and approachable: "Most sculpture is up on a pedestal in a psychologically different space. I am determined to have it inhabit ordinary space, to let people in, around, and among the objects."[38]

That determination, however, leaves him no choice but to create sculpture on a human scale and install it at the level of the street, with all the spatial and compositional problems that decision entails. Sometimes he has addressed this problem by placing works like *Girl in Nature* or *Kent State: Abraham and Isaac* in smaller, sheltering spaces; sometimes a work like the Buffalo *Restaurant* will bring its environment with it. But in his most successful sculptures, Segal has not so much solved the problems of space and scale as changed the terms of the problem.

As was the case in Youngstown, Segal is seldom given the chance to choose a site or even consult with architects and groundskeepers in designing the location for a sculpture. With his usual resourcefulness, Segal has turned this liability to his advantage. "If I work with a project, I'm really at the mercy of how good the architect is," he says. "I'm really better off if it's the work of the collective unconscious... Everything that men make — like a city street — is a collective art object. People can give you all kinds of economic reasons for all the high rises in New York, but no single person planned how it feels to walk in those streets. America is full of unconscious artworks. All I'm doing is waltzing with it."

Segal's public sculpture is the product of a new concept of space — a space that has less to do with traditional formal problems and three dimensions than with the sociological, cultural, and economic environment of a work. Segal says, "If I'm going to be honest about the derivation of the idea, John Cage's silence was devoted to sharpening your perception and tuning in to the quality of the real sounds you heard in a real place, where nothing was planned, where everything was 'normal' — normal moments in your life. Now take the idea of sound and add to that what you see, and what you hear. You must decide to accept the vibrancy of an unconsciously made object like the modern American city." For Segal, the space an outdoor work inhabits is no longer simply a matter of its height, width, and depth; rather, it is a total environment of sights, sounds, and smells, all the allusions and resonances of a monument's site.

Segal contrasts his conception of space with the symbolic and psychological frame of empty space — parks or piazzas — surrounding traditional European outdoor sculpture. The empty plaza around a public sculpture — "the equivalent of the frame around a painting" — is echoed in the white walls, waxed floors and bare spaces of the contemporary gallery — "a vision of Utopian perfection." In the gallery, Segal remains primarily concerned with manipulating the play of voids and masses in the utopia that the pristine space affords. But on the street, his interest shifts to the coloristic, symbolic, thematic, emotional, and formal devices with which he can make his sculpture reflect not only the appearance of a site, but also its social, economic, political, and mythic associations. Indoors, Segal composes on a three-dimensional picture plane; outdoors, he discards the frame.

Segal's argument for the inclusion of more life in public art is the logical outgrowth of his longstanding interest in environmental art and the ideas of Kaprow and Cage. But his real aim is one common to all artists, representational or abstract, who practice what he calls "the realism that sucks out the spirit." Segal remembers a recent bus ride up Riverside Drive in New York City. Looking out the left-hand windows, he could see, stretching for block after block, the broad green lawns and graffiti-covered historical sculptures of Riverside Park. Block after block: nineteenth century *Beaux-Arts* monuments, generals on horseback, figures by Saint-Gaudens, Neoclassical arches, stranded on the lawns like flotsam on a dirty beach, mute witness to the grandeur of the large metropolitan city in the last century. Then, at 155th Street, the bus turned a corner onto Broadway: "All of a sudden, it looked like a contemporary collage — the Spanish grocery stores, the iron gratings, the swervy, jagged marks of the graffiti. Everything feels like it's part of a modern painting or sculpture. There's a quality of space that is purely twentieth century. The time has its own individual order." When he is given a site like the Youngstown mall, Segal seeks to isolate that individual order, to extract the spirit of an unconsciously fashioned, public space.

112 **Girl Looking Through Window.** 1972. (Cat. 126)
Plaster and mixed media, 96 × 36 × 24 in.
Museum Boymans-van Beuningen, Rotterdam.

113 **The Curtain.** 1974. (Cat. 138)
Plaster and mixed media, 84 × 39 × 32 in.
National Collection Fine Arts, Smithsonian
Institution, Washington, D.C.

Since *The Steelmakers,* Segal has preferred to pursue more personal themes in his public works, many of which return to the motifs that he has investigated throughout his career. He says, "The thing I like about these outdoor sculptures is that I can skip all over the map with subject matter; the form can be completely different in each piece. I can tackle a whole different set of problems each time. It's incredible how open-ended the whole thing becomes."

As public sculpture becomes more dependent on the personal interests of the sculptor, it poses new challenges for artist and audience alike. While avoiding controversies like those surrounding *Gay Liberation* or *Kent State,* in which the public responded to the events depicted rather than to the artworks, much of Segal's recent work, in its reticence and privacy, runs the opposite risk of making little impression on the general viewer at all. If the public artwork is to avoid the commemorative function of the traditional monument, and yet remain public in more than just name, it must appeal to a wide audience through psychological insight, aesthetic delight, and, as Segal would insist, the revelation of the spirituality of physical experience. It is a mark of his profound humanism and emotional insight that out of his private preoccupations with forms like windows and benches, and such aesthetic interests as the expression of movement in plastic form, Segal can create public art with a genuine popular appeal.

The window is among the most persistently recurring formal motifs in Segal's work. Beginning with some of his early oils, and continuing through such sculptures as *Girl Looking Through a Window* (1972) and *The Curtain* (1974), Segal has engaged in an ongoing investigation of the psychological and spatial tensions established by the window jamb and the framed glance. A broad picture window played a prominent role in *The Restaurant,* his first public work; and more recent bronzes have further explored the levels of significance in casements and dormers. The 1979 *Man in a Toll Booth,* cast in white bronze for the collection of the Newark Art Museum, interns a solemn, introspective figure within the confines of an actual Art Deco toll booth, which once stood at the entrance to the Holland Tunnel. The weight and

112

116

domineering dimensions of the toll booth suggest a prison as much as a shelter, and the incarcerated figure remains vulnerable despite the bronze walls around him.

In *Girl in Kimono Looking through Window*, cast two years later for the plaza outside a Philadelphia office building erected by Norman Wolgin near Independence Hall, the window becomes a diaphanous membrane between two worlds. The figure in the toll booth was confined in a claustrophobic, centripetal space; in the Philadelphia work, the sash does not enclose the woman, but defines a line of confrontation — a psychological window of vulnerability, in which the spectator is as exposed as the mute bronze figure.

Of course, Segal is not the first artist to draw on the romantic and psychological associations of the window. His treatment of the theme owes something to Kaspar David Friedrich's *Woman at the Window*, with its exploitation of the formal and symbolic properties of the divisions between panes of glass; and Segal's compositions also recall the dramatic tension and compositional clarity that windows suggesting romantic escape from oppressive circumstances, bring to so many of Edward Hopper's canvases. Segal has another formal explanation for the persistent attraction of the motif to contemporary artists: "The first thing you learn in art school is that the conception of a Renaissance painting is that of a window on the world... If you're born now and you're going to consider what kind of artwork you're going to make, [you ask] is the flatness of your canvas plane the wall or is it a window? Wrestling with that idea, I think it's absolutely inevitable that dozens of modern artists would be dealing with the theme of the window."[39]

Segal's theory may be the best explanation for his own predilection for sashes and sills: the box of the sash provides a format as rigid as a frame, and forces the spectator to confront the work frontally, as if it were a painting on canvas rather than a three-dimensional form. Yet perhaps the most arresting aspect of Segal's windows, particularly when they appear in public works, is their inversion of the mind. The windows in Segal's sculpture do not reveal a landscape embodying the depicted individual's mental life; they simply divide one world from another, the

113

114 **Girl in Kimono Looking Through Window.** 1980. (Cat. 168)
Bronze, glass and plastic, 96 × 43 × 30 in.
Collection Mr. and Mrs. Norman Wolgin, Philadelphia, Pa.

115 **Man in Toll Booth.** 1979. (Cat. 163)
Bronze: 108 × 43 × 43 in; figure: 74 in. high.
Newark Museum, Newark, New Jersey.

115

space of the audience from the art-space of the plaster or bronze figure. The spectator is no longer outside looking in; rather, he is staring across a gap at a figure so securely absorbed in its own life that it paradoxically becomes more life-like than art-like. The psychological states of the figures enclosed in Segal's tableaux are no more scrutable than our own; their final effect is to make the spectator more aware of his own perceptive act and, by extension, of his voyeuristic glances at passersby. The dramas of communication enacted in *The Restaurant*, *Man in a Toll Booth*, and *Woman Looking Through a Window*, make these works especially appropriate for city streets, where so many personal contacts are daily made and lost.

Windows are not the only thematic and organizational motifs that have captured Segal's imagination. "If you see someone sitting on a bench," he says, "it's like looking at Cézanne's *Mount St. Victoire*, or it's like looking at some other landscape or still life — there's the purely aesthetic aspect. But there are hundreds of thousands of people sitting around like that in New Jersey. And on bus rides, everyone starts reading their *Times* and after ten minutes they're semi-comatose. It's like enforced Zen meditation."

In his public works, Segal has consistently demonstrated his sensitivity to both the aesthetic and the social functions of the bench. The essential characteristic of the bench, which distinguishes it from chairs and stools, is that it accommodates more than one person. In *Gay Liberation*, Segal made use of the resolutely gregarious nature of the park bench to offer an implicit invitation to the hostile or uncertain viewer to join the figures, and thus mitigate the presumptive threat posed by their sexual proclivities. The device is one of the most familiar in Segal's repertoire: his first two works made prominent use of a chair and a restaurant booth, and, since then, benches have appeared in a number of tableaux. In the gallery plasters, the motif works effectively to further Segal's enduring desire to obscure the boundaries between art and life. But in public the bench comes into its own. Amid the rush of the city, the bench is traditionally an oasis of rest; it is urban, but personal and individualized. By joining

such a public object to the sculptural art objects, and then returning the prop to its natural environment, Segal breaks down any rigid hierarchical distinction between the "artistic" bronze figures and other objects encountered in the daily life of the city dweller. Without resorting to vaudeville tactics or sacrificing aesthetic quality, he successfully foregoes the high-art pretensions of much public sculpture, and subverts the sanctity of bronze.

The park bench makes one of its most dramatic and effective appearances in the 1981 work, *Three People on Four Benches*. Segal once compared the composition of one of his tableaux to the visual structure of sheet music: "It's like looking at a musical score of Bach. We listen to the music, and we can get a mental image of a clear structure. So, the quickest visual way is to look at a musical score. You can see the dots and the intervals between them and how they pile up. That clue from the music, the spaces between things and the proportions of the bulks are very much like structured music (in the sculpture)."[40] The description seems particularly appropriate to *Three People*, in which the figures are positioned like grace notes on a staff defined by the benches. Seen from the street, the sidewalk, or the air the delicate, juxtaposed balance of the seated bronzes is at once a clearly defined spatial structure, and the visual analogue of Baroque counterpoint.

Three People was originally designed for a new Justice Center in Cleveland, Ohio, and for Pepsico's corporate sculpture garden in Purchase, New York. Unrelieved even by landscaping, and raised above the level of the street, the stark, monolithic façade of the Justice Center's northern exposure seemed an especially unpromising site for so intimate and unaffected a sculpture. Undeterred, Segal decided on a strongly horizontal design that would not compete with the scale of the architecture. Since the site provided no spatial, social, or cultural environment, Segal created a tableau that brings a world with it. The park benches in *Three People* does double duty, both inviting the passerby and shaping the space the sculpture occupies. The work succeeds so well as a self-contained yet accessible outdoor monument that Segal has made an exception to his insistence on

116 **Three People on Four Benches.** 1979. (Cat. 164)
Bronze and aluminum, 52 × 144 × 58 in.
A.P.: Pepsico Sculpture Gardens, Purchase, New York.
1/3: Cuyahoga County Justice Center, Cleveland, Ohio.
2/3: Martin Z. Margulies, Grove Isle, Fla.
3/3: Sidney Besthoff, New Orleans, La.

116

117 **Blue Girl on Park Bench.** 1980. (Cat. 169)
Painted plaster and painted aluminum, 51 × 78 × 44 in.
Collection Melvin Golder, Melrose Park, Pa.

117

site-specificity, and recast it in white bronze for a plaza in New Orleans and a private collection in Florida. *Three People* is a sculpture that, without sacrificing its artistic integrity or formal identity, effortlessly adapts to different sites and readily offers itself to the aesthetic, psychological, and physical delectation of its audience.

In contrast to the human and formal tensions of the grouping in *Three People on Four Benches*, and offsetting its phantomic whiteness, Segal's intensely chromatic *Blue Girl on Park Bench* attempts a less complex expression of human solitude and isolation. The sense of the figure's commonplace reality is so emphatic and irrefutable that it tends to mask the poetics of the piece. The visual poem detonates belatedly as we disengage from brute fact and slip off into a poetic dream-space with this haunting girl, so inappropriately dipped in an anesthetizing cerulean, sky-blue fluid. She inhabits an attenuated moment of waiting removed from time and place, as much the product and occasion of reverie as she is of observation.

Most critics have dwelt upon Segal's banal realism, or on his environmental cunning in assembling a convincing mosaic of object fragments registering drab urban existence in all its longueurs and oppression. But Segal can also be placed in an obsessive native romantic tradition which acknowledges the American dream, no matter how shoddy. Like Hopper, and perhaps with something of the tragic sense of Eugene O'Neill and Tennessee Williams, he confronts a depersonalizing modern world by offering the illusion and promise of better things to come — a spectrum of denied hopes that range from the gently maudlin to the apocalyptic. The artistic strategy may seem a bit threadbare and unfashionable today, but it can still be gripping, and takes its place in an honorable historical continuity of realist painting and sculpture dating back to the late-nineteenth century.

In Segal's non-heroic figure we may also recognize something of the bored urban mass-man whom Baudelaire first discovered, and Flaubert despised — the human flotsam left behind in the great cities after the decline of the romantic movement. Questioned about his forlorn figure on the bench and its source, Segal remembers that it was based on actual scenes encountered on his frequent commuting trips to New York from his home in New Brunswick, New Jersey. He takes an equally dim view of people on benches whether found in the metropolis or the suburbs. He has described a town near his own, for example, which is, in effect, a collage of decayed architectural styles, as "an embalmed Victorian corpse." He thus seems to mark out affinities with the late nineteenth-century French artists and poets who detested the torpor and enervation of small town life: Flaubert's horror of the provinces, or Redon's despair at the *bêtise* of his native Bordeaux, in whose remembered citizenry he discerned visages of "idiocy and vice," as one critic suggests, images that later became the basis for his mournful fantasies contrived in the liberated, Bohemian atmosphere of cosmopolitan Paris.

Without a trace of bitterness or sarcasm, Segal identifies the personages of his particular public theater by relating them to the life he has observed around him:

Outside New York there is no culture, only a vacant landscape. People go on living. They go bowling; they commit adultery. It is truly amazing in America how many square miles there are with no life of the mind. The people are restless, moody, forever dissatisfied. They cannot quite put their finger on their discontent, but they know something is wrong.

The combination of uneventful lives and an unappeased hunger for something better has been both a powerful social vision and a favorite artistic theme in American arts and letters since the twenties. It persists at a more generalized, poetic level for Segal even in the age of affluence. It is, he admits, more attuned to psychological than sociological truths. "I deal with the specifics of each person's nature," he avers. "I let the smell of the specific lead me to universals." He disdains an art of explicit facile shortcuts to a statement of the human condition.

Segal's model for the girl on the bench was a friend who posed informally in his studio, where he positioned and repositioned her to capture the exact, telling gestures he sought. He purchased a park bench and repainted it black to balance the vivid colors of garment, flesh, handbag and shopping bag he already had in mind. The geometry of the bench accentuated and framed the architecture of the human figure in its lattice. The choice of color was more complicated, in part a reversion to the lush painterliness of his expressionist canvases of the late fifties, revived only intermittently in the sculpture of the sixties. The palette was also inspired by a recent trip to Venice where the alternately faded and fluorescent, gaudy façades of the delicate Italian architecture impressed him. He bought Venetian pigment in powder form after he observed Italian masons mixing the powder with cement to repair a deteriorating façade. He thinks of his creation as a composite of "chunks of colored architecture." The livid blue of the figure, her features and garments is broken by the inconsistent "flash of a flesh-colored hand," and by the brilliant magenta shopping bag and the Lethean shades of the bench — a mythic scene somehow despite the Mondrianesque geometry and pattern of the simplistic color sequence.

In the early seventies Segal made an important change in his technical methods, abandoning his external plaster molds, and casting from inside the body molds in hydrostone. The images gained a far more life-like semblance and nuance, and probably that called forth a compensating color invention. Interestingly, making the actual body mold in plaster only takes a matter of hours, while the reconstruction of the figure from the segmented castings involves "weeks and months" of work. When Segal's model departed, and the plaster castings were taken from inside her negative mold, Segal was left with five or six sections which had to be reassembled in a life-like and convincing attitude. The final delicate balance of gestural nuance, and formal and psychological tension was achieved and invented not simply recorded mechanically. The process of physical reconstruction also proved risky and unpredictable. Segal has described the process:

I had to rebuild the figure and piece it together by using more wet plaster. And when I put in wet plaster, the forms tend to get away. They want to dissolve. I could have been left with a blob. I have to nudge the pieces together when they are wet and floppy. I fight gravity, to build the form architecturally.

The considerable technical effort required professional skill, physical dexterity and intense concentration. The result is something between a replica, *à la* Mme. Tussaud, and a golem, an effigy of startling force and magical powers rooted in the world we know but distanced by its virulent primary colors. The figure attains the grave composure that is the mark of highly formal art rather than genre realism. In terms of contemporary culture and psychology, the figure is both ourselves and "the other," a metaphor for artist and audience, isolation and community, probably best evoked by Baudelaire's ambivalent salutation to his readers in the preface to his *Les Fleurs du Mal: "Hypocrite lecteur, — mon semblable, — mon frère."* ("Hypocrite reader! — My twin! — My brother!")

Not all of Segal's repeated themes involve formal motifs like windows or benches: many of his tableaux reveal an enduring fascination with the depiction of movement, and, particularly, of moments of arrested action, or tensed exertion. His figures, dignified and solemn, seem to resist the temptation to engage in frivolous activity; nonetheless, certain works convey an exhilarating sense of movement, and Segal has been able to retain this kinetic energy in the spaces of public sites and the medium of bronze. Perhaps the most dramatic of his installations, *The Circus Fliers*, cast in plaster in 1980, occupies center stage in the Butler Square West development — a converted nineteenth century factory building in downtown Minneapolis. The theme is not new to Segal: in 1971, he cast a *Man on the Flying Trapeze*, and, the next year, a *Girl on a Swing*. But the Minneapolis work is far more complex and accomplished than these earlier attempts. *The Circus Fliers* hangs from the ceiling of a four-story atrium traversed by wooden beams two feet square — buttresses that swing across the space with the panache of high top showmen. When Segal first saw the raw wood beams and the high ceiling, he was determined to "waltz with" the space. The unique and demanding character of the site makes his success all the more noteworthy: *The Circus Fliers* is a ballroom extravaganza.

Segal cast two figures, one male, one female, which he suspended from the ceiling of the atrium with steel cables. The tensed interplay between these

119 **Man on the Flying Trapeze.** 1971. (Cat. 110)
Plaster, wood, metal and rope, 72 × 36 in.
Wadsworth Atheneum, Hartford.

120 **Girl on Swing.** 1972. (Cat. 120)
Plaster, metal and rope, 42 × 18 × 68 in. (variable heighs).
Galerie Onnasch, Cologne.

121 **The Dancers.** 1971. (Cat. 111)
Bronze, 72 × 144 × 96 in.
1/5: Collection Seymour Schwebber, King's Point, New York.
2/5: National Gallery of Art, Washington, D.C.
3/5: Collection Mr. and Mrs. Perry R. Bass, Fort Worth, Texas.

119

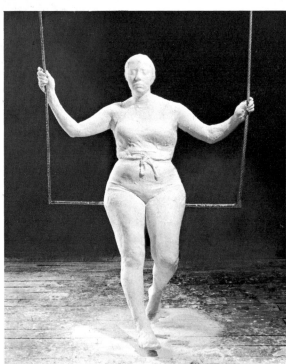

120

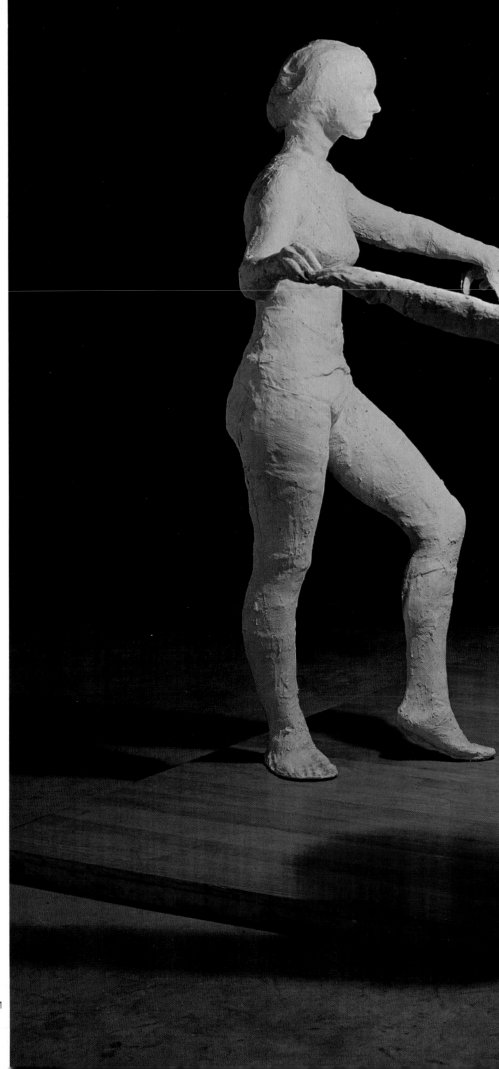

121

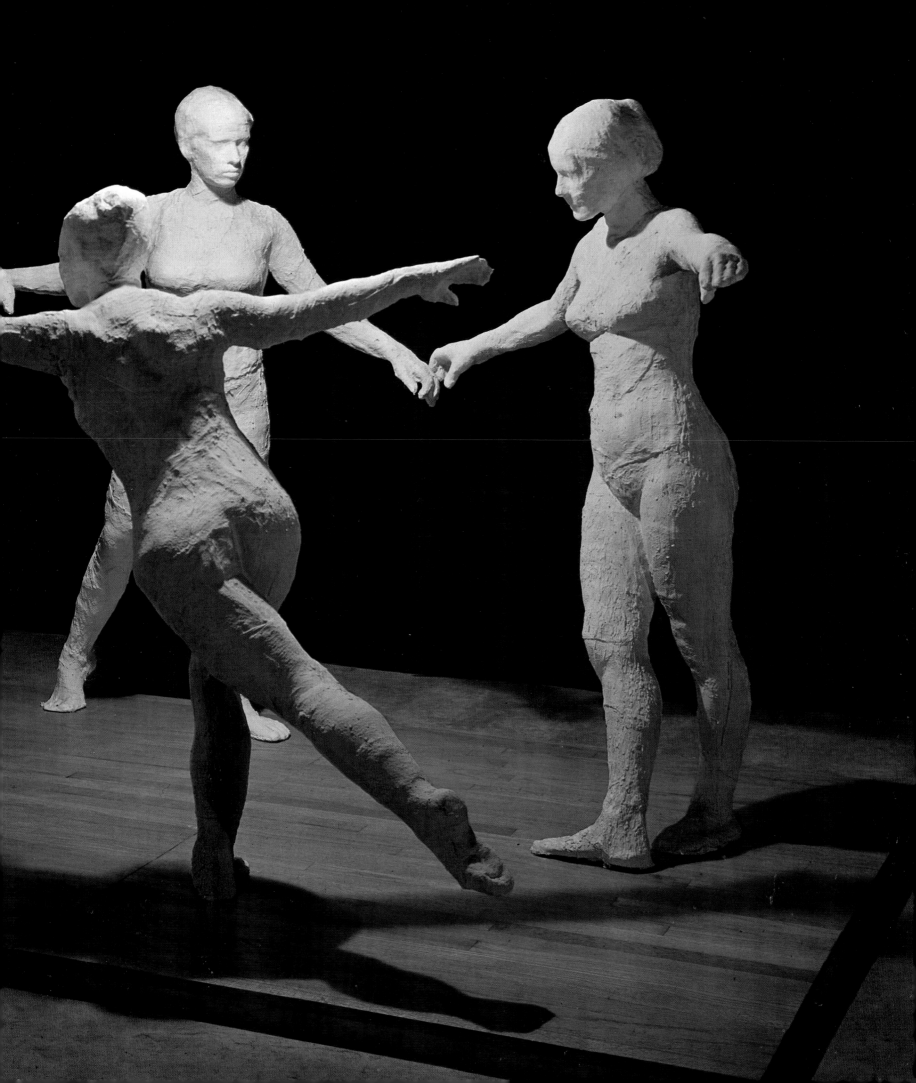

figures as they swing on trapezes across the giddy height, mimics the flight of the massive joists across the vault. Space is looped, laced, penetrated and dissolved. The effect on the spectator, weary from a day of shopping or sitting in an office, must be one of pure visual delight.

Bronze might seem to be temperamentally unsuited to the depiction of movement. But in a recent cast made from an improvisation on his earlier work in plaster, *The Dancers,* Segal has succeeded in capturing the animation and agility of the ballerina's trained muscles. In 1982 the artist made two casts of the figure group — Segal's first bronzes which were not intended as public sculpture. They now belong to a private collector in Long Island, and have been lent to The Whitney Museum of American Art for its new public exhibition space at the Philip Morris, Inc. Sculpture Court in New York. The tight circle of dancers obviously refers to Matisse, but, although they share the energy of Matisse's revelers, their poise and dignity owe more to the introspective, absorbed performers of Degas. Although the figures lack any accompanying environment, the centrifugal composition unites them in a spiraling circle of nimble movement.

Created for an artworld audience, *The Dancers* is an expression of the fascinations and delights of the artist's private life. In *The Commuters*, Segal addressed the different challenge of interpreting the familiar iconography of the American scene in response to the demands of a particular site. And the location of the tableau, the lobby of the Port Authority Bus Terminal in mid-town Manhattan, was a particularly demanding one.

In 1980, Segal was selected from a field of over one hundred artists to execute a work for the newly renovated terminal. This was one site he did not have to inspect: "The Port Authority terminal is forever on my mind," says Segal. "A lot of my mental life has been spent there."[41] From the beginning of his career, Segal has commuted from New Jersey by bus to Manhattan, and the terminal has provided the inspiration for almost a dozen works, including *The Bus Driver* (1962), *The Bus Riders* (1962), *The Bus Station* (1965), and *To All Gates* (1971).

123

124

122

Although the site readily suggested the theme of the work, the location assigned him in the terminal tested Segal's ingenuity. The sculpture was to be placed in an area of open floor space, surrounded by ticket windows and benches, and illuminated from above by a circle of bright lights — "I've never used so many lights in my life," he says. Resolved to harmonize his work with "all the arbitrary, man-made, man-designed moves in the space," he created a spare tableau of three white bronze figures, typical habitués of the terminal, queuing to board a bus. Arranged on a diagonal axis in ascending heights, the figures convey an insistently horizontal movement that projects the path of their arrested progress. The surroundings of the Port Authority provide the most authentic environment conceivable for these ghostly commuters, locked in the same motions as their hastening viewers.

Like all of Segal's public sculptures, *The Commuters* will experience the particular difficulties of contemporary art in communicating to a wide audience. Paradoxically, the ease with which the spectator can grasp the realistic imagery and narrative content of Segal's works makes them all the more susceptible to being dismissed or ignored, as if their aesthetic, psychological, and cultural significance could be comprehended in a fleeting glance. Segal prefers to trust to the sensibility and patience of his audience: "I feel that there's enough intelligence and sensitivity in a large part of the population that I'm foolish if I try to talk down to anybody. I have to assume that they're smart enough and they're sensitive enough to have these feelings and ideas. I can't be responsible for the range of response — I don't know if I want to be a leader. I'd rather let people make up their own stories, have their own responses."

Of course, such idealism has its risks. Segal's art is as much indebted to the modernist tradition as is the abstract sculpture of a Richard Serra or Tony Smith, and it is inevitable that many compositional accomplishments and art-historical allusions will pass unnoticed before the uneducated eye. On the other hand, Segal's experience with *Kent State: Abraham and Isaac* and *Gay Liberation* betrays the social frag-

125

mentation that makes a return to the classical commemorative monument a dubious option at best.

Segal's most powerful and disturbing figure group, *The Holocaust,* represents his most challenging public sculpture. It was commissioned by San Francisco's Committee for a Memorial to the Six Million Victims of the Holocaust, after Segal's maquette was selected from an open competition. Interestingly, and rather poignantly, the selection committee included concentration camp survivors in addition to art specialists and for them his baldly explicit composition of piled up corpses, framed by a solitary living witness, who stands looking vacantly through a barbed wire enclosure, offered the most gripping and eloquent testimony to the Nazi slaughter of the Jews. Segal had in the early sixties steered clear of emotional public issues, regarding his sculpture as an essentially private and intimate statement, despite its obvious cultural and environmental implications which gave definition to individual existence. However, by 1967, at the height of the Viet Nam turmoil, he clearly engaged in a form of social commentary when he created *The Execution.* Allowing for some striking pose reversals, that grouping anticipates many of the telling compositional features of *The Holocaust.* Indeed, this sixties ''protest'' against events in Viet Nam revived the traditional art-historical theme of a Massacre of the Innocents, a venerable and familiar image of martyrdom. Originally he had envisioned for this early work a *mise-en-scène* of heaped up concentration camp victims, inspired by some of the classic newsphotos of the carnage. Ultimately, he chose to abandon the allegory because it seemed too personal and poignant. In fact, it even posed some of the same gruesome problems he later encountered in making *The Holocaust,* including the unnerving decision of whether to make casts from the actual dead in the morgue for the work, in its first conception.

Segal decided that the disorderly effect of mass murder that he had observed in photos of the German death camps could not be captured literally, and instead he settled on a small number of ten victims for *The Holocaust,* carefully choreographing their recumbent positions, and thus reducing his first grandiose vision to a more simple and controlled scheme.

He encouraged his models to assume positions that they felt were imaginatively right, usually working with two figures at a time, and marking out the previous simulated corpse positions carefully on his studio floor. He then composed the group in tandem, in a way designed to neutralize the disturbing sense of chaos and meaninglessness in the piled corpses, and to restore human meanings and a kind of ritualized grief by emphasizing geometry and formal decorum. The tense formal ordering thus achieved only increased the emotional impact of the scene. Picasso's classical stylization of *Guernica*'s massacre victims and even more aptly, the heaped up corpses he depicted in his tragic grisaille, *The Charnel House,* also inspired by death camp photography, create a similar patterned and interlocking cluster effect that intensifies the emotional power of these allegories of martyrdom.

Segal's fictive corpses in plaster splay out on the ground in the form roughly of a star or a cross, with religious and allegorical implications. One of the two women, lying on the stomach of a man, with her legs outstretched to the upper left of the composition, holds a partly-eaten apple in her hand. She is an ample, earthly figure, suggesting nature's abundance even in death, a Persephone image of renewal. ''I became as interested in Eve's sensuality as anything else,'' Segal has stated in an interview. ''It has to do with survival.'' But perhaps the critical figure in the work is the lone survivor in the foreground, strangely detached from the chilling scene, and dressed in those ''famous striped prison pajamas,'' in Segal's words. It is he who gives the event a mythic definition and, in effect, reenacts for all of us the suffering and perceiving part of the tragic action as he broods over the grisly scene. Resigned yet noble, he recalls Tiresias, the blind and suffering seer whom Sophocles uses in Antigone to reveal the truths which other mortals find difficult to contemplate and live with. The stoical calm and statuesque dignity of Segal's figure are also strangely reminiscent of Donatello's life-size sculptures, and its quietude contrasts violently with the tensions and the variety of poses in which the more hectic dead are frozen, creating a kind of pinwheeling and layered composite of limbs convulsed in

126 **The Execution.** 1967. (Cat. 71)
     Plaster, wood, metal and rope, 96 × 132 × 96 in.
     Vancouver Art Gallery.

126

death. Segal decided live beings rather than cadavers would portray the state of death more effectively. He cast his figures from friends and relations, after he had studied photographs of the concentration camps. What struck him most vividly from these celebrated and intimidating visual archives of war horrors was the disorder of the heaped corpses:

"I must have looked at one thousand photographs," he said, "and I was struck by the obscenity of the disorder, the heaping of the bodies. In most countries, there is a ritual order at funerals. The corpses are carefully composed, and there is a ritual of grieving. Here was a decision by a modern state to perform official murder of an entire race. The indignity of the heaping, the total disregard for death, spoke of the insanity."

The fateful figure in the prison pajamas was modeled from Martin Weyl, Director of the Israel Museum and an actual concentration camp survivor, whom Segal selected to deepen and fix his own sense of commitment, and to give the composition authenticity. Weyl's ambiguous, self-absorbed pose distances the dreadful events that have taken place behind him, and it also intercedes with and relieves the viewers' painful exposure to the horrifying incident, but without resolving the problem of evil, or alleviating the memory of the mass murder of millions of innocent victims. With his subtle figural and formal strategies Segal managed to restate freshly, and most eloquently, a plausible symbolic scene from the great tragedy of modern history. He linked even this enormity of aberrant behavior to his other more privatist work which often characteristically illuminates the human condition from a sobering, ethical perspective, and with a comparable originality of form and thought.

The warm reception for Segal's public art indicates that an alternative exists to facile acceptance and philistine rejection of meaningful sculptural forms. The popularity of so many of his sculptures demonstrates that, despite the public's admitted ignorance of technical and formal issues, a general audience can identify with the psychological, philosophical, and spiritual insighs of serious works of art, both public and private. In large part, Segal's success can be ascribed to his desire to confront his subject matter on its own terms, and his willingness to research and finally capture the tempo and life of a site in the sculpture occupying it. Perhaps equally important is the artist's unaffected, natural empathy with, and intuitive perception of, the daily worries, joys, and aspirations of the common man.

Today, Segal remains optimistic about the future of public art: "Something rings true about it. People are hungry for some common belief. Everyone wants to feel attached to something larger than themselves. They want to have faith in something." Through the example of his consistently original and accomplished career in public sculpture, and with the growing popular response to many of his works, Segal has done as much as any contemporary artist to justify this optimism.

NOTES

1. Christopher B. Crosman and Nancy E. Miller, "A Conversation with George Segal," *Gallery Studies 1* (Buffalo: Buffalo Fine Arts Academy, 1977), p. 11.

2. Donald Thalacker, *The Place of Art in the World of Architecture* (New York: Chelsea House Publishers, 1980) p. 15.

3. Crosman, p. 12.

4. Ibid, p. 12.

5. Ibid, p. 12.

6. Ibid, p. 15.

7. Donald Thalacker, p. 15.

8. Crosman, p. 15.

9. Ibid, p. 16.

10. "Testimony of George Segal, Sculptor," United States Senate Committee on Governmental Affairs, Subcommittee on Civil Service and General Services, first session, (September 25, 1979) p. 7.

11. Nancy Tobin Willig, "Segal Sculpture Installed at Fed. Bldg.," Buffalo *Courier Express* (May 28, 1976).

12. Douglas Mazanec, "Inside George Segal," *Northern Ohio Live*, Vol. I, No. 18 (June 1-14, 1981), p. 29.

13. Crosman, p. 17.

14. Greenwich catalogue, p. 36.

15. Jan van der Marck, *George Segal* (New York: Harry N. Abrams, 1975), p. 242.

16. "Try again in twenty years," *Art News* (November 1978), p. 6.

17. Ibid, p. 6.

18. Carole Nelson, "Ghostly Presences: Sculptor 'mummifies' subjects in wet plaster," Baltimore *Sun* (November 28, 1978).

19. Grace Glueck, "Princeton to Get Sculpture Rejected by Kent State," *New York Times*, Nov. 18, 1978.

20. Malcolm N. Carter, "George Segal," *Saturday Review*, Vol. VIII, No. 5 (May 1981), p. 30.

21. John Perreault, "George Segal: Plastered People," Village *Voice* (October 24, 1974).

22. James M. Saslow, "A Sculpture without a Community: *Christopher Street*, Vol. V, No. 4 (February 1981), p. 27.

23. Glueck, "Homosexual-Liberation Statue Is Planned for Sheridan Square," *New York Times* (July 21, 1979).

24. Richard Goldstein, "Greenwich Village is Not Amused," Village *Voice* (September 10-16, 1980).

25. Saslow, p. 28.

26. Ibid. pp. 24, 26.

27. Sherryl Connelly, "A tale of a park, a sculpture, and a Village," *Daily News* (October 7, 1980).

28. Edith Evans Asbury, "Sculpture Planned for 'Village' Brings Objections," *New York Times* (August 28, 1980).

29. Saslow, p. 30.

30. "Reader's Views on the Gay Pride Statues," *Villager* (September 11, 1980).

31. John Beardsley, *Art in Public Places* (Washington: Partners for Livable Places, 1981), pp. 71, 72.

32. Paula L. Cizman, "Segal's World," *Books and Arts* (November 23, 1979), p. 21.

33. Mazanec, p. 30.

34. Cizman, p. 21.

35. Louis Zona, "A Segal Comes to Youngstown," p. 14.

36. Ibid, p. 12.

37. "Sculpture," *The New Yorker* (October 27, 1980), p. 45.

38. Mazanec, p. 29.

39. Crosman, p. 12.

40. Ibid, p. 16.

41. Van der Marck, p. 204.

ILLUSTRATIONS

ENVIRONMENTAL SCULPTURE

127 Woman in Red Jacket. 1958. (Cat. 2)
     Plaster, 71 × 30 × 24 in.
     Collection of the artist.

128 **Woman on a Chair**. 1961. (Cat. 4)
Plaster, modeled by hand.
Collection of the artist.

129 **Lovers on a Bench**. 1962. (Cat. 10)
Plaster, wood and metal, 48 × 60 × 36 in.
Collection Dr. and Mrs. Hubert Peeters, Bruges, Belgium.

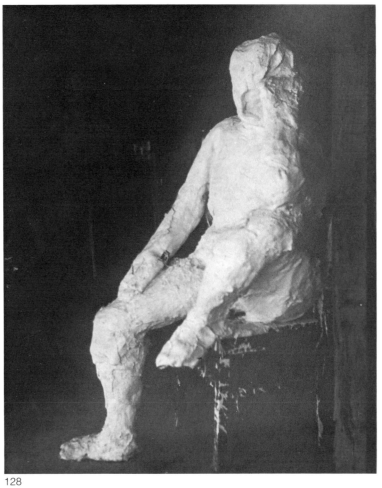

128

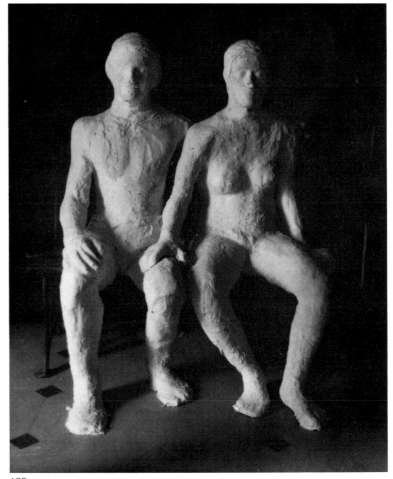

129

130 **Woman Painting Her Fingernails.** 1962. (Cat. 11)
Plaster, wood, glass, mirror, cloth and nail polish, 55 × 35 × 25 in.
Collection Mrs. Fann Schniewind, Neviges, Germany.

131 **The Bus Riders.** 1962. (Cat. 12)
Plaster, metal and vinyl, 74 × 48 × 108 in.
Hirshhorn Museum and Sculpture Garden,
Smithsonian Institution, Washington, D.C.

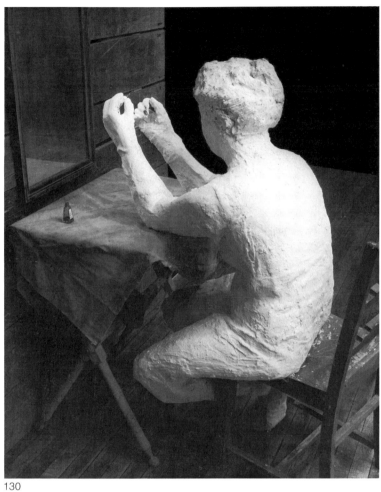

130

131

132 **Lovers on a Bed I.** 1962. (Cat. 13)
Plaster, wood, metal, mattress and cloth, 48 × 54 × 70 in.
Collection Mrs. Robert B. Mayer, Chicago.

133 **Woman Leaning Against a Chimney.** 1963. (Cat. 16)
Plaster and cinder block, 90 × 28 × 16 in.
Collection Mr. and Mrs. R. Matthys, Ghent.

134 **Gottlieb's Wishing Well.** 1963. (Cat. 17)
Plaster and pinball machine, 65 × 25 × 76 in.
Private collection, Brussels.

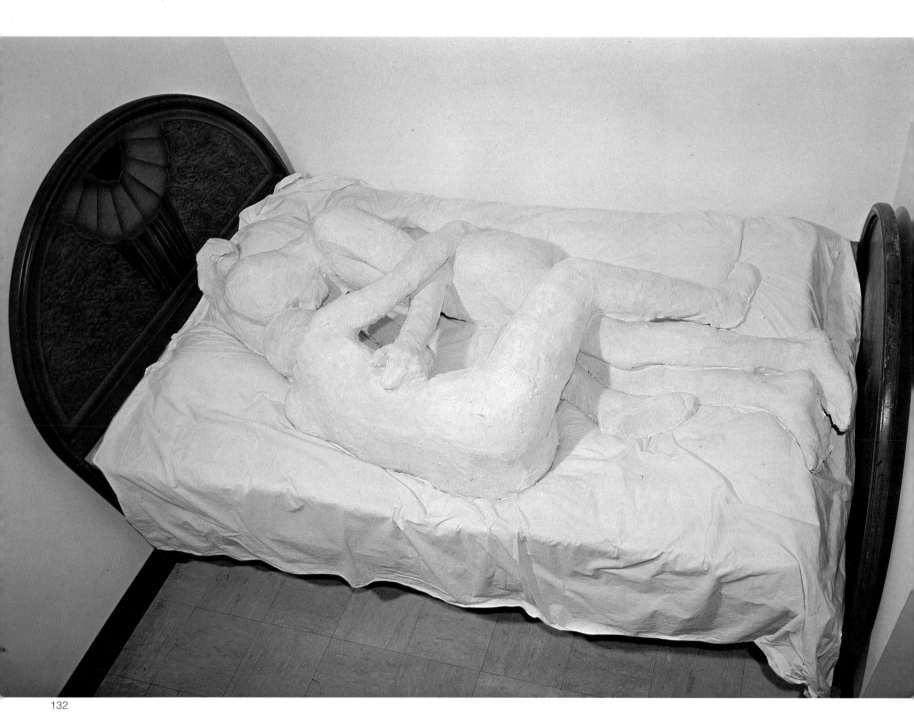

132

133

134

135 **Woman Fastening Her Bra.** 1963. (Cat. 18)
Plaster, wood and mirror, 72 × 18 × 30 in.
Collection Mr. and Mrs. Morton G. Neumann, Chicago.

136 **The Artist's Studio.** 1963. (Cat. 19)
Plaster, wood, metal, paint and mixed media, 96 × 72 × 108 in.
Harry N. Abrams Family Collection, New York.

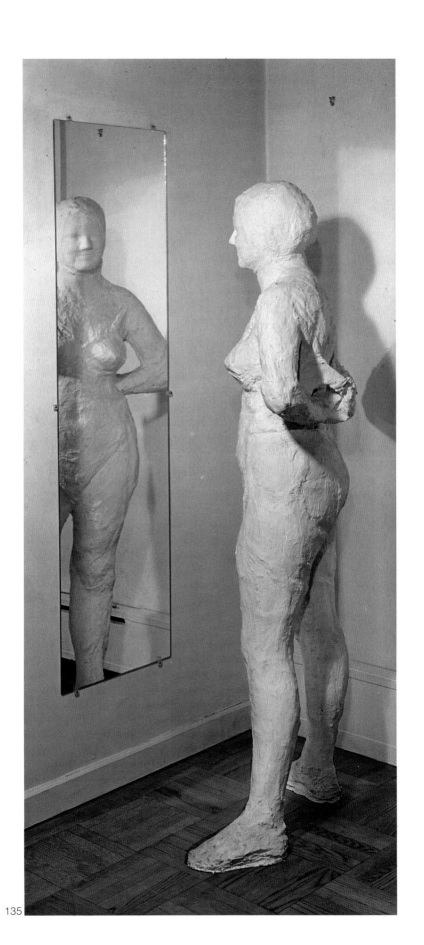

135

137 **The Farm Worker.** 1963. (Cat. 20)
Plaster, wood, glass and imitation brick, 96 × 96 × 42 in.
Collection Reinhard Onnasch, Berlin.

138 **Man Leaning on a Car Door.** 1963. (Cat. 21)
Plaster, wood and metal, 96 × 48 × 30 in.
Staatsgalerie Stuttgart, Stuttgart.

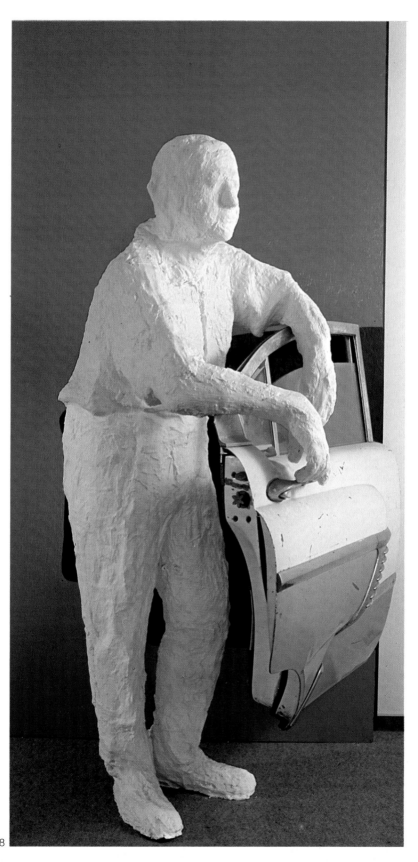

137   138

139 **Woman on a Bed.** 1963. (Cat. 22)
Plaster, canvas and wood, 50½ × 77 × 56¼ in.
Seattle Museum of Art, Seattle, Wash.
Gift of Mr. and Mrs. Bagley Wright.

140 **Woman on a Church Pew.** 1964. (Cat. 27)
Plaster, wood and paper, 42 × 60 × 24 in.
Collection Mr. and Mrs. Leonard J. Horwich, Chicago.

141 **Woman in a Doorway I.** 1964. (Cat. 28)
Plaster, wood, glass and aluminum paint, 113 × 63¼ × 18 in.
Whitney Museum of American Art, New York.

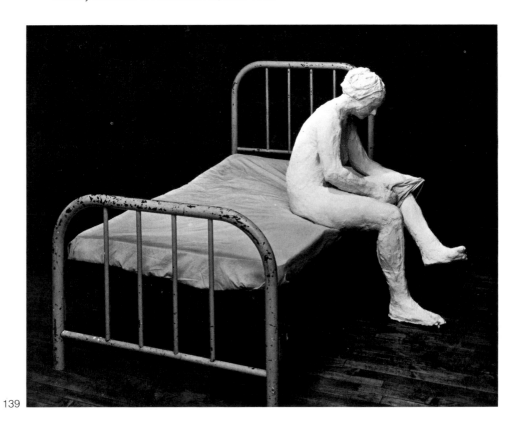

139

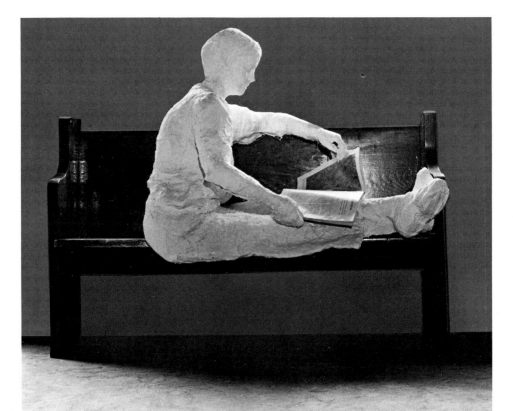

140

142

142 **Richard Bellamy Seated.** 1964. (Cat. 29)
Plaster and metal, 54 × 48 × 48 in.
Collection Mr. and Mrs. Adam Aronson, Saint Louis.

143 **Girl on a Green Kitchen Chair.** 1964. (Cat. 30)
Plaster and wood, 50 × 32 × 24 in.
Collection Frederick R. Weisman, Beverly Hills.

144 **Woman in a Red Wicker Chair.** 1964. (Cat. 32)
Plaster and wicker, 48 × 32 × 42 in.
Collection Vivian Tyson, New York.

143

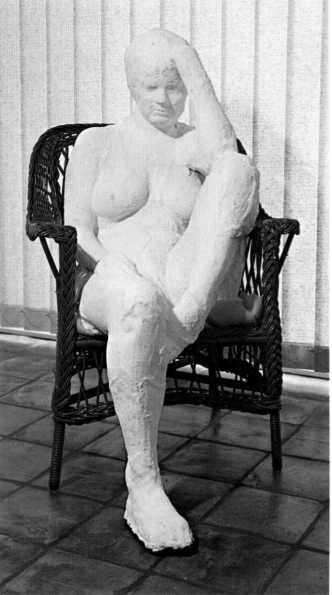

144

145 **The Tar Roofer.** 1964. (Cat. 31)
Plaster, wood, metal and tar paper, 84 × 96 × 79 in.
Gewebesammlung der Stadt Krefeld, Germany.

146 **Couple at the Stairs.** 1964. (Cat. 33)
Plaster, wood and metal, 120 × 104 × 96 in.
Museum Boymans-van Beuningen, Rotterdam.

147 **Woman in a Doorway II.** 1965. (Cat. 34)
Plaster and wood, 96 × 72 × 96 in.
Stedelijk Museum, Amsterdam.

145

146

147

148 **Woman Washing Her Foot in a Sink.** 1965. (Cat. 35)
Plaster, wood, metal and porcelain, 60 × 48 × 36 in.
Wallraf-Richartz-Museum, Cologne (Ludwig Collection).

149 **Woman Brushing Her Hair.** 1965. (Cat. 36)
Plaster, wood and plastic, 40 × 24 × 46 in.
Walker Art Center Minneapolis, Minn. (Gift of Mrs. Julius Davis).

150 **The Actress.** 1965. (Cat. 37)
Plaster and wood, 72 × 36 × 48 in.
Hirshhorn Museum and Sculpture Garden,
Smithsonian Institution, Washington, D.C.

149

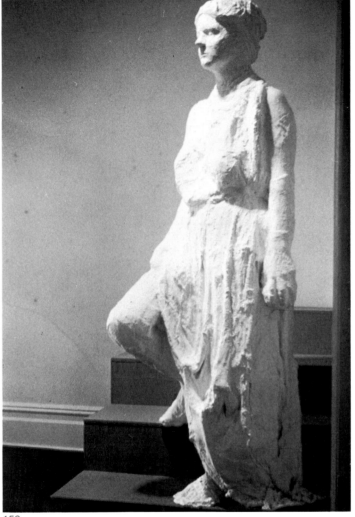

150

151 **Robert and Ethel Scull.** 1965. (Cat. 38)
     Plaster, wood, canvas and cloth, 96 × 72 × 72 in.
     Collection Mr. and Mrs. Robert C. Scull, New York.

152 **Couple on a Bed.** 1965. (Cat. 39)
     Plaster and metal, 47 × 81 × 50 in.
     Art Institute of Chicago (Mrs. Robert B. Mayer Collection).

152

153 **Old Woman at a Window.** 1965. (Cat. 40)
Plaster, wood, glass, chrome and board, 96 × 36 × 48 in.
Collection Mr. and Mrs. Melvin Hirsh, Beverly Hills.

154 **Vera List.** 1965. (Cat. 41)
Plaster and metal, 52 × 27 × 40 in.
The Albert A. List Family Collection, New York.

155 **The Bus Station.** 1965. (Cat. 42)
Plaster, wood and plastic, 96 × 48 × 24 in.
Collection Howard and Jean Lipman, New York.

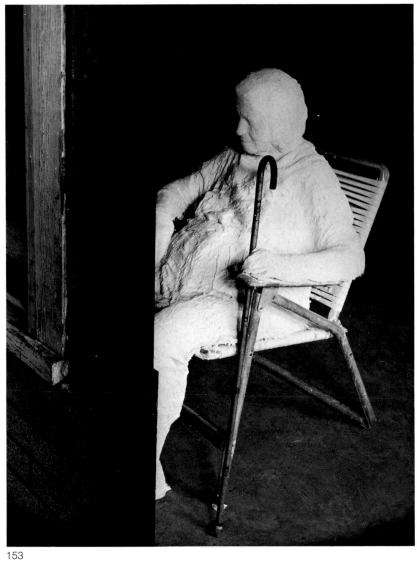

153

154

156 and 157 **The Butcher Shop.** 1965. (Cat. 43)
Plaster, metal, wood, vinyl, Plexiglas and other objects,
94 × 99¼ × 48 in.
Art Gallery of Ontario, Toronto (Gift from the Women's
Committee Fund, 1966).

158 **Woman Listening to Music I.** 1965. (Cat. 44)
Plaster, wood and hi-fi set, 72 × 96 × 72 in.
Collection Spencer Samuels and Co., Ltd., New York.

159 **Sunbathers on a Rooftop.** 1963-1967. (Cat. 55)
Plaster, wood, metal, glass and tar, 30 × 144 × 78 in.
Collection Dr. Giuseppe Panza di Biumo, Milan, Italy.

160 **Ruth in Her Kitchen** (Final Version). 1964-1966. (Cat. 46)
Plaster and wood, 50 × 72 × 60 in.
Von der Heydt Museum, Wuppertal, Germany.

158

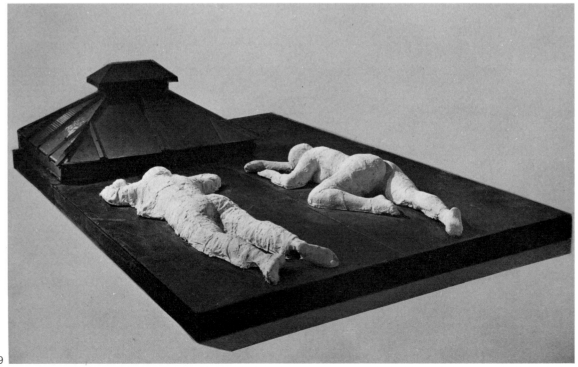

159

160

161 **The Diner.** 1964-1966. (Cat. 47)
Plaster, wood, metal, Formica, Masonite and fluorescent light,
102 × 108 × 87 in.
Walker Art Center, Minneapolis.
(Note: The relationship of the two figures has been changed
from the original.)

162 **The Shower Curtain.** 1966. (Cat 48)
Plaster, 69 × 47 × 16 in.
Private collection.

163 **Pregnant Woman.** 1966. (Cat. 49)
Plaster, wood and canvas, 46 × 23½ × 32 in.
Collection *Playboy* Magazine, Chicago.

162

163

161

164 **The Costume Party** (Final version). 1965-1972. (Cat. 118)
Acrylic on plaster, metal, wood and mixed media, 72 × 144 × 108 in.
Sidney Janis Gallery, New York.

165 **Walking Man.** 1966. (Cat. 50)
Plaster, wood and painted metal, 85 × 58 × 34 in.
Collection Mrs. Norman B. Champ, Jr., Saint Louis.

164

166 **The Billboard.** 1966. (Cat. 51)
   Plaster, wood, metal and rope, 189 × 117 × 20 in.
   South Mall Project, Albany.

167 **The Truck.** 1966. (Cat. 52)
   Plaster, wood, metal, glass, vinyl, and film projector, 66 × 60 × 53 in.
   Art Institute of Chicago (Mr. and Mrs. Frank G. Logan Fund).

167

168 **Legend of Lot.** 1966. (Cat. 53)
Plaster, 72 × 96 × 108 in.
Kaiser Wilhelm Museum, Krefeld, Germany (Lauffs Collection).

169 **The Motel Room.** 1967. (Cat. 59)
Plaster and wood, 72 × 78 × 72 in.
Collection P. Janlet, Brussels.

168

170 **The Photobooth.** 1966. (Cat. 54)
     Plaster, wood, metal, glass, fluorescent and
     incandescent light, 72 × 73 × 29 in.
     Collection Martin Z. Margulies, Bay Harbour, Fla.

171 **The Movie Poster.** 1967. (Cat. 60)
     Plaster, wood and photograph, 74 × 28 × 36 in.
     Collection Kimiko and John Powers, Aspen, Colorado.

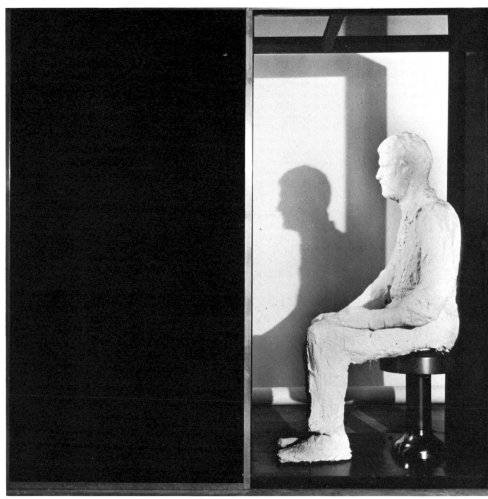

170

171

172 **Girl Washing Her Foot on a Chair.** 1967. (Cat. 61)
Plaster and wood, 48 × 24 × 46 in.
Collection Mr. and Mrs. E. A. Bergman, Chicago.

173 **Girl on Chair, Finger to Mouth.** 1967. (Cat. 62)
Plaster and wood, 52 × 42 × 16 in.
Collection Mr. and Mrs. Morton G. Neumann, Chicago.

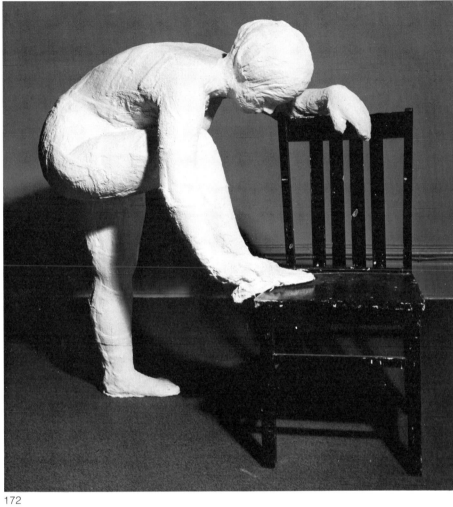

172

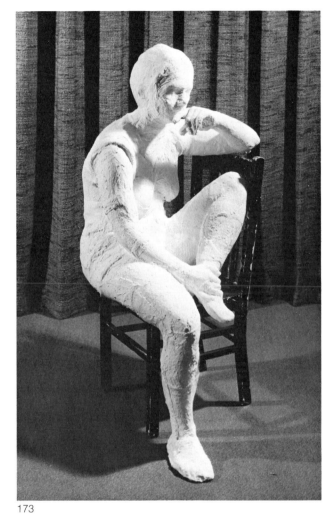

173

173

174

174 **The Moviehouse.** 1966-1967. (Cat. 57)
Plaster, wood, plastic and incandescent lights,
102 × 148 × 153 in.
Musée National d'Art Moderne, Paris (on loan from
Centre National d'Art Contemporain, Paris)

175 **The Laundromat II** (Original Version). 1966-1967. (Cat. 58)
Plaster, metal and plastic, 47 × 97 × 43 in.
Collection Reinhard Onnasch, Berlin.

176 **The Laundromat II** (Late Version). 1966-1970. (Cat. 94)
Plaster, metal and plastic, 72 × 72 × 30 in.
Collection Reinhard Onnasch, Berlin.

177 **Seated Girl.** 1967. (Cat. 63)
Plaster, wood and metal, 52 × 42 × 16 in.
Private collection.

175

176

178 **Girl Putting on an Earring.** 1967. (Cat. 64)
Plaster and wood, 50 × 40 × 40 in.
Collection Joan Avnet, New York.

179 **Girl Undressing.** 1967. (Cat. 65)
Plaster and wood, 63 × 34 × 22 in.
New Jersey State Museum, Trenton
(The Governor of New Jersey Purchase Award).

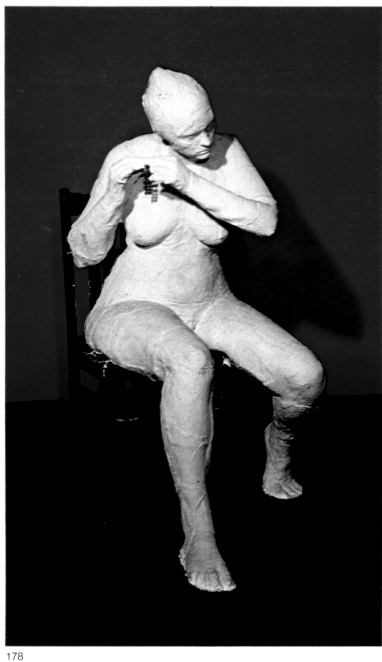

178

179

180 **Girl Putting Up Her Hair.** 1967. (Cat. 66)
Plaster and wood, 53 × 24 × 26 in.
Neue Galerie, Aachen (Ludwig Collection).

181 **Circus Girl.** 1967. (Cat. 67)
Plaster, wood and plastic, 51 × 32 × 35 in.
Collection Mrs. Miriam Keller, Stuttgart.

180

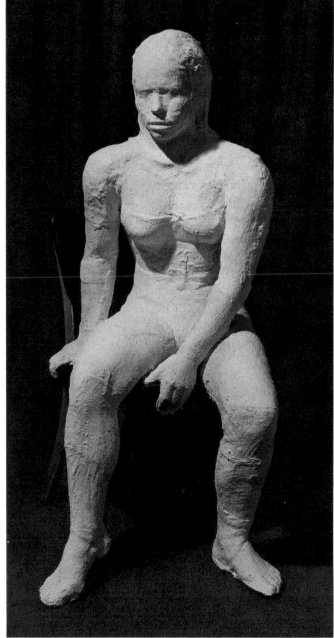

181

179

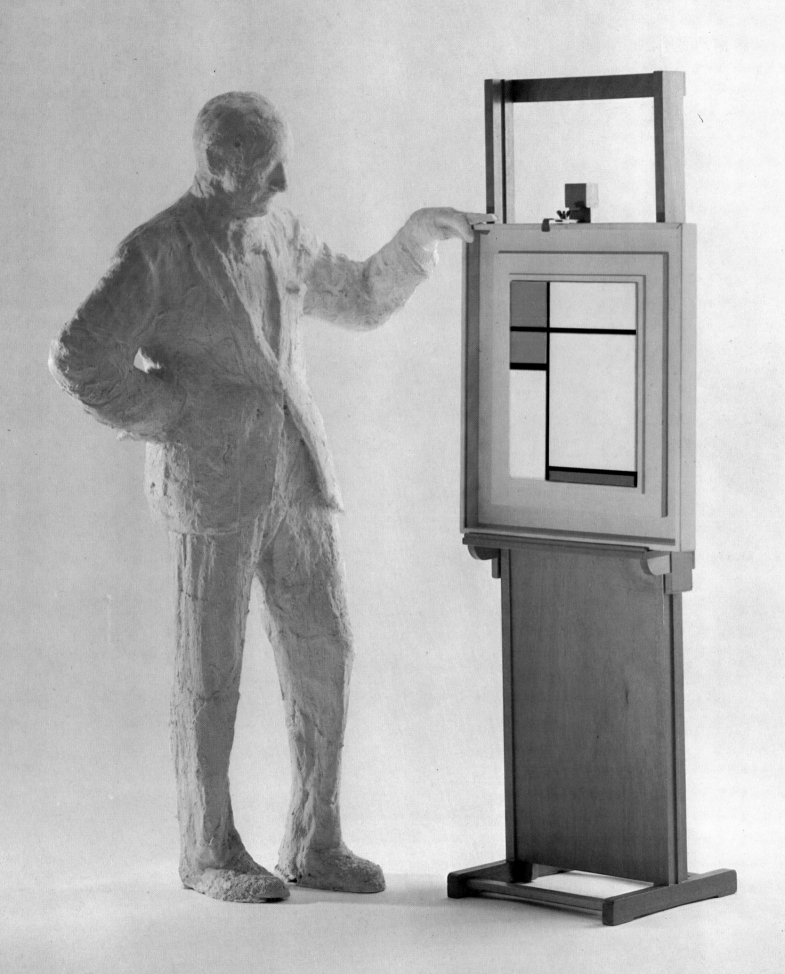

182 Sidney Janis with Mondrian's
"Composition" of 1933, on an Easel.
1967. (Cat. 68)
Plaster, wood, metal and canvas,
67 × 50 × 33 in.
The Museum of Modern Art, New York
(Sidney and Harriet Janis Collection).

183 Man Leaving a Bus. 1967. (Cat. 69)
Plaster, painted metal, glass,
chrome and rubber, 88½ × 39 × 33½ in.
Harry N. Abrams Family Collection,
New York.

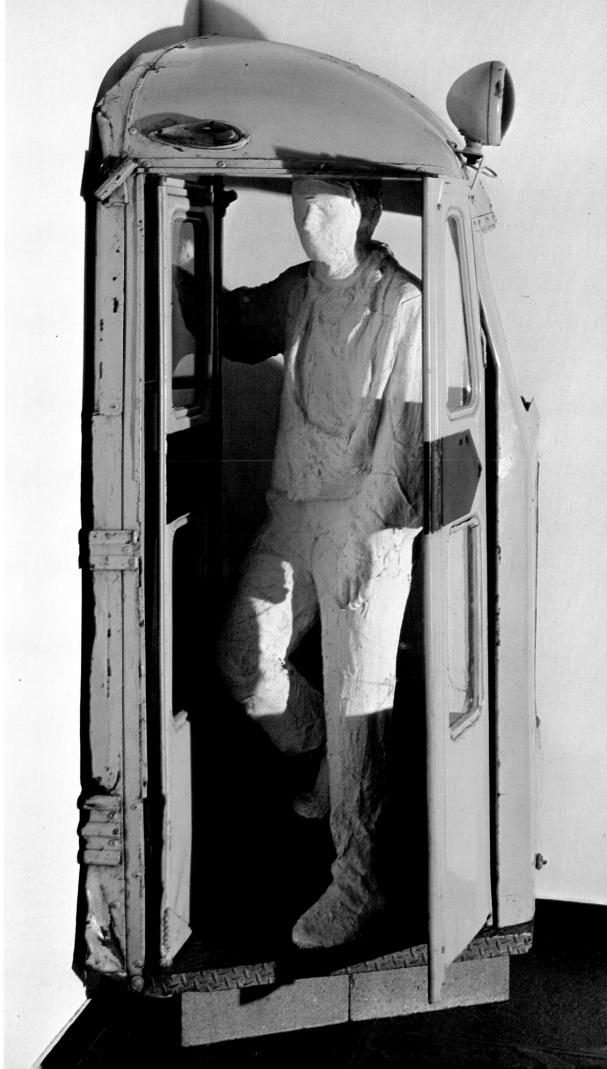

182   183

184 **Restaurant Window I.** 1967. (Cat. 70)
Plaster, wood, metal and plastic, 96 × 138 × 69 in.
Wallraf-Richartz-Museum, Cologne (Ludwig Collection).

185 **John Chamberlain Working.** 1965-1967. (Cat. 56)
Plaster, metal, plastic and aluminum paint, 69 × 66 × 56 in.
The Museum of Modern Art, New York (Promised Gift of Carroll
Janis and Conrad Janis).

186 **The Execution.** 1967. (Cat. 71)
Plaster, wood, metal and rope, 96 × 132 × 96 in.
Vancouver Art Gallery.

184

185

187 **Man Leaning Against a Wall of Doors.** 1968. (Cat. 72)
Plaster, wood and paper, 120 × 80 × 36 in.
The Hudson River Museum, Yonkers, New York
(Gift of Geigy Pharmaceuticals, Division of
Geigy Chemical Corporation).

188 **Man Leaning Against a Wall of Doors.** 1968. (Cat. 73)
(Back of doors, with billboards.)
Plaster, wood and paper, 120 × 80 × 36 in.
The Hudson River Museum, Yonkers, New York
(Gift of Geigy Pharmaceuticals, Division of
Geigy Chemical Corporation).

188

189 **Girl Putting on Her Shoe.** 1968. (Cat. 74)
Plaster, wood and plastic, 37 × 24 × 48 in.
Collection Mr. and Mrs. William S. Paley, New York.

190 **Man in a Chair.** 1968. (Cat. 75)
Plaster, aluminum, plastic and glass, 42 × 24 × 42 in.
Collection Thomas Benenson, New York.

191 **The Shower Stall.** 1968. (Cat. 76)
Plaster and metal, 78 × 34 × 43 in.
Private collection, Italy.

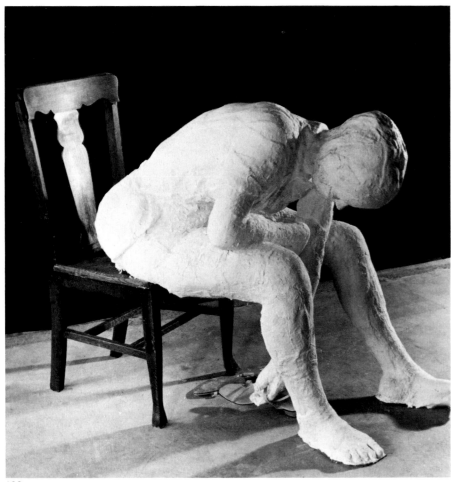

189

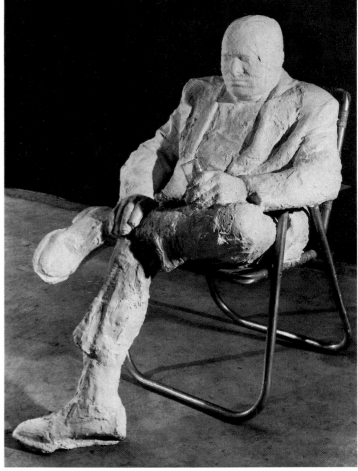

190

192　**Self-Portrait with Head and Body.** 1968. (Cat. 77)
Plaster and wood, 66 × 32 × 42 in.
Collection Carter Burden, New York.

193　**Artist in His Studio.** 1968. (Cat. 78)
Plaster, wood, paper and pastel, 96 × 120 × 108 in.
Collection Reinhard Onnasch, Berlin.

194 The Subway. 1968. (Cat. 79)
Plaster, metal, glass, rattan, incandescent light and
electrical parts, 90 × 115 × 53 in.
Collection Mrs. Robert B. Mayer, Chicago.

195 Girl Holding a Cat. 1968. (Cat. 80)
Plaster and wood, 48 × 17 × 32 in.
Collection Mrs. Helen Segal, New Brunswick, N.J.

194

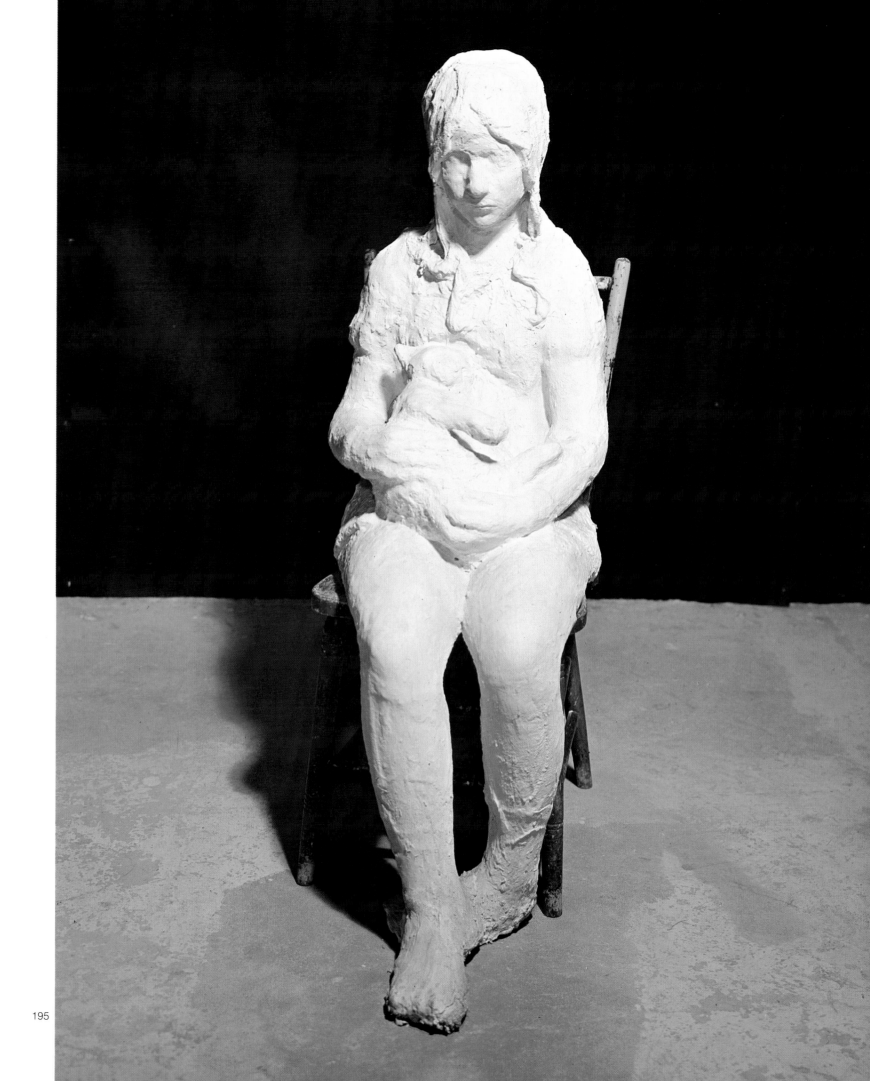

196 **Girl Sitting Against a Wall I.** 1968. (Cat. 81)
Plaster, wood and glass, 84 × 96 × 37 in.
Staatsgalerie, Stuttgart.

197 **The Parking Garage.** 1968. (Cat. 82)
Plaster, wood, metal, electrical parts and light bulbs, 120 × 152 × 48 in.
Newark Museum, New Jersey.

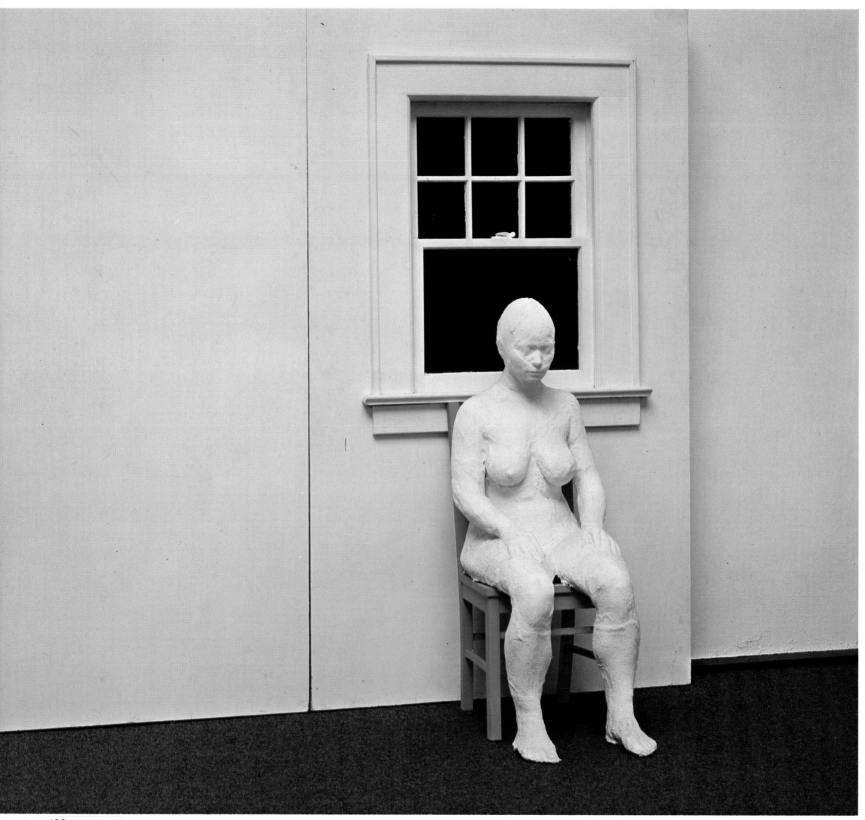

196

198 **Girl on a Chaise Lounge.** 1968. (Cat. 83)
Plaster and metal, 36 × 24 × 72 in.
Collection Irma and Norman Braman, Miami, Florida.

199 **Construction Tunnel.** 1968. (Cat. 84)
Plaster, wood and metal, 168 × 60 × 93 in.
The Detroit Institute of Arts (Founders Society Purchase)

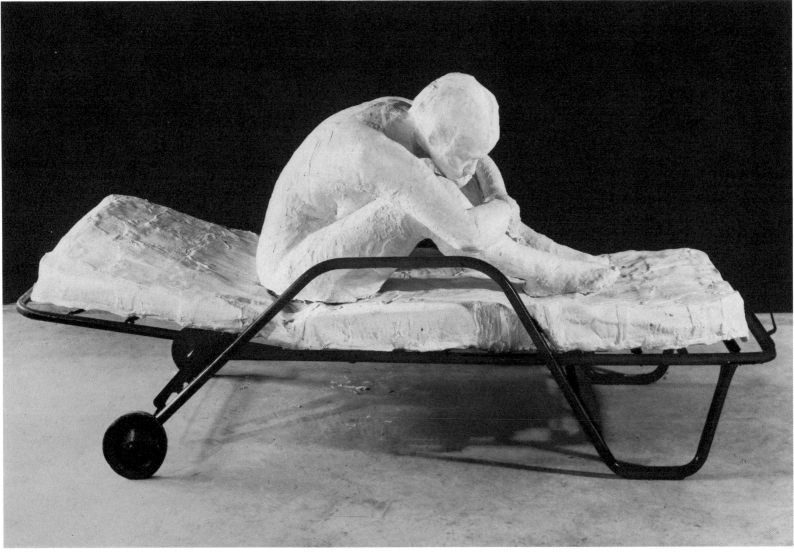

198

199

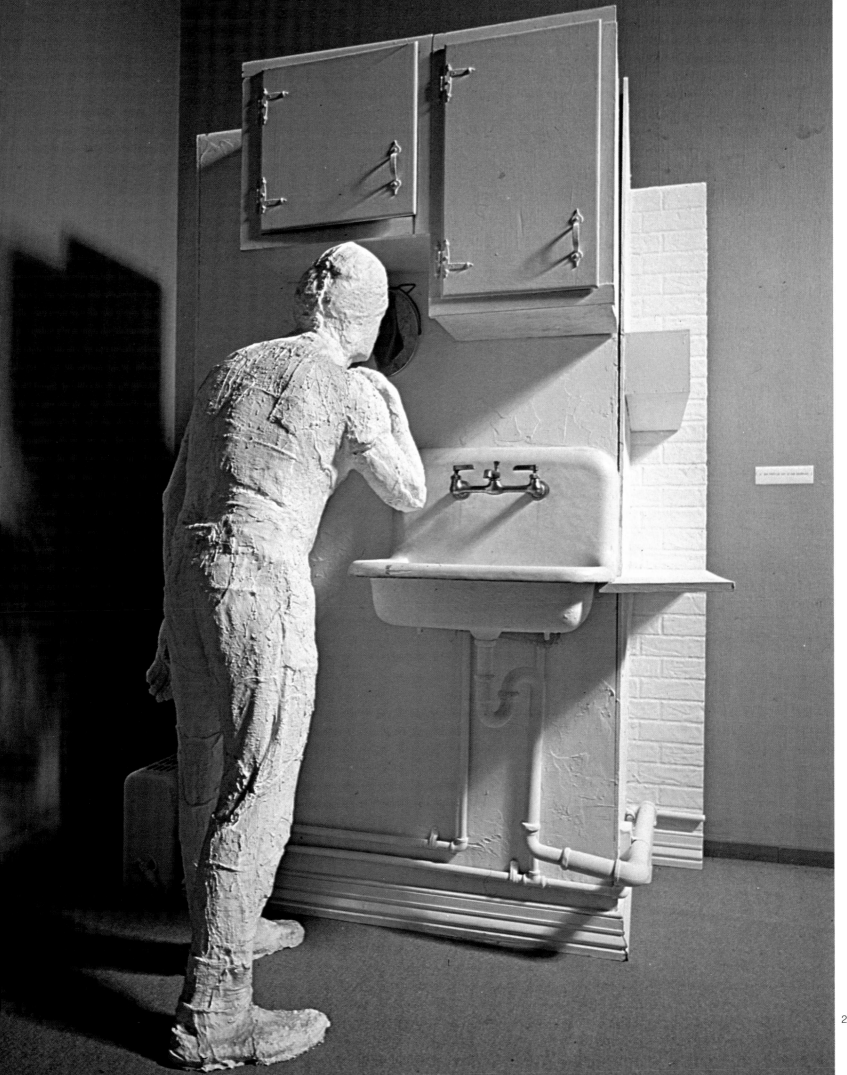

200 **The Artist in His Loft.** 1969. (Cat. 86)
Plaster, wood, metal, glass and porcelain, 90 × 69 × 60 in.
Collection Reinhard Onnasch, Berlin.

201 **Girl Putting on Mascara.** 1969. (Cat. 87)
Plaster, wood and plastic, 52 × 36 × 21 in.
Suermondt Museum, Aachen (Ludwig Collection).

202 **Seated Girl, Hands Clasped.** 1969. (Cat. 88)
Plaster and wood, 52 × 36 × 21 in.
Private collection, Paris.

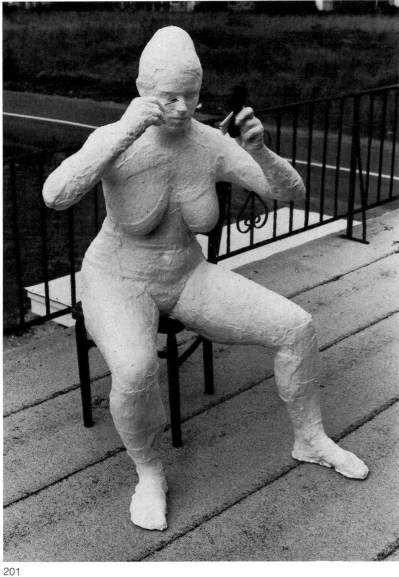

201

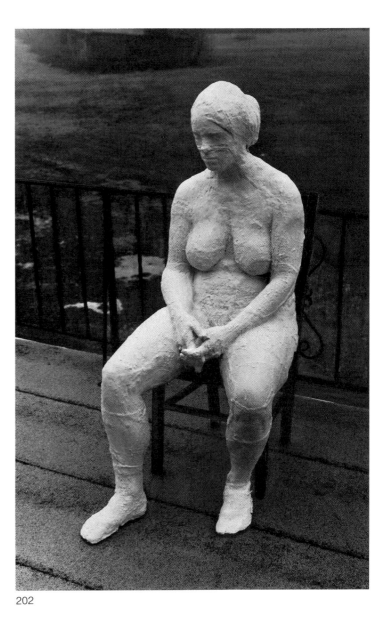

202

203 **The Girl on the Flying Trapeze.** 1969. (Cat. 89)
Plaster, metal and rope, 96 × 60 × 24 in.
Collection Mrs. Robert B. Mayer, Chicago.

204 **Man in a Chair (Helmut von Erffa).** 1969. (Cat. 90)
Plaster and wood, 50 × 29 × 36 in.
Collection Dr. Giuseppe Panza di Biumo, Milan, Italy.

205 **The Tightrope Walker.** 1969. (Cat. 91)
Plaster, metal and rope, 78 × 204 × 60 in.
Museum of Art, Carnegie Institute, Pittsburgh.

203

204

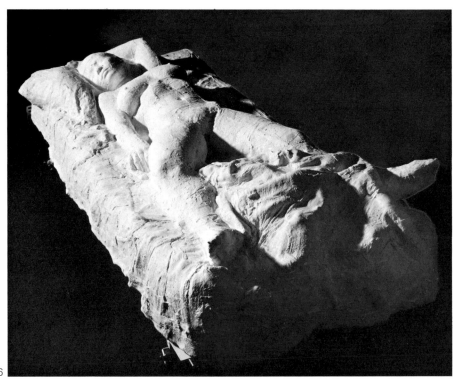

206

207

206 **Sleeping Girl.** 1969. (Cat. 92)
Plaster and metal, 22 × 73 × 33 in.
Private collection, Cologne.

207 **Girl Looking into Mirror.** 1970. (Cat. 99)
Plaster, wood and mirror, 72 × 28 × 27 in.
Collection Frederick R. Weisman, Beverly Hills.

208 **The Store Window.** 1969. (Cat. 93)
Plaster, wood, plastic and aluminum, 96 × 104 × 36 in.
Milwaukee Art Center (Gift of Friends of Art, 1970).

209 **Girl Sitting Against a Wall II.** 1970. (Cat. 100)
Plaster, wood and glass, 91 × 60 × 40 in.
Collection Akron Art Institute, Akron, Ohio.

210 **Man on a Scaffold.** 1970. (Cat. 101)
Plaster, metal and wood, 144 × 96 × 60 in.
Whereabouts unknown.

211 **Man on a Ladder.** 1970. (Cat. 102)
Plaster, wood, metal, plastic and fluorescent light, 108 × 108 × 57 in.
Neue Galerie, Aachen (Ludwig Collection).

209

210

212 **Lovers on a Bed II.** 1970. (Cat. 103)
Plaster and metal, 48 × 72 × 60 in.
Collection Phillip Johnson, New York.

213 **Girl Walking Out of the Ocean.** 1970. (Cat. 104)
Plaster and wood, 84 × 60 × 28½ in.
Private collection, Brussels.

214 **Alice Listening to Her Poetry and Music.** 1970. (Cat. 105)
Plaster, wood, glass and tape recorder, 96 × 96 × 33 in.
Staatsgalerie Moderner Kunst, Munich.

215 **The Brick Wall.** 1970. (Cat. 106)
Plaster, wood and plastic, 96 × 152 × 42 in.
Gatodo Gallery, Tokyo, Japan.

216 **The Dentist.** 1966-1970. (Cat. 95)
Plaster, metal, glass, plastic, aluminum paint, rubber and dental cement, 81 × 53 × 53 in.
Sidney Janis Gallery, New York.

217 **Girl Washing Her Hair at a Sink.** 1971. (Cat. 112)
Plaster, wood, metal and porcelain, 62 × 60 × 30 in.
Indiana University Art Museum, Bloomington (Gift of Mr. and Mrs. Henry R. Hope and Dr. Richard
D. Youngman and purchased with the aid of funds from the National Endowment for the Arts).

218 **The Aerial View.** 1970. (Cat. 107)
Plaster, wood, plastic, incandescent and fluorescent light, 96 × 105 × 48 in.
The Art Museum of the Atenaeum, Helsinki (Collection Sara Hilden).

216

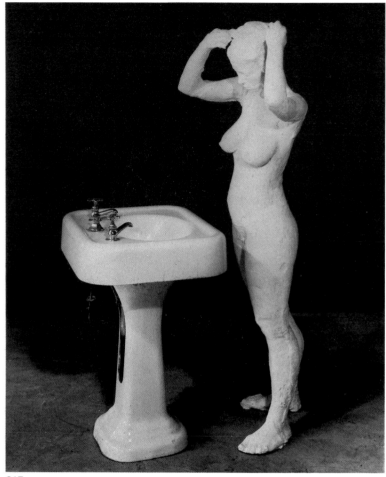

217

219 **The Bar.** 1971. (Cat. 113)
   Plaster, wood, metal, glass, plastic, neon light and television, 96 × 102 × 36 in.
   Collection Martin Z. Margulies, Grove Isle, Florida.

220 **Girl Leaning Against a Doorway.** 1971. (Cat. 114)
   Plaster, wood, plastic and incandescent light, 108 × 56 × 48 in.
   Tokyo Central Museum, Japan.

219

221 **Man Standing on a Printing Press.** 1971. (Cat. 115)
Plaster, wood and metal, 96 × 96 × 24 in.
Des Moines Register and Tribune Company, Des Moines, Iowa.

222 **Man Installing Pepsi Sign.** 1972. (Cat. 121)
Plaster, wood, plastic, metal and fluorescent light, 112 × 96 × 54 in.
Collection Reinhard Onnasch, Berlin.

223 **Man in Green Doorway.** 1972. (Cat. 122)
Plaster, wood and porcelain, 85 × 38 × 29 in.
Collection Gilbert B. Silverman, Southfield, Michigan.

222

223

221

224 **Woman Listening to Music II.** 1972. (Cat. 123)
Plaster, wood, hi-fi set, record, 72 × 96 × 72 in.
Courtesy Sidney Janis Gallery, New York.

225 **Gertrude: Double Portrait.** 1972. (Cat. 124)
Plaster, wood, plastic and super-8 film, 96 × 144 × 72 in.
Collection of the artist.

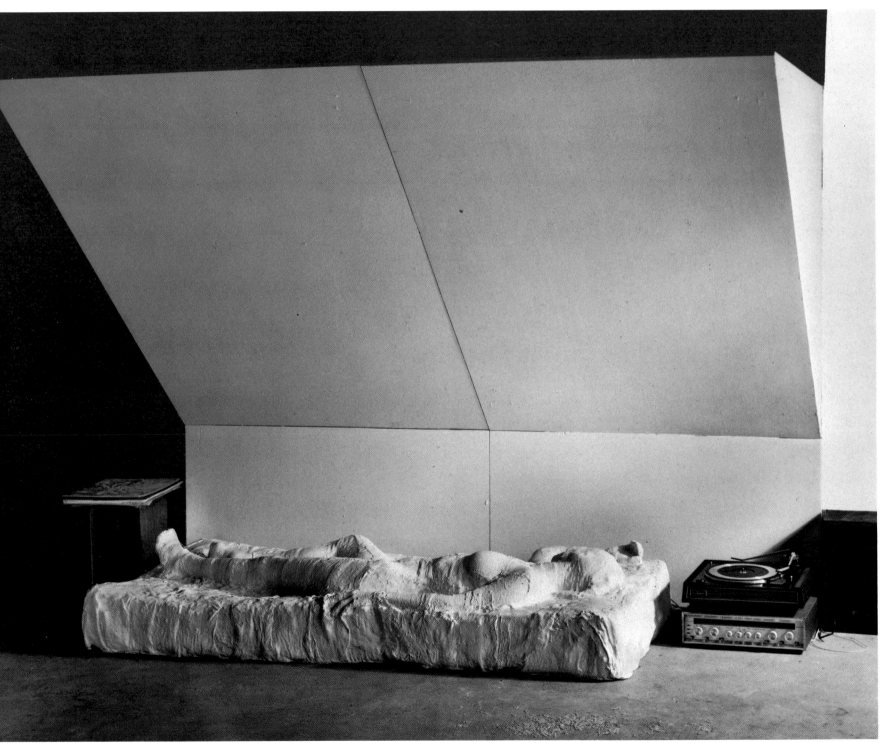

224

225

226 **Girl with Arm on a Chair.** 1972. (Cat. 125)
Plaster, 33 × 18 × 14 in.
Collection M. Riklis, New York.

227 **Restaurant Table Still Life.** 1971. (Cat. 116)
Plaster, wood and metal, 35 in. high × 36 in. diameter.
Courtesy Sidney Janis Gallery, New York.

228 **Girl Looking Through Window.** 1972. (Cat. 126)
Plaster and mixed media, 96 × 36 × 24 in.
Museum Boymans-van Beuningen, Rotterdam.

226

227

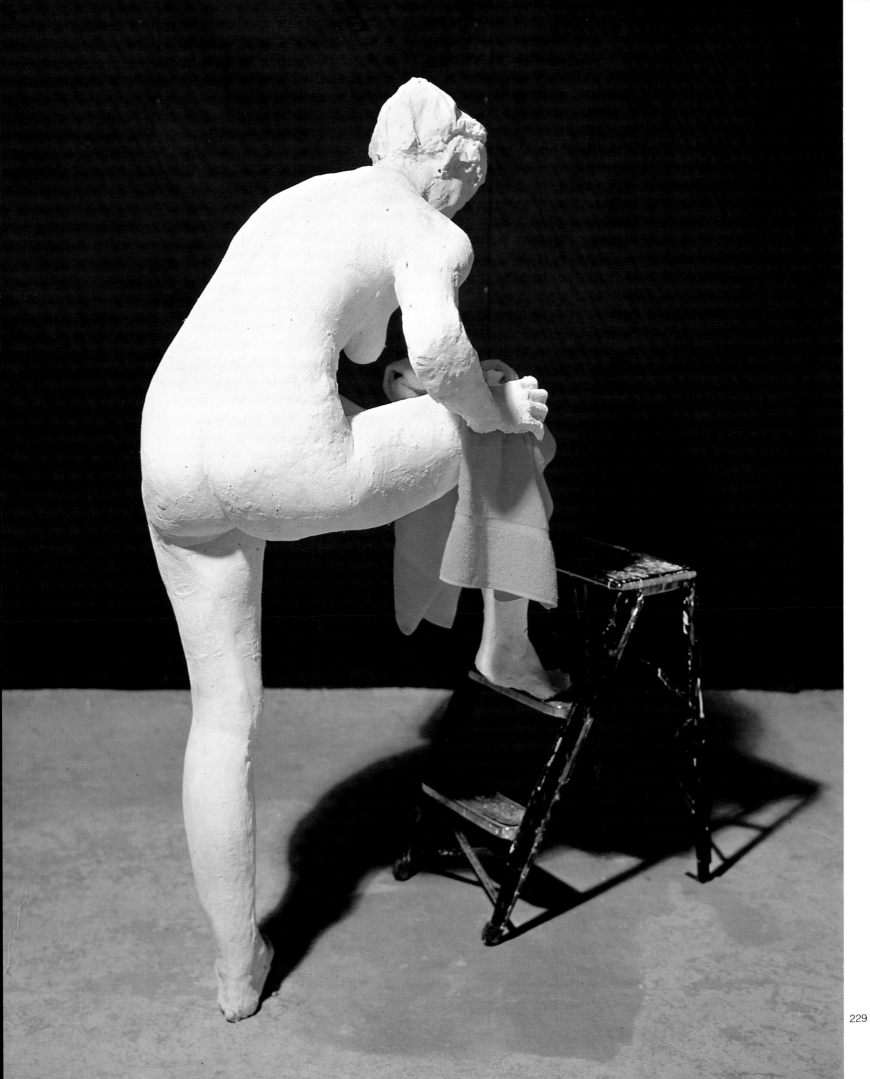

229 **Girl Drying Her Knee.** 1973. (Cat. 129)
Plaster, aluminum and cloth, 59 × 24 × 44 in.
Collection Ercole Lauro, Naples.

230 **Girl on Red Wicker Couch.** 1973. (Cat. 130)
Plaster, mixed media, 35 × 80 × 58 in.
Hopkins Center Art Gallery, Dartmouth College, Hanover, New Hampshire.

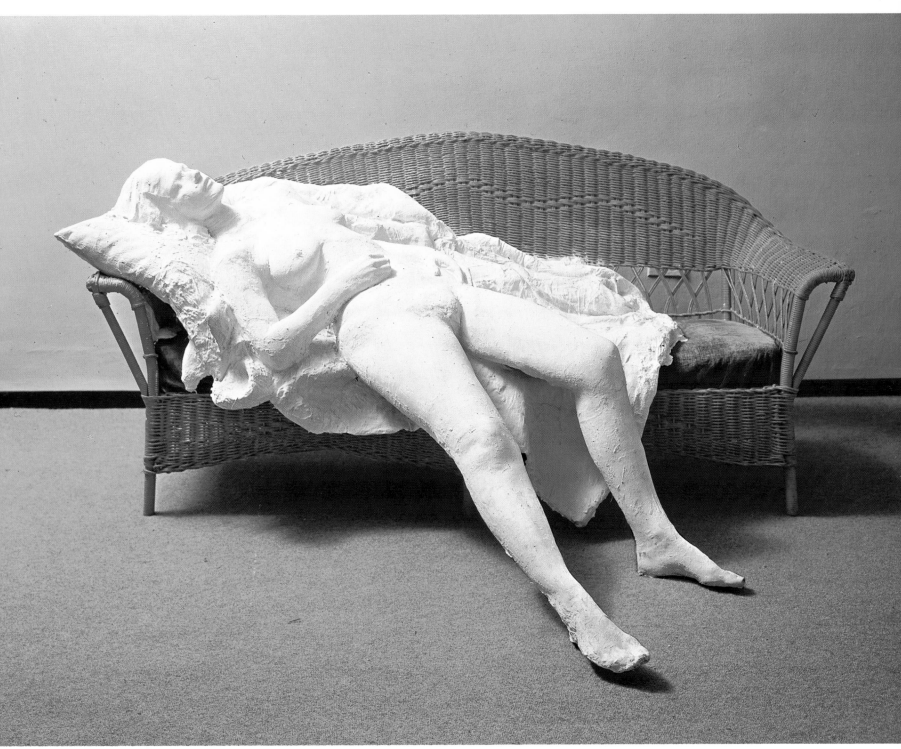

230

231 and 232 **Girl on Bed III.** 1973. (Cat. 131)
      Plaster, 22 × 81½ × 40 in.
      Courtesy Sidney Janis Gallery, New York.

231

232

233 **Corice in Shower.** 1973. (Cat. 133)
Plaster, ceramic tile and wood,
67 × 22½ × 24 in.
Collection Arman, New York.

234 **Waitress Pouring Coffee.**
1973. (Cat. 134)
Plaster, wood, metal and porcelain,
96 × 42 × 34 in.
Shiga Museum of Art, Japan.

233

234

235 **Girl on Red Chair with Blue Robe.** 1974. (Cat. 136)
Plaster, wood and acrylic, 96½ × 48 × 45 in.
Collection Leonard and Gloria Luria, Miami, Florida.

236 **Girl Next to Bathroom Column.** 1974. (Cat. 137)
Plastic and ceramic tile, 64¼ × 29¼ × 16½ in.
Courtesy Sidney Janis Gallery, New York.

237 **The Curtain.** 1974. (Cat. 138)
Plaster and mixed media, 84 × 39 × 32 in.
National Collection Fine Arts, Smithsonian Institution, Washington, D.C.

238 **The Rock.** 1974. (Cat. 139)
Plaster prototype, 114 × 120 × 36 in.
Courtesy Sidney Janis Gallery, New York.

239 **Exit.** 1975. (Cat. 140)
Plaster, wood, plastic and electric light, 84 × 72 × 36 in.
Philadelphia Museum of Art (Gift of the Friends of the Philadelphia Museum of Art).

239

240 **Girl on Bed.** 1973. (Cat. 132)
Plaster and metal, 50½ × 79½ × 35¾ in.
Collection Harry Torczyner, New York.

241 **Girl Putting on Scarab Necklace.** 1975. (Cat. 141)
Plaster, wood, metal and glass, 84 × 45 × 45 in.
Collection Mission of Iran.

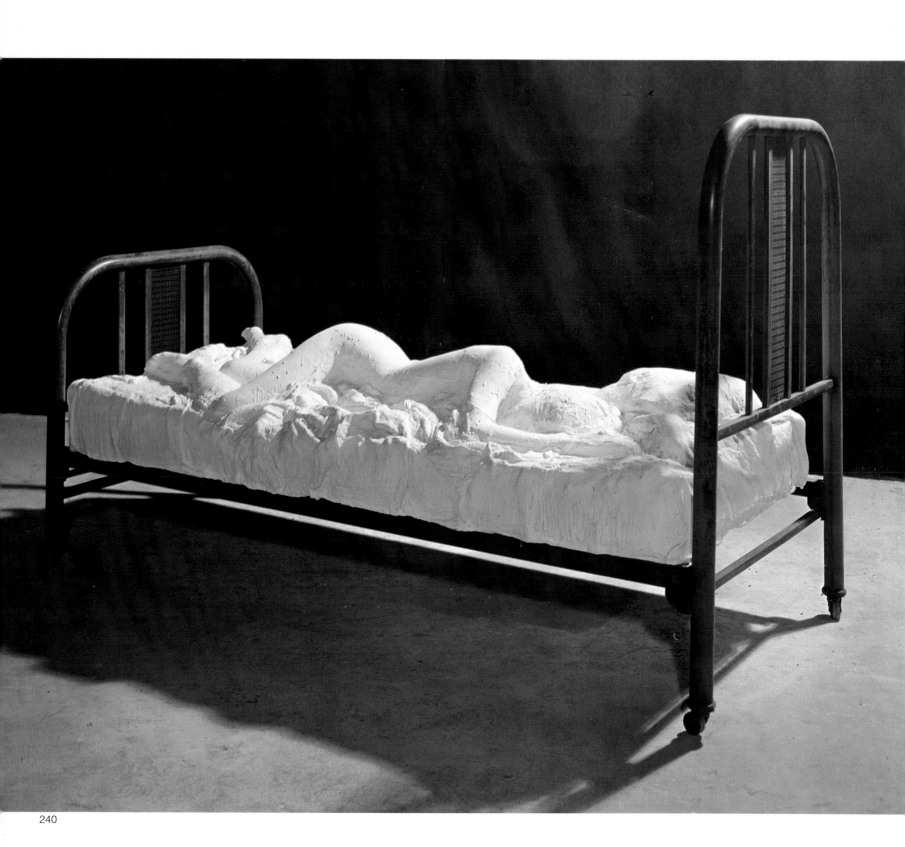

240

241

242 **The Corridor.** 1975. (Cat. 142)
Plaster and wood, 84 × 84 × 48 in.
Tamayo Museum, Mexico City, Mexico.

243 **Man on Wood Scaffold.** 1976. (Cat. 146)
Plaster, wood and metal, 144 × 60 × 120 in.
Courtesy Sidney Janis Gallery, New York.

244 **Claire Entering Doorway.** 1976. (Cat. 147)
Plaster and painted wood, 92 × 38 × 33 in.
Private collection, Brussels.

245 **Black Girl Behind Red Door.** 1976. (Cat. 148)
Painted plaster and wood, 82 × 38 × 24 in.
Collection Madame Landau, Paris.

246 **Post No Bills.** 1976. (Cat. 149)
Work destroyed.

BILLS

247 **Couple on Black Bed.** 1976. (Cat. 150)
Painted plaster and wood, 44 × 82 × 60 in.
Collection Sydney and Frances Lewis Foundation, Virginia.

248 **Red Girl Behind Red Door.** 1976. (Cat. 151)
Painted plaster and wood, 91 × 50 × 25 in.
Collection Irma and Norman Braman, Miami, Florida.

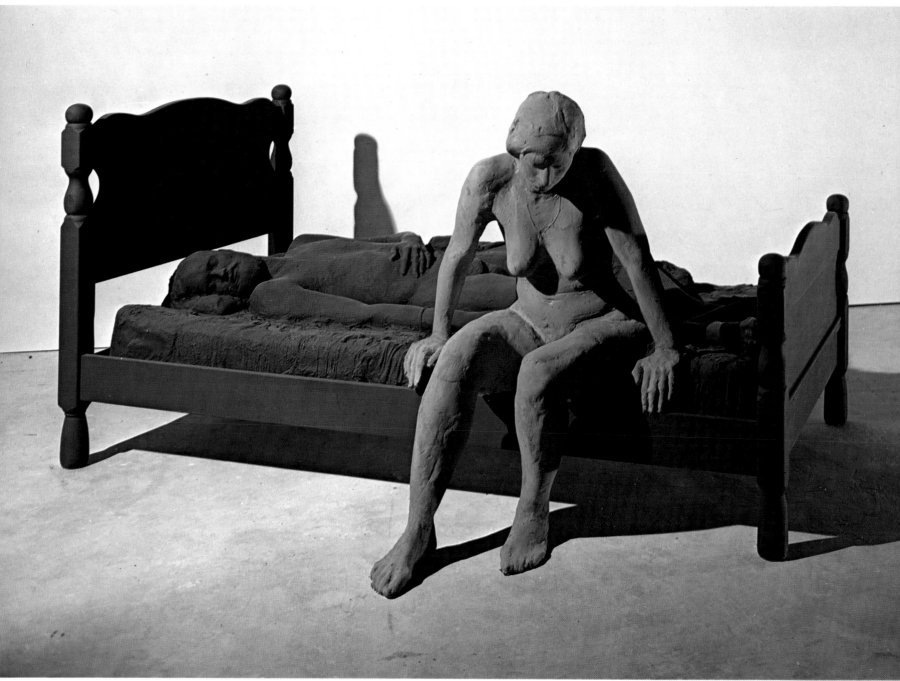

247

249 **Blue Girl on Black Bench.** 1977. (Cat. 152)
Plaster, wood and paint, 42 × 72 × 36 in.
Collection Martin Z. Margulies, Grove Isle, Florida.

250 **Go-Go Dancer.** 1978. (Cat. 160)
Plaster, wood, mirror, electric lights and vinyl, 108 × 59 × 48 in.
Collection Irma and Norman Braman, Miami, Florida.

249

251 **Street Meeting.** 1977. (Cat. 154)
Painted plaster and painted wood, 96 × 95 × 52 in.
Collection Bruce and Judith Eissner, Marblehead, Mass.

252 **Couple in Open Doorway.** 1977. (Cat. 153)
Painted plaster, wood and metal, 96 × 69 × 52 in.
Courtesy Sidney Janis Gallery, New York.

253 **Flesh Nude Behind Brown Door.** 1978. (Cat. 159)
Painted plaster, painted wood and metal, 96 × 60 × 40 in.
Courtesy Sidney Janis Gallery, New York.

252

253

254 **Blue Girl in Front of Black Doorway.** 1977. (Cat. 155)
Painted plaster, painted wood, metal, 98 × 39 × 32 in.
Collection Leonard and Gloria Luria, Miami, Florida.

255 **Blue Girl Behind Blue Door.** 1977. (Cat. 156)
Painted plaster, painted wood, metal, 96 × 53 × 23 in.
Courtesy Sidney Janis Gallery, New York.

256 **Appalachian Farm Couple-1936.** 1978. (Cat. 161)
Plaster, wood, metal and glass, 108 × 90 × 36 in.
Neuberger Museum, Purchase, New York.

257 **Three People on Four Benches.** 1979. (Cat. 164)
Plaster, wood and metal, 52 × 144 × 58 in.
Courtesy Sidney Janis Gallery, New York.
Bronze:
1/3: Cuyahoga County Justice Center, Cleveland, Ohio.
2/3: Martin Z. Margulies, Grove Isle, Florida.
3/3: Sydney Besthoff III, New Orleans, La.
A.P.: Pepsico Sculpture Gardens, Purchase, N.Y.

254

255

256

257

258 **Man Looking Through Window.** 1980. (Cat. 171)
Plaster, plastic, wood and glass, 96 × 37 × 28 in.
Courtesy Sidney Janis Gallery, New York.

259 **Girl in White Wicker Chair.** 1980. (Cat. 172)
Plaster and wicker chair, 40 × 40 × 69 in.
Collection Eli Broad, Los Angeles, Ca.

260 **Hot Dog Stand.** 1978. (Cat. 162)
Painted plaster, painted wood, plastic, metal and electric lights,
108 × 72 × 84 in.
San Francisco Museum of Modern Art, San Francisco, Ca.

258

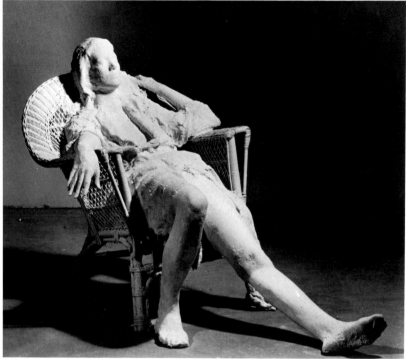

259

260

261 **The Hustle: The Four-Hand Pass.** 1980. (Cat. 173)
Plaster, wood, plastic, video-tape and sound/studio, 96 × 144 × 192 in;
figures 68 × 38 × 38 in.
Courtesy Sidney Janis Gallery, New York.

262 **Woman on a Bench II.** 1980. (Cat. 174)
Painted plaster and painted wood, 47 × 47 × 40 in.
Collection Dr. and Mrs. Paul Todd Makler, Philadelphia, Pa.

261

262

263 **Helen with Apples II.** 1981. (Cat. 182)
Painted plaster, 96 × 48 × 42 in.
Portland Museum of Art, Portland, Oregon.

264 Earlier Version of **Helen with Apples.** 1981 (No longer extant). (Cat. 183)
Painted plaster and wood, 96 × 48 × 42 in.

265

265 **Woman Standing in Blue Doorway.** 1981. (Cat. 184)
Painted plaster and wood, 82 × 55 × 33 in.
Courtesy Sidney Janis Gallery, New York.

266 **Blue Woman in Black Chair.** 1981. (Cat. 185)
Painted plaster and metal, 52 × 26 × 44 in.
Huntington Art Gallery, University of Texas at Austin, Texas.

267 **Woman in White Wicker Chair.** 1982. (Cat. 186)
Plaster and wood, 45 × 37 × 52 in.
Collection Shaindy and Bob Fenton, Ft. Worth, Texas.

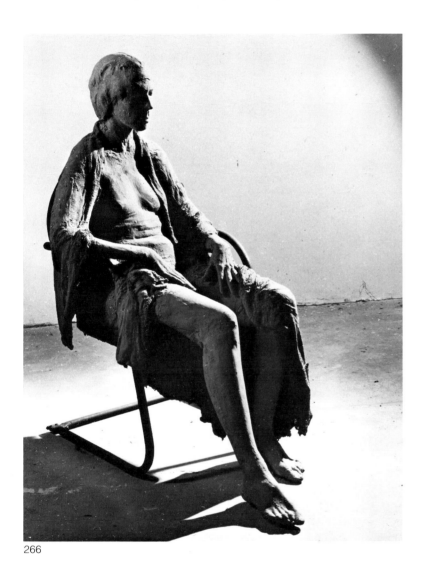

266

267

268 **Seated Woman with Dangling Shoe.** 1982. (Cat. 187)
Plaster and wood, 49 × 17 × 37½ in.
Courtesy Sidney Janis Gallery, New York.

269 **Cézanne Still Life No. 1.** 1981. (Cat. 176)
Painted plaster, wood and metal, 27 × 30 × 14 in.
Courtesy Sidney Janis Gallery, New York.

270 **Cézanne Still Life No. 5.** 1982. (Cat. 180)
Painted plaster, wood and metal, 37 × 36 × 29 in.
Collection Sydney and Frances Lewis Foundation, Richmond, Va.

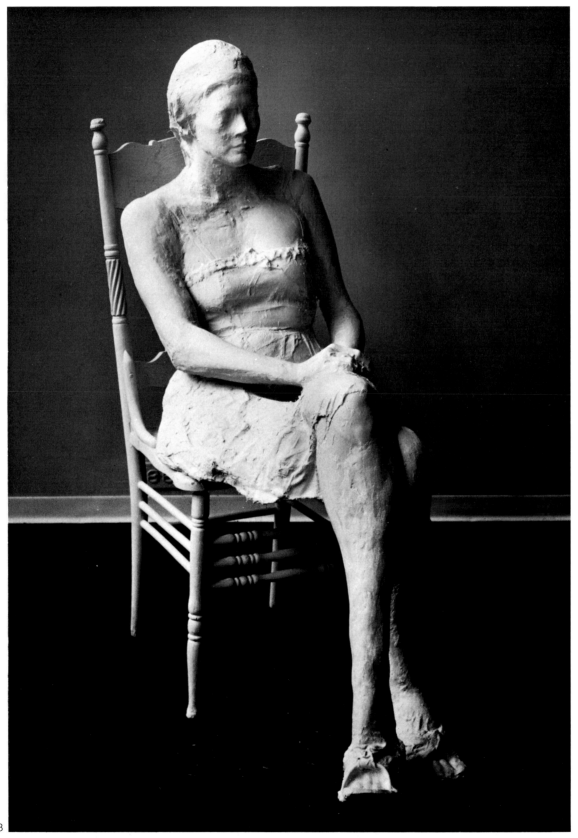

268

269

270

271

272

271 **Woman in Front of Corrugated Wall.** 1980. (Cat. 175)
Plastic, wood and painted plaster, 106 × 76 × 24 in.
Courtesy Sidney Janis Gallery, New York.

272 **Japanese Couple Against Brick Wall.** 1982. (Cat. 188)
Painted plaster and wood, 96 × 95 × 27½ in.
Courtesy Sidney Janis Gallery, New York.

273 **Machine of the Year.** 1983. (Cat. 191)
(**Time** Magazine Cover).
Plaster, wood, plastic and mixed media, 96 × 144 × 96 in.
Collection Time-Life, New York.

273

274 **Nude in Doorway.** 1983. (Cat. 192)
Plaster and wood, 37 × 22½ × 12 in.
Courtesy Sidney Janis Gallery, New York.

275 **Woman in Coffee Shop.** 1983. (Cat. 193)
Painted plaster, wood, metal and plastic, 86 × 62 × 52 in.
Collection Frederich Weisman, Los Angeles, Ca.

276 **Saul Steinberg with Rubens Painting.** 1983. (Cat. 194)
Plaster and wood, 92 × 36¾ × 26 in.
Courtesy Sidney Janis Gallery, New York.

277 **Resting Dancer.** 1983. (Cat. 195)
Plaster, wood and flourescent lights, 96 × 82½ × 48 in.
Courtesy Sidney Janis Gallery, New York.

274

276

275

278

278 **Two Bathers.** 1983. (Cat. 196)
Plaster and wood, 68½ × 36 × 22 in.
Courtesy Sidney Janis Gallery, New York.

279 **Morandi's Still Life.** 1983. (Cat. 197)
Plaster, wood and acrylic paint, 16 × 24 × 14¼ in.
Courtesy Sidney Janis Gallery, New York.

280 **Paint Cans with Barn Wood.** 1983. (Cat. 198)
Plaster, wood and acrylic paint, 12¾ × 24 × 11 in.
Courtesy Sidney Janis Gallery, New York.

279

280

281 **Rush Hour.** 1983. (Cat. 199)
Plaster, 96 × 96 × 192 in.
Courtesy Sidney Janis Gallery, New York.

282 **Jacob and the Angels** (Work in progress). 1984. (Cat. 200)
Plaster, wood and plastic and rock, 132 × 144 × 76 in.
Courtesy Sidney Janis Gallery, New York.

281

BAS-RELIEFS

283

283 **Girl Buttoning her Raincoat.** 1970. (Cat. 207)
Plaster, wood and plastic, 24 × 48 × 15 in.
Collection Kenneth Newberger, Highland Park, Ill.

284 **The Coffee Shop** (Box). 1969. (Cat. 204)
Plaster, wood, metal, plastic and cloth, 60 × 24 × 12 in.
Collection I. Lechien, Brussels.

285 **The Open Door** (Box). 1969. (Cat. 205)
Plaster, wood and metal, 60 × 24 × 12 in.
Collection of the artist.

286 **Woman on Chair** (Box). 1969. (Cat. 206)
Plaster, wood and windowshade, 60 × 24 × 12 in.
Private collection.

284

285

286

287 **The Embrace.** 1971. (Cat. 208)
Plaster, 39 × 36 × 10½ in.
Collection Tove Dalmau, New York.

288 **Couple Embracing.** 1972. (Cat. 209)
Plaster, 30 × 36 × 10½ in.
Collection Adam Aronson, St. Louis, Missouri.

289 **Girl in the Shower.** 1972. (Cat. 210)
Plaster, ceramic tile, chrome, 42 × 28 × 10 in.
Galerie Kriwin, Brussels.

287

289

288

290 **Artist's Daughter.** 1972. (Cat. 211)
Plaster and wood, 28 × 26 × 12 in.
Collection Mrs. Helen Segal, New Jersey.

291 **The Clock.** 1972. (Cat. 213)
Plaster, wood and electric clock, 33½ × 24½ × 17½ in.
Abrams Family Collection, New York.

292 **Girl with Folded Arms.** 1972. (Cat. 212)
Plaster, 48 × 36 × 15 in.
Collection Mr. and Mrs. Burton Hoffman, Stamford, Conn.

290

292

291

293 **The Bather.** 1972. (Cat. 214)
Plaster, 36½ × 28 × 8 in.
Courtesy Sidney Janis Gallery, New York.

294 **Girl in Gray Corner.** 1973. (Cat. 217)
Plaster, 48 × 48 × 15 in.
Collection Mr. and Mrs. Fred Greenberg, New Rochelle, N.Y.

295 **Girl with Clasped Hands.** 1973. (Cat. 218)
Plaster, 33¼ × 17¾ × 18 in.
Courtesy Sidney Janis Gallery, New York.

294

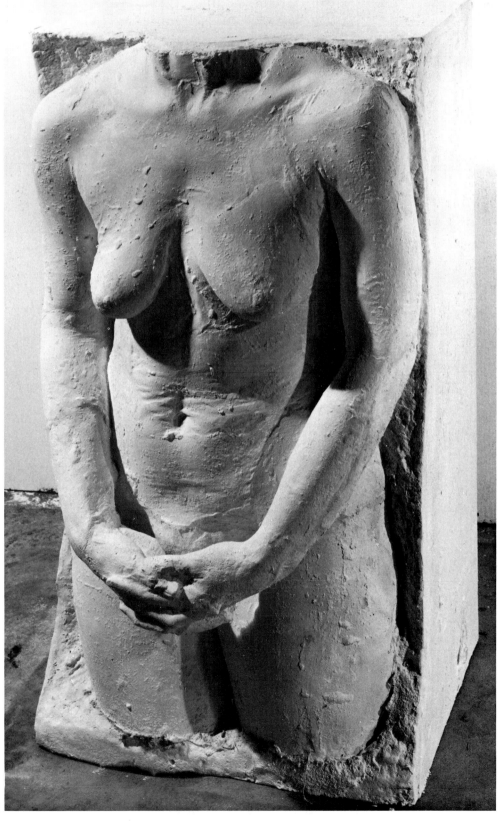

295

296 **His Hand on Her Back.** 1973. (Cat. 219)
Plaster, 42 × 29 × 12 in.
Collection Mission of Iran.

297 **Standing Girl Looking Right.** 1973. (Cat. 220)
Plaster, 42 × 28 × 13 in.
Galerie HM, Brussels.

296

297

298 **Girl Against a Post.** 1973. (Cat. 221)
Plaster, 60 × 21 × 20 in.
Pennsylvania Academy of the Fine Arts.

299 **Still Life with Red Ball.** 1973. (Cat. 222)
Plaster, 37 × 16³/₄ × 8¹/₂ in.
Courtesy Sidney Janis Gallery, New York.

298

299

300 **Girl in Doorway.** 1973. (Cat. 223)
Plaster, 56 × 29 × 10½ in.
Courtesy Sidney Janis Gallery, New York.

300

301 **Girl in Robe I.** 1974. (Cat. 224)
Plaster, 33 × 14½ × 8 in.
Courtesy Sidney Janis Gallery, New York.

302 **Girl in Robe II.** 1974. (Cat. 225)
Plaster, 29½ × 18 × 9½ in.
Collection Mr. and Mrs. Phil Gersh, Beverly Hills, Ca.

303 **Girl in Robe III.** 1974. (Cat. 226)
Plaster, 36¼ × 18 × 9 in.
Collection D. Makler Gallery, Philadelphia, Pa.

304 **Girl in Robe IV.** 1974. (Cat. 227)
Plaster, 32¾ × 18¼ × 8½ in.
Collection Westdeutsche Spielbanken, Munich.

305 **Girl in Robe V.** 1974. (Cat. 228)
Plaster, 34¼ × 18¼ × 12½ in.
Collection Westdeutsche Spielbanken, Munich.

306 **Girl in Robe VI.** 1974. (Cat. 229)
Plaster, 25¾ × 16 × 7 in.
Collection Jonathan Goodson, Los Angeles, Ca.

301

303

305

302

304

306

307 **Girl Emerging from Tile Wall.** 1974. (Cat. 230)
Plastic and ceramic tile, 39 × 16³/₈ × 10 in.
Collection Barry Boonshaft, Quakertown, Pa.

308 **Nude Turning.** 1974. (Cat. 231)
Plaster, 37³/₄ × 33¼ × 14 in.
Collection Mr. and Mrs. Albert A. List, New York.

309 **Girl Entering Doorway.** 1974. (Cat. 232)
Plaster, 33 × 23 × 14½ in.
Collection Montedison U.S.A., New York.

308

307

309

310 **Girl Seated on Gray Chair.** 1974. (Cat. 233)
Plaster, wood and plastic, 36 × 26¹⁄₈ × 20³⁄₄ in.
Courtesy Sidney Janis Gallery, New York.

311 **The Blue Robe.** 1974. (Cat. 234)
Plaster and cloth, 49 × 36³⁄₄ × 14¹⁄₂ in.
Courtesy Sidney Janis Gallery, New York.

310

311

312 **Crouching Woman.** 1975. (Cat. 242)
Plaster, 28 × 22½ × 16 in.
Collection Mrs. J. Bellet, Pompton Lakes, NJ.

313 **Portrait of Suzy Eban.** 1974. (Cat. 235)
Plaster, 36½ × 17¼ × 11½ in.
Collection Mr. and Mrs. Abba Eban.

314 **Portrait of Tove-Lin Dalmau.** 1974. (Cat. 236)
16 × 18 × 7½ in.
Collection Tove-Lin Dalmau.

312

313

314

315 **Girl Leaving Shower.** 1974. (Cat. 237)
Plaster and ceramic tile, 73½ × 25½ × 17½ in.
Collection Mr. William Paley, New York.

316 **The Couple.** 1974. (Cat. 238)
Plaster, 42 × 24 × 25 in.
Courtesy Sidney Janis Gallery, New York.

315

316

317 **Seated Girl: Chin on Wrist.** 1974. (Cat. 239)
Plaster, 36¹/₈ × 30¹/₄ × 21¹/₄ in.
Private collection, Tokyo, Japan.

317

318 **Her Arm Crossing His.** 1975. (Cat. 243)
Plaster, 40¼ × 18¼ × 12 in.
Witte Memorial Museum, San Antonio, Texas.

319 **Her Hand on His Thigh.** 1975. (Cat. 244)
Plaster, 39 × 17¼ × 15 in.
Collection Mr. Jay Bennett, New York.

318

319

320 **Girl Pinning Up Her Hair** (Version II). 1973-1975. (Cat. 240)
Plaster and ceramic, 39 × 36¹/₂ × 9³/₄ in.
Courtesy Sidney Janis Gallery, New York.

321 **Girl in Shower with Washcloth.** 1975. (Cat. 245)
Plaster, wood and plastic, 36 × 27 × 13 in.
Courtesy Sidney Janis Gallery, New York.

320

321

322 **Girl with Blue Door and Black Jamb.** 1975. (Cat. 246)
Plaster and painted wood, 47 × 20 × 15 in.
Collection Lenore Gold, Atlanta, Georgia.

323 **The Orange Door.** 1975. (Cat. 247)
Plaster and wood, 46 × 28 × 22 in.
Collection Eileen Rosenau, Bryn Mawr, Pa.

322

323

324 **The Gray Door.** 1975. (Cat. 248)
Plaster and wood, 41 × 26 × 17 in.
Collection David W. Doupe, M.D., Erie, Pa.

325 **Blue Girl Behind Black Door.** 1975. (Cat. 249)
Painted plaster, painted wood and metal, 42 × 22 × 13 in.
Collection Harry Torczyner, New York.

324

325

326 **Summer Place: Robin.** 1975. (Cat. 250)
Plaster, wood and plastic, 36 × 27 × 13 in.
Collection Mr. and Mrs. Harold Ladas, New York.

327 **Blue Girl Next to Green Door Frame.** 1975. (Cat. 251)
Painted plaster and wood, 34 × 27 × 12 in.
Courtesy Sidney Janis Gallery, New York.

328 **Girl Next to Chimney** (Version I). 1975. (Cat. 252)
Plaster, wood and plastic, 32 1/2 × 40 × 11 1/2 in.
Courtesy Sidney Janis Gallery, New York.

326

327

329 **Girl on Blanket, Arm Over Eyes.** 1975. (Cat. 253)
Plaster, 60 × 48 × 18 in.
Courtesy Sidney Janis Gallery, New York.

330 **Embracing Couple.** 1975. (Cat. 254)
Plaster, 34 × 30³/₄ × 11¹/₂ in.
Martin Friedman, Walker Art Center, Minneapolis, Minn.

329

330

331 **Seated Woman: Floor Piece.** 1975. (Cat. 255)
Plaster, 25 × 23 × 29 in.
Courtesy Sidney Janis Gallery, New York.

332 **Two Torsos.** 1975. (Cat. 256)
Plaster, 41 × 30 × 9 in.
Collection Robert Weiss, Chicago, Ill.

331

332

333 **Kissing Her Cheek.** 1975. (Cat. 257)
Plaster, 28 × 24 × 11 in.
Birmingham Museum of Art, Birmingham, Ala.

334 **Hands on Chair** (Revised Version). 1975. (Cat. 258)
Plaster, 29 × 22 × 11½ in.
Courtesy Sidney Janis Gallery, New York.

335 **Bus Stop.** 1975. (Cat. 259)
Plaster and wood, 25 × 19 × 5 in.
Courtesy Sidney Janis Gallery, New York.

333

334

335

336 **Lying Woman: Floor Piece.** 1975. (Cat. 260)
Plaster, 14 × 38 × 27 in.
Courtesy Sidney Janis Gallery, New York.

337 **Girl Touching Her Waist and Thigh.** 1975. (Cat. 261)
Plaster, 31 × 16 × 9 in.
Courtesy Sidney Janis Gallery, New York.

338 **Girl Seated Next to Birch Tree.** 1975. (Cat. 262)
Plaster and wood, 43 × 33 × 23 in.
Collection Jesse Shanok and Toby Forur, New York.

336

337

338

339 **Green Girl Next to Green Wall.** 1975. (Cat. 263)
Painted plaster and wood, 26 × 18 × 8 in.
Courtesy Sidney Janis Gallery, New York.

340 **Portrait of Henry.** 1976. (Cat. 266)
Plaster, 18 × 40 × 11 in.
Israel Museum, Jerusalem (Gift of Henry Geldzahler).

341 **Girl Behind Chair and Bedpost.** 1975. (Cat. 264)
Painted plaster and wood, 35 × 28 × 16 in.
Courtesy Sidney Janis Gallery, New York.

339

340

341

342 **Brown Girl.** 1977. (Cat. 268)
Painted plaster, 35 × 12 × 10½ in.
Courtesy Sidney Janis Gallery, New York.

343 **Magenta Girl, Blue Door Frame.** 1977. (Cat. 269)
Painted plaster and wood, 43½ × 22½ × 8 in.
Courtesy Sidney Janis Gallery, New York.

344 **Flesh Nude in Blue Field I.** 1977. (Cat. 270)
Painted plaster, 33½ × 67½ × 8 in.
Courtesy Sidney Janis Gallery, New York.

342

343

344

345 **Flesh Nude in Blue Field II.** 1977. (Cat. 271)
Painted plaster and wood, 37³/₄ × 16¹/₂ × 7¹/₂ in.
Courtesy Sidney Janis Gallery, New York.

346 **Girl Sitting on Bed with Bedpost.** 1977. (Cat. 272)
Painted plaster and painted wood, 32 × 29 × 20¹/₂ in.
Collection R. Looker, Carpentaria, California.

345

346

347 **Magenta Girl on Green Door.** 1977 (Cat. 273)
Painted plaster and painted wood, 72¹/₂ × 23 × 12 in.
Collection Dr. Milton D. Ratner Family Collection.

348 **Red Girl Next to Blue Doorway.** 1977. (Cat. 274)
Painted plaster, 42³/₄ × 23 × 8¹/₈ in.
Courtesy Sidney Janis Gallery, New York.

349 **Blue Girl Against Barn Wall.** 1977. (Cat. 275)
Plaster and painted wood, 50 × 30 × 15 in.
Collection Mr. and Mrs. Jack Friedland, Gladwine, Pa.

347

348

349

350 **Two Girls Next to Tree.** 1977. (Cat. 276)
Painted plaster and painted wood, 48 × 35 × 12 in.
Collection Howard Estrin, New Jersey.

351 **Black Girl, Black Doorframe.** 1978. (Cat. 277)
Painted plaster and painted wood, 35 × 18 × 12¹/₂ in.
Collection Mrs. R. D. Murray, Princeton, New Jersey.

352 **Girl Looking Out of Window.** 1979. (Cat. 280)
Painted plaster and painted wood, 51 × 21 × 22 in.
Courtesy Sidney Janis Gallery, New York.

350

352

351

353 **Girl on Blanket, Full Figure.** 1978. (Cat. 278)
Plaster, 76 × 42 × 12 in.
Columbus Museum of Art, Columbus, Ohio.

354 **Pregnant Series: Seven Stages.** 1978. (Cat. 279)
Plaster, No. 1, 2, 3: 28¹/₂ × 18 × 8 in.; No. 4, 5, 6, 7: 28¹/₂ × 18 × 10 in.
Courtesy Sidney Janis Gallery, New York.

353

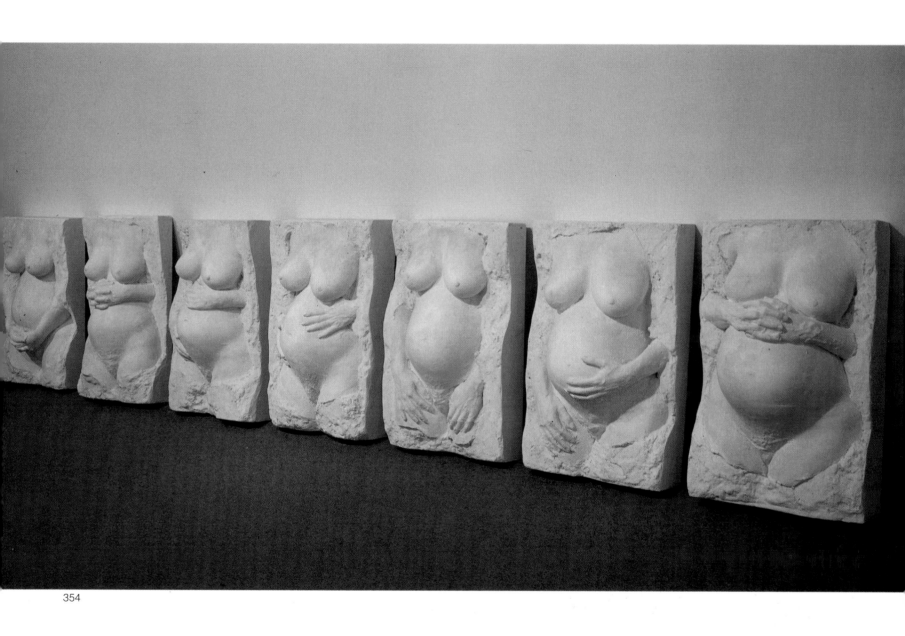

354

355 **Blue Girl in Black Doorway.** 1979. (Cat. 281)
   Painted plaster and painted wood, 64 × 24 × 20 in.
   Collection Dr. and Mrs. Harold Joseph, St. Louis, Missouri.

356 **Girl for the Whitney Museum.** 1979. (Cat. 282)
   Fiberglass edition, 19¹/₂ × 9¹/₄ × 7¹/₂ in.
   Courtesy Sidney Janis Gallery, New York.

357 **Blue Girl in Front of Blue Doorway.** 1980. (Cat. 284)
   Painted plaster and painted wood, 52 × 36 × 15 in.
   Courtesy Sidney Janis Gallery, New York.

355

356

358 **Diana (Red Column).** 1981. (Cat. 285)
Painted plaster and painted wood, 48 × 32 × 12 in.
Courtesy Sidney Janis Gallery, New York.

359 **Suzanne.** 1981. (Cat. 286)
Painted plaster and wood, 36 × 23 × 15 in.
Courtesy Sidney Janis Gallery, New York.

360 **Woman Straddling Orange Chair.** 1982. (Cat. 290)
Painted plaster, 36 × 24 × 19½ in.
Courtesy Sidney Janis Gallery, New York.

361 **Penny.** 1981. (Cat. 287)
Painted plaster and painted wood, 32 × 31½ × 12 in.
Courtesy Sidney Janis Gallery, New York.

358

359

360

361

362 **Seated Woman on Red Chair.** 1981. (Cat. 288)
Painted plaster, 36 × 36 × 20 in.
Courtesy Sidney Janis Gallery, New York.

362

363 **Woman Eating Apple.** 1981. (Cat. 289)
Painted plaster and wood, 38 × 38 × 8 in.
Courtesy Sidney Janis Gallery, New York.

364 **Woman Looking into Mirror.** 1982. (Cat. 291)
Painted plaster, wood, plastic and ceramic tile, 48 × 32 × 20 in.
Courtesy Sidney Janis Gallery, New York.

363

FRAGMENTS

365 **Figure VIII.** 1969. (Cat. 292)
Plaster, 37 × 20 × 10 in (casting of 8).
Collection Giovanni Agnelli,
Torino, Italy.

366 Seated Torso with Arm Between Legs. 1970. (Cat. 293)
Plaster, 16 × 13¼ × 8½ in.
Courtesy Sidney Janis Gallery, New York.

367 Lovers I. 1970. (Cat. 294)
Plaster, 26 × 18 × 6½ in.
Courtesy Sidney Janis Editions.

368 Girl Resting. 1970. (Cat. 295)
Plaster, 15 × 15 × 11 in.; edition of 75.
Courtesy Sidney Janis Editions.

369 Lovers II. 1970. (Cat. 296)
Plaster, 36 × 24 × 24 in.
Collection Ms. Renee Lachonsky, Brussels.

366

367

368

369

370 **Studio Wall.** 1970. (Cat. 297)
Plaster.
Studio installation, photo credit Hans Namuth.

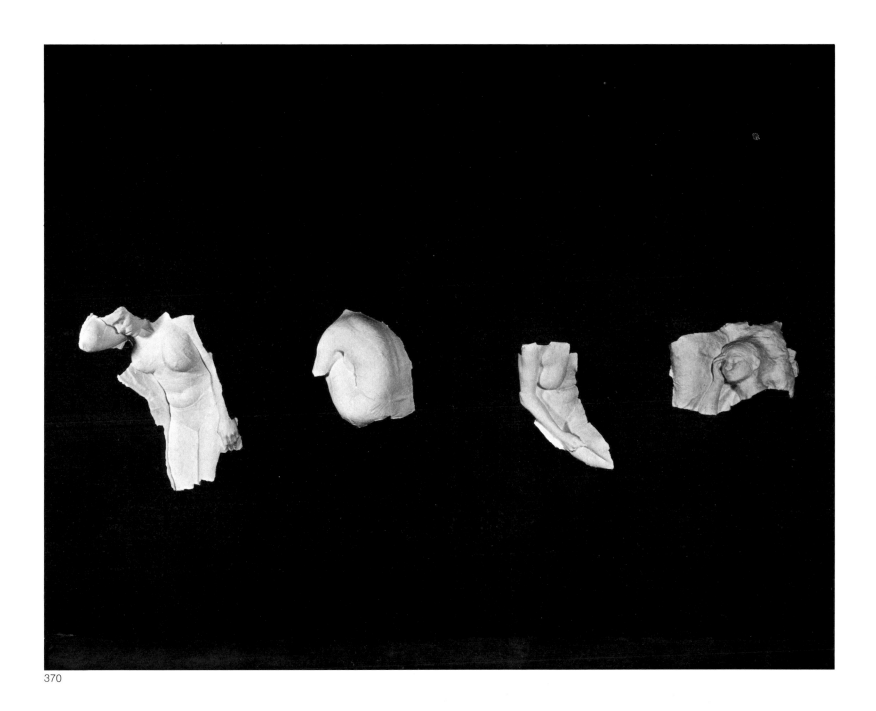

370

371 **Nude Stretching (Right) Hands on Thighs (Center) Back III (Left).** 1971. (Cat. 298)
Plaster.
Installation view of George Segal exhibition, Sidney Janis Gallery,
April-May 1971.

372 **Hand fragment. Number 4.** 1974. (Cat. 299)
Painted plaster, 16 × 11 in.
Courtesy Sidney Janis Gallery, New York.

373 **Two Hands and Dress Buckle.** 1978. (Cat. 302)
Painted plaster, 14 × 14 × 5 in.
Collection Mr. and Mrs. Alfonso Albarelli, Philadelphia.

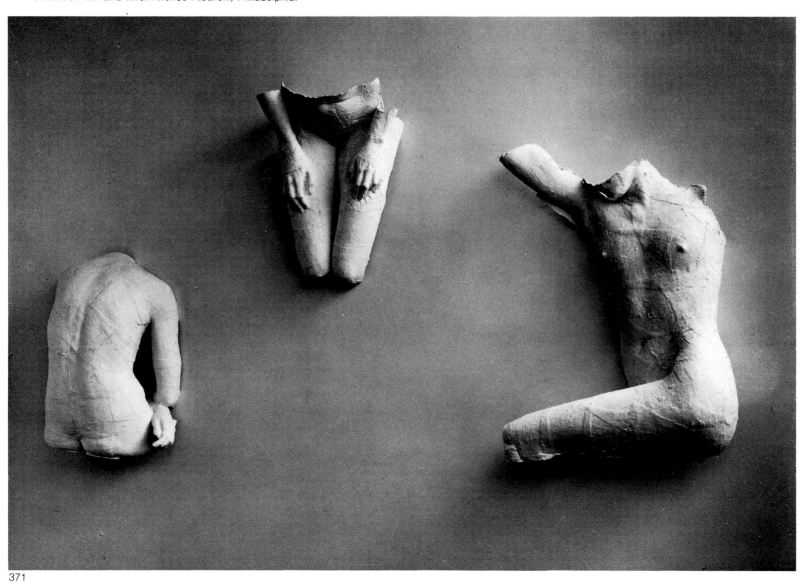

371

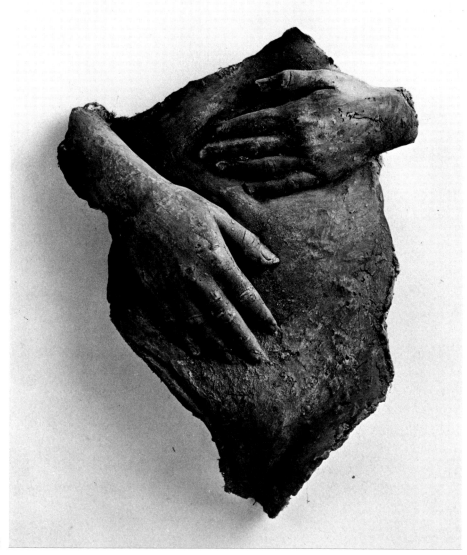

372

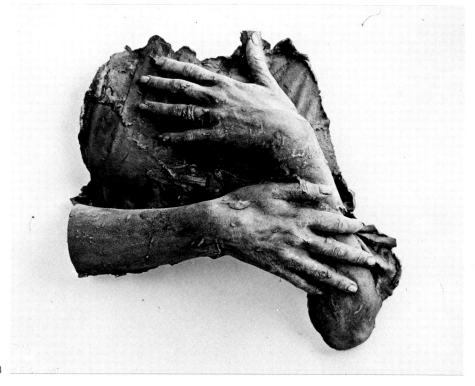

373

374 **Hand on Stomach.** 1978. (Cat. 303)
Painted plaster, 16 × 10 × 4¹/₂ in.
Courtesy Sidney Janis Gallery, New York.

375 **Right Hand Holding Left Wrist.** 1978. (Cat. 304)
Painted plaster, 14 × 11 × 6 in.
Collection William J. Hokin, Chicago, Illinois.

376 **Hands Entwined on Lap.** 1978. (Cat. 305)
Painted plaster, 11 × 16 × 7 in.
Collection Mr. and Mrs. Thomas and Strauss, New York.

377 **Two Hands on Blue Lap.** 1978. (Cat. 306)
Painted plaster, 11 × 12 × 4¹/₂ in.
Collection Mr. and Mrs. Steven Marcus, Milwaukee, Wis.

374

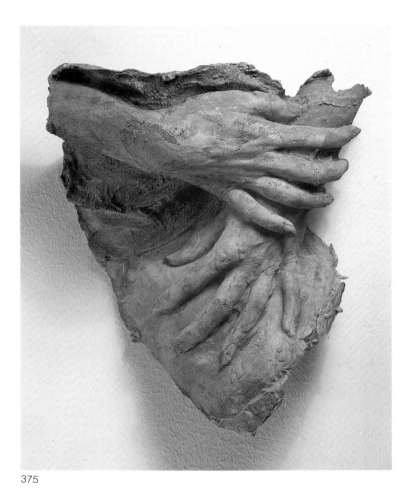

375

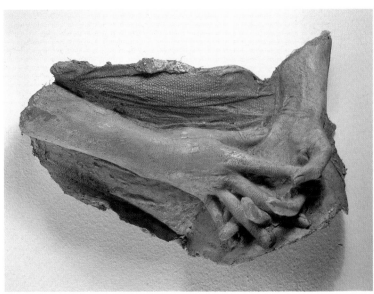

376

377

378 **Two Hands Over Breast.** 1978. (Cat. 307)
Painted plaster, 12 × 10 × 4¹/₂ in.
Courtesy Sidney Janis Gallery, New York.

379 **Girl on Wicker Chair.** 1980. (Cat. 311)
Painted plaster, 39 × 24 × 16 in.
Courtesy Sidney Janis Gallery, New York.

380 **Blue Girl in Blue Wicker Chair.** 1979. (Cat. 308)
Painted plaster, 22 × 17 × 8 in.
Collection Jerome Stone, Chicago, Illinois.

378

379

380

381 **Body Fragment No. 1.** 1980. (Cat. 312)
Painted plaster, 22¼ × 14 in.
Collection Herbert Kohl, Milwaukee, Wis.

382 **Flesh Girl in Blue Wicker Chair.** 1979. (Cat. 309)
Painted plaster, 33 × 18 × 15 in.
Courtesy Sidney Janis Gallery, New York.

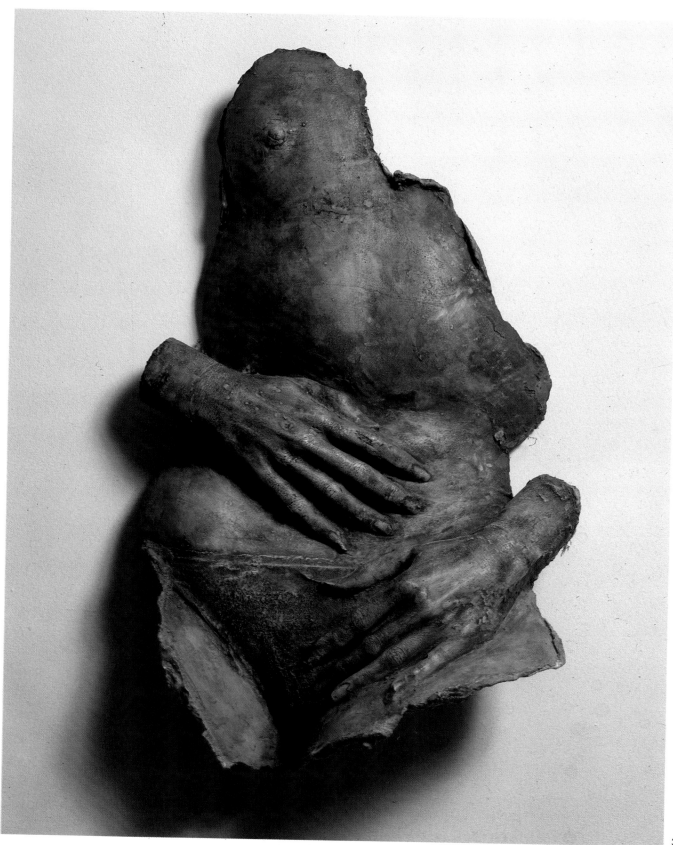

381

382

OILS ON CANVAS

383

383 **Old Testament Moon.** 1958-1959. (Cat. 323)
Oil on canvas, 48 × 96 in.
Collection of the artist.

384 **Chicken Man.** 1957. (Cat. 319)
Oil on canvas, 72 × 96 in.
Collection of the artist.

385 **Woman in Chair.** 1959. (Cat. 326)
Oil on canvas, 48 × 72 in.
Collection of the artist.

386 **Turkish Delight.** 1960. (Cat. 329)
Oil on canvas, 72 × 96 in.
Collection of the artist.

387 **Woman in Restaurant Booth.** 1960. (Cat. 330)
Oil on canvas, 72 × 96 in.
Collection of the artist.

388 **The Blow.** 1960. (Cat. 331)
Oil on canvas, 72 × 96 in.
Collection of the artist.

389 **Woman in Phone Booth.** 1960-1961. (Cat. 332)
Oil on canvas, 72 × 96 in.
Private collection.

384

385

387

388

386

389

WORK ON PAPER

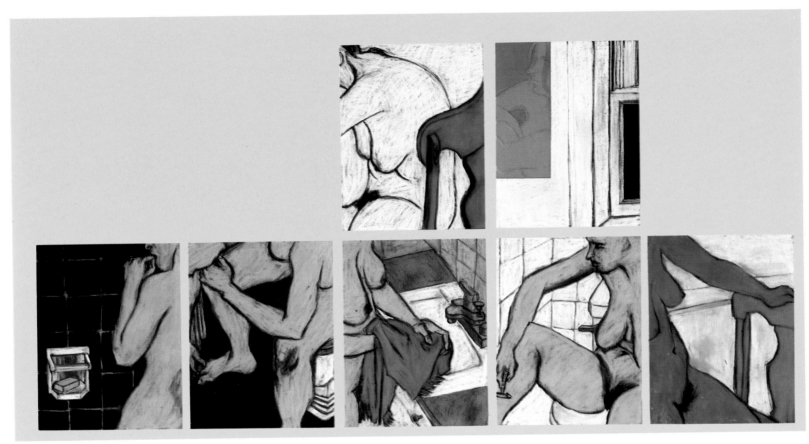

390

390 **Untitled.** 1968-1970. (Cat. 339)
Pastel, 19 × 25 in. each.
Courtesy Sidney Janis Gallery, New York.

391 **Untitled Pastels.** 1968-1970. (Cat. 340)
Pastel, 19 × 25 in. each.
Courtesy Sidney Janis Gallery, New York.

392 **Blue Jean Series: Three Figures in Red Shirts: Two Front, One Back.** 1975. (Cat. 342)
4-color aquatint, 44⁷/₈ × 85¹/₁₆ in. Ed. 35.
Published by 2RC, Rome, Italy, Courtesy Sidney Janis Gallery, New York.

393 **Untitled.** 1972. (Cat. 341)
Pastel, 24¹/₂ × 18¹/₂ in.
Courtesy Sidney Janis Gallery, New York.

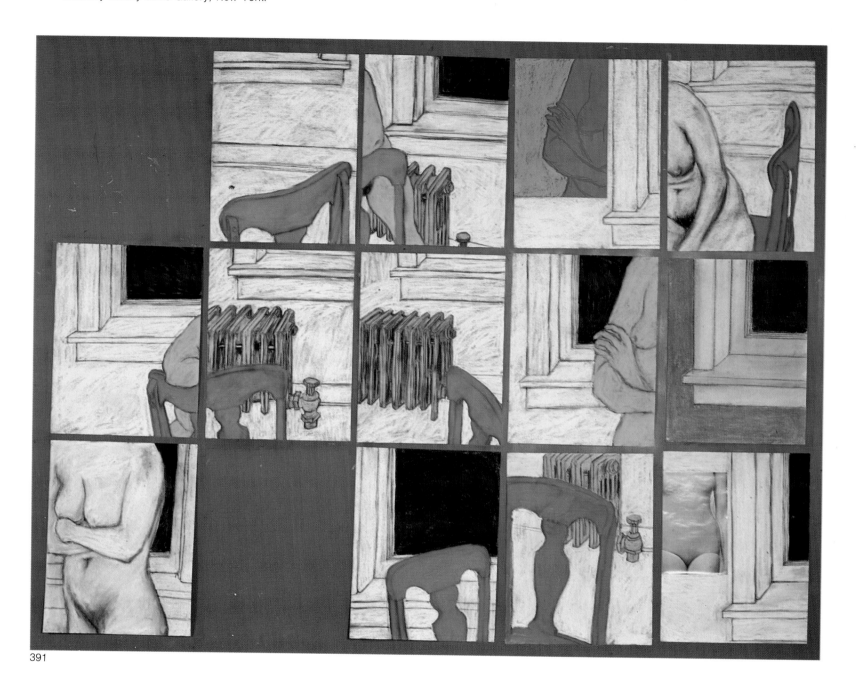

391

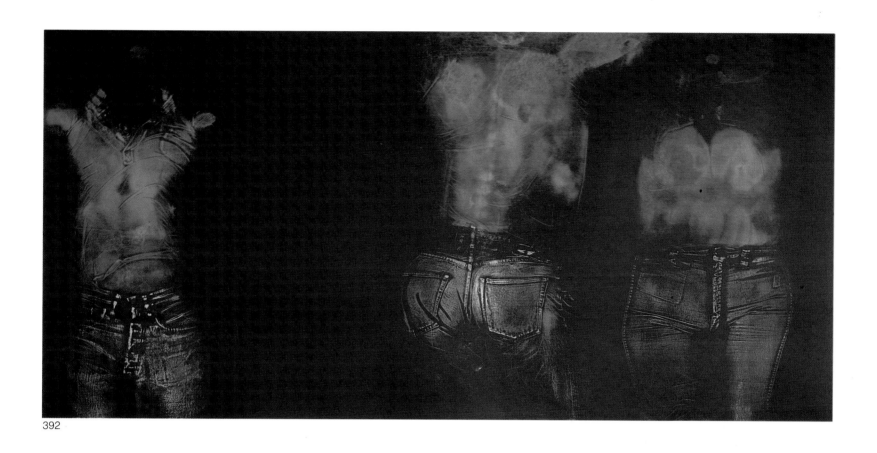

392

393

394 **Girl in Robe No. 1-5.** 1981. (Cat. 343)
   Pastel on paper, 18 × 12 in.
   No. 1: Collection Mr. and Mrs. Martin Bucksbaum, Des Moines, Iowa.
   No. 2: Collection Bob Wagoner, San Antonio, Texas.
   No. 3-5: Courtesy Sidney Janis Gallery, New York.

395 **Helen.** 1982. (Cat. 344)
   Ink on paper, 18 × 12 in.
   Collection Mr. and Mrs. Jay Wright, Piermont, New Hampshire.

394

BIBLIOGRAPHY: CRITICAL RECEPTION

Asterisk indicates a particularly relevant entry.

1956

A description of the installation of Segal's paintings, along with works by Allan Kaprow, in the Z and Z Delicatessen in New Brunswick; of anecdotal interest primarily (New Brunswick (N. J.) *Daily Home News,* Saturday, Sept. 22, 1956).

Nude in Kitchen (Cat. 314)

1957

One paragraph review of the Hansa Gallery show in New York (May 6-25) associating Segal's early paintings with Bonnard, Matisse, Degas, and Lautrec, primarily for their similarity in handling color (*Art News,* May, 1957).

Provincetown Interior I (Cat. 315)

1958

Reviews of Hansa show (Feb. 17-March 8): John Ashbery describes Segal's paintings as "unmorbid Expressionism. The figures are powerfully situated in space, sometimes swung into the canvas like an axe, cleaving it into two areas of hot, contrasting color." (*Art News,* Vol. LVI, No. 10, Feb. 1958)); Robert Dash calls him "a painter of enormous energy and convincing power." (*Arts,* Feb. 1958.)

Nude (Cat. 201)

1959

Review of the show at the Hansa Gallery (Feb. 2-21), where sculpture makes its first appearance in the form of life-size figures constructed from burlap impregnated with plaster and molded on an armature of chicken wire; "Their effect is of swiftly improvised immediacy, with the arrested movement of a Pompeian dog." (*Art News,* Feb. 1959.)

1960

Reviews of a show of paintings at the Green Gallery, New York (Nov. 15-Dec. 10) are generally unfavorable; Sidney Tillim criticizes his work for slovenliness, and labels Segal's figurative expressionism as "method acting" on canvas (source unknown); a review in *Art News* "wonders what would have been the result if the artist had worked these stimulating compositions with a little more deliberation." (Nov. 1960.)

1962

In his review of the "New Realists" show at the Sidney Janis Gallery (Oct. 31), Brian O'Doherty called Segal's early tableaux "the find of the exhibition." O'Doherty linked Segal with a trend he considered mere entertainment and journalism — Pop Art. (*New York Times,* Oct. 31, 1962.)

Woman in a Restaurant Booth (Cat. 6)

As early as the New Realists show, many critics realized that Segal offered something different from the commercial obsessions of Pop Art; Irving Sandler's review of the Janis show recognized Segal as "a special case" (New York *Post,* Sunday, Nov. 18, 1962); Harold Rosenberg observed: "Segal is the only exhibitor who uses the new illusory combination to create a new feeling rather than as a commentary on art." (*The New Yorker,* Nov. 24, 1962, pp. 161-167.)

1963

* "Mallary, Segal, Agostini: The Exaltation of the Prosaic," by Martin Friedman, *Art International,* Vol. VII, No. 8 (Nov. 10, 1963) offers a perceptive article that distinguishes Segal from the Pop artists. Unlike the latter, who incorporate objects as a commentary on the commodity fetishism of contemporary culture, Segal finds deeper, timeless, humanistic value in his confrontations of human casts and objects. Friedman compares Segal's sculpture with classic tragedy and Greco-Roman mythology, and also identifies the importance of composition and spatial relationships in heightening the effect of Segal's figures. The essay is unique among contemporary efforts to assess Segal, which either grouped him with Pop artists Oldenburg and Lichtenstein, or included him in new movements such as "Neo-Dada."

* "Pop Art: A Dialogue," a transcription of a discussion between George Segal and Sidney Tillim (*Arts Magazine* critic in *Eastern Arts Quarterly,* Vol. II, No. 1, Sept.-Oct. 1963). Tillim makes the point that Segal approaches sculpture as if it were painting: rather than dealing with space in terms of volumes and voids, he sets up tableaux that frame three-dimensional objects as if they were projected

from a surface. Segal analyzes his own work as a rejection of both flat Abstract Expressionist space and Renaissance perspective. Instead of these alternatives, he turned to a literal volume which did more than fill space — it became a "presence."

The Gas Station (Cat. 23)

1964

Brian O'Doherty locates Segal in the group of artists (Marisol, Wesselmann, Kienholz) who worked to erase the distinctions between art and life. The "arty" elements in a Segal piece — his plaster casts — become significant in the presence of brute objects (bedsteads, doors, tables, etc.). In the process, art and reality are equated. (The *New York Times*, Sunday, March 22, 1964). Irving Sandler addresses this issue in a review of Segal's *Gas Station* at the Greene Gallery. The size of the piece, says Sandler, forces the viewer to experience it as a real environment. This experience heightens the tension between the realism of the casts and their eerie, ghostlike presence. (New York *Post*, March 22, 1964.)

* "The Sculpture of George Segal" by Ellen H. Johnson, *Art International*, Vol. VIII, No. 2 (March 20, 1964), pp. 46-49). This interesting discussion of Segal's work makes the following points: against the doubting Thomases, Johnson shows that Segal does employ skill and technique in creating his casts, which are more than just copies. Johnson discusses the nature of plaster as a lowly, anti-art material; Segal's tableaux are three-dimensional Cubist paintings; his use of light is fundamentally coloristic and painterly.

Allan Kaprow describes the objects in Segal's environments as physical presences on equal terms with the cast figures. He observes about Segal's chairs, tables, razors, and windows: "Their magic lies in their existential necessity, their blunt actuality and their sense of belonging, both to each other and to the silent personages among them." (*Art News*, Vol. LXII, No. 10, Feb. 1964, p. 30 ff.)

* "An Interview with George Segal," by Henry Geldzahler in *Artforum* (Nov. 1964), pp. 26-29. A very short interview, important because Segal substantiates many of the things critics have been saying about his work. Segal acknowledges the influence of Kaprow's Happenings, the pictorial and planar relationships between objects in his works, the use of light as color, and his attempt to make composition trigger emotional revelation.

Segal on capturing the essence of his subjects: "Of all the clues projected by a person, I think I trust most qualities of bone structure and how that person holds his or her body in many situations. Then, too, people seem to accumulate certain kinds of objects over the years and move more comfortably through them in a space of their own making. The final joke may be on me. After pursuing the intangibility of spirit so long, I find I must deal with it by trying to encase it in uncompromisingly real objects." *The Artist's Reality: An International Sculpture Exhibition*, exhibition catalogue, New School Art Center, New York, Oct. 14-Nov. 14, 1964, unpaginated.)

* "George Segal," Henry Geldzahler, *Recent American Sculpture*, exhibition catalogue, The Jewish Museum, New York, Oct. 15-Nov. 29, 1964, p. 25. A good, brief elucidation, elegantly phrased. Geldzahler surveys the important topics — the influence of Happenings, the divergence from Pop, the difference from social realism, and the "choreographic notation" embodied in Segal's installations — and adds a few novel observations of his own.

Writing in 1964, Ursula N. Eland attempts to accommodate Segal's work to the familiar stereotype of Pop Art. This thin and superficial account is important only for what its failed attempt at pop classification reveals about the nature of Segal's art. ("George Segal," Ursula N. Eland, *Gallery notes*, The Buffalo Fine Arts Academy and the Albright-Knox Art Gallery, Volume XXVII, Number 2, Spring 1964, unpaginated.)

1965

Segal did not stop drawing; his pastels were well received by an anonymous Herald Tribune critic, who called them "exquisitely composed

Untitled (Cat. 339)

figure drawings, in luminous pastels, reminiscent of the Fauves." (New York *Herald Tribune*, May 8, 1965.)

Review by Grace Glueck of the Segal show at Janis in the *New York Times*, Oct. 24, 1965. She quotes Segal: "The gestures have to be psychologically true to the subjects. I also consider them in relation to the space of the whole composition... I find that very exciting — to take a piece of real space and compose it just as severely as a painting."

John Canady cites Segal as one of those creative, talented artists, who took Pop Art beyond its limits. Segal, Rauschenberg, and Kitaj did more than entertain; they re-introduced figurative art into the avant-garde. (*New York Times*, March 7, 1965.)

* "An interview with George Segal," by Katherine Molnar and Elizabeth Palin, in the *Argomag*, Winter 1965, pp. 9-14. The sophistication of this interview belies its inclusion in a high school literary magazine. Segal discusses the use of pictorial space in his sculpture, his coloristic handling of light, his concern for sculpture as generalized gesture rather than strictly accurate duplication of particular detail, and his reasons for working in plaster.

George Segal, quoted in the catalogue for *The New American Realism* exhibition at the Worcester Art Museum, Feb. 18-April 4, 1965, says: "If you see a *thing*, how you feel about it and your whole host of inner reactions have something to do with that thing. You can't help impressing your own humanity on it once you regard it."

In his *Nine Pastels* Series (1964-65), shown in his one-man show at Janis (Oct. 4-30), Segal began experimenting with the fragmented bodies and arbitrary boundaries he developed later in his sculpture.

1966

The influence of Kaprow's Happenings is seen in Segal's success with "environmental art."

The Truck (Cat. 52)

The Truck, with its continuous projection of traffic on the inside windshield, won the top jury award and a prize of $5,000 for its appearance in the 68th American Exhibition at the Art Institute of Chicago ("Art: A Surrounding of 'Environments'", by Hilton Kramer, *New York Times*, August 27, 1966).

Legend of Lot (Cat. 53)

* Rosalind Krauss, in a review of the "Erotic Art" show at Janis, interprets erotic representational art in general as a parody of art seriously concerned with examining and challenging our ways of seeing and perceiving. Erotic art is only voyeurism, and as such imitates our normal habits without enriching them. Krauss takes Segal's literary *Legend of Lot* as symbolic of the spectator's visual act and, in the case of Lot's wife, of the result of reducing perception to voyeurism. (Rosalind Krauss, review of Janis' "Erotic Art" exhibition, *Artforum,* Dec. 1966.)

1967

Segal explains his move to sculpture as an attempt to make boundaries precise, and hence

to gain greater control over the spatial relationships in his work: "I could carve space by choosing and placing. Space became a total aesthetic area which I could enter — as an intensely felt, internal experience...." (Cited in "George Segal's 'Portraits in Plaster'" by Barbara Gold, Baltimore *Sun*, Nov. 5, 1967).

Lighting and arrangements are important to the effect of a Segal work. He suggests that for best results they should be seen in their original home in his chicken coops. (Cited in "Twentieth Century Period Pieces" by Ricki Washton, *Arts,* Feb. 1967.)

Couple at the Stairs (Cat. 33)

Writing about the 1964 piece, *Couple at the Stairs*, Segal says: "I've been both voyeur and participant in this situation." The urge to look, and to make the audience the artist's conspirator, is fundamental to Segal's work. ("Three individuals combine to make an 'excellent show'", by Robert Fulford in Toronto *Daily Star*, Jan. 14, 1967.)

Lawrence Alloway makes the familiar comparison of Segal's creations to "the mood of human isolation" in Hopper's paintings, specifically comparing Hopper's *Nighthawks* and Segal's *Gas Station* (p. 37), ("Art as Likeness," *Arts Magazine,* May 1967, pp. 34-39).

* "The Sense of 'Why not?': George Segal on his art," *Studio International,* Vol. CLXXIV, (Oct. 1967), pp. 147-49. Segal explains the reason for only making life size sculpture, and for never dressing his figures with real clothing. His interest, he says, lies in the confrontations and dialogue between individuals, and not in the solipsistic introspection of the Abstract Expressionist: "I don't want to report the world as a reflection of my own blood vessels."

* "George Segal as Realist," by Robert Pincus-Witten, *Artforum* (Summer 1967), pp. 84-87. A thorough survey of criticism to date, original for its emphasis on the humanistic and figurative value in Segal's work: "Segal's achievement above all else has been to replenish an ancient and honorable stream run dry in the mid-twentieth century.... His work is infinitely more profound and human than that of the general run of Pop artists with whom he has been affiliated.... Segal occupies an isolated and tenuous position in modern art. What he does is harder." (p. 87).

Robert Pincus-Witten: "...above all else, Segal is a lover, and his work has always closely reflected his personal relationships. From the first, his sculpture has been cast from friends and acquaintances." ("George Segal," Robert Pincus-Witten, *Dine Oldenburg Segal: Painting/Sculpture,* exhibition catalogue, Art Gallery of Ontario, Toronto, Jan. 14-Feb. 12, 1967, and Albright-Knox Art Gallery, Buffalo, New York, Feb. 24-March 26, 1967, p. 58.)

The justification for a 1967 exhibition, combining the works of Oldenburg, Dine, and Segal, depended on a distinction between those Pop artists — Warhol and Lichtenstein — who incorporate real objects in a cool, parodic art, and those "hot" artists, particularly those represented in the show, who incorporate ordinary objects in their work for expressive and emotional reasons. (Preface, Brydon Smith, in *Dine Oldenburg Segal: Painting/Sculpture,* exhibition catalogue, Art Gallery of Ontario, Toronto, Jan. 14-Feb. 12, 1967, and Albright-Knox Art Gallery, Buffalo, New York, Feb. 24-March 26, 1967, p. 58.)

Segal on composition: "The peculiar shape and qualities of the actual empty air surrounding the volumes becomes an important part of the expressiveness of the whole piece. The distances between two figures or between a figure and another object becomes crucial. My pieces often don't end at their physical boundaries." Emily Rauh adds: "The selection of objects and the placement of them in relation to the figure are as carefully worked out as in any Dutch seventeenth century genre painting.'' (''George Segal,'' Emily S. Rauh, *7 for 67: Works by Contemporary American Sculptors,* City Art Museum of Saint Louis, Oct. 1-Nov. 12, 1967, unpaginated.)

1968

When Segal creates his archetypical proletarian figures, he is struggling with ''phantoms, demons and internal fantasies that border on nightmare. My specific activity is picturing the phantom — picturing it exorcises it.'' (''Segal and Whitman: The life styles of two artists,'' Michaela Williams, Chicago *Daily News,* April 20, 1968.)

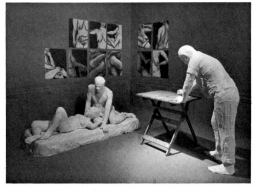

Artist in His Studio (Cat. 78)

* ''Plebeian Figures, Banal Anecdotes: The Tableaux of George Segal,'' Hilton Kramer, *New York Times,* Dec. 15, 1968. Kramer admits that Segal's *The Artist in His Studio* does raise familiar questions about the relation between reality and representation, albeit in a crude and anecdotal manner. Otherwise, Kramer considers Segal's exhibition at the Sidney Janis Gallery frivolous and uninventive; for him Segal is a vulgarized Hopper and his success reveals the inordinate influence of wealthy, decadent patrons and the inability of the general public to distinguish good art from bad.

A review of Segal's show at Janis (Dec. 4, 1968-Jan. 4, 1969) in *Arts Magazine* notes the rich coloristic effects of black and white in *The Artist in His Studio,* and suggests a continuity between Segal's painting and sculpture (by P.T., Nov. 1968, p. 57).

* ''Plaster Caste,'' John Perreault, *Art News* (Nov. 1968), pp. 54 ff. Perreault argues that Segal is a ''poetic realist'': his sculptures communicate through the gestures of their

bodies, like dancers, and, in their timelessness, reveal the universal in the particular.

Segal's work has by this date become so well known that the phrase ''Segal-like plaster dummies'' occurs without apology or comment in a New Yorker theater review by Brendan Gill (*The New Yorker,* April 27, 1968, p. 84).

* ''George Segal'' by Phyllis Tuchman, in *Art International,* Vol. XII, No. 7 (Sept. 20, 1968), pp. 51-53. This short article goes beyond a lucid synopsis of critical perspectives to make several original observations. Tuchman considers Segal's tableaux a reversal of Renaissance perspective: one does not discern an illusion of depth on a canvas plane, but the illusion of a picture plane and perspective order in three-dimensional objects. Tuchman further draws an enlightening comparison between Segal's attitudes and existential thought. The introductory quotation by Segal and his admission of the influence of Giotto, Poussin, and Goya are also revealing.

Hedy Backlin-Landman, Curator of American Art at the Art Museum, Princeton University, in the catalogue for the exhibition ''George Segal'' (Sept. 19-Nov. 3, 1969) makes the observation: ''George Segal's works are clearer statements in favor of the essential humanity of art than any of his contemporaries have cared to make; they exist because we exist.''

The Chicago Museum of Contemporary Art published the first attempt to document the entirety of Segal's œuvre, in conjunction with their exhibition of twelve Segal tableaux. Jan van der Marck, the catalogue's author, offers few original insights, but his perspective is to be recommended for its emphasis on Segal's humanism and concern for attitude and emotion. (Introduction, Jan van der Marck, *George Segal: 12 Human Situations,* exhibition catalogue, Museum of Contemporary Art, Chicago, April 12-May 26, 1968.)

1970

* ''George Segal,'' by Ernesto J. Ruiz de la Mata, San Juan *Star,* May 31, 1970. A short article interesting for its comparison of Segal's eroticism to the writings of Henry Miller.

Segal: ''Plaster is bold and wet and clean. It has its own life under fingers. It changes every second.'' (''The Frozen Images of George Segal,'' by George McCue, St. Louis *Post-Dispatch,* Dec. 13, 1970.) A report on Segal's methods, primarily.

In recognition of his prominence in the art world, Segal received an honorary Doctor of Fine Arts degree from Rutgers University, where he had earned his masters. (''Rutgers to Honor Nobel Laureates, Cahill,'' no byline, New Brunswick (New Jersey) *Home News,* May 19, 1970); his figures turn up, apparently without the need for explanation or attribution, in a trade magazine advertisement announcing the merger of two electronics firms (*Electronic News,* May 18, 1970); and on the cover of the *Current Medical Digest,* illustrating a story on drug abuse (*Current Medical Digest,* Vol. XXXVII, No. 4, April 1970.)

John Canady raises the question of the ''ethics'' of Segal's casting technique, and then dismisses it as absurd. The power of Segal's work is sufficient to disarm any suspicion of aesthetic depravity. (''Odd Thing to Worry About, Ethics,'' *New York Times,* June 7, 1970).

* Review by Lawrence Alloway, *The Nation* (June 8, 1970), p. 702. This short piece clarifies the important issue of the ''sculptural'' status of Segal's figures: their pictorial origin is evident in the density and continuity of their surfaces, which display none of the voids and spatial penetration common to sculpture. Alloway also discusses Segal's talent for depicting typical actions that evoke the universal in the particular.

The catalogue for the Figures/Environments exhibition organized by the Walker Art Center, quotes Segal on his use of space: ''I pay a terrific amount of attention to the geometry and proportion of the naturalistic setting. What I can't find I construct. I use the premise of walking into a real space, intensifying it by working very carefully with the space between the figures and objects surrounding them.'' Aside from this quote, Martin Friedman's comments about ''proletarian classicism'' are less interesting than the suggestive, if undeveloped, premise of the exhibition. Segal is grouped with other contemporary artists who express ''recent attitudes about the figure, beyond those found in traditional techniques.'' The other artists are Red Grooms, Alex Katz, Duane Hanson, Paul Thek, Jann Haworth, Lynton Wells, and Robert Whitman; their differences from Segal are at least as important as their similarities. (''George Segal,'' Martin Friedman, *Figures/Environments,* exhibition catalogue, Walker Art Center, Minneapolis, Minnesota, May 15-June 13, 1970, pp. 16-18.)

Woman on Chair (Box) (Cat. 206)

1971

One of the less formalist critics of Segal was Jules R. Bemporad, an Air Force psychiatrist. Bemporad compared the box enclosing Segal's fragmentary figures to the interpersonal relationships that "box in" the depressed patient. He suggests that *Woman on a Chair* sold successfully in multiple editions because its purchasers identified with the sculpture's mental state. ("Therapist questions classical analytic theory of depression," *Roche Report: Frontiers of Clinical Psychiatry*.)

In a review of Segal's 1971 Janis Gallery show, John Canaday compares the sculptor to Degas. Both artists appear to re-create life without comment. "But both are uncanny masters in their special way of selecting a pose, in adjusting the angle of a head, of showing how a body sags into rest or the way it moves into action." ("Plaster People and Plastic Cuties," *New York Times*, April 25, 1971.)

By 1971, the conventional critical wisdom considered Segal's plaster mold depictions of the human condition, "the quiet horror of the totally familiar." Whether the critic felt this was finally a "bland, unconvincing" critique, or "brilliant and moving," the conception of Segal's intent was the same. (Review by Marjorie Welsh, *Manhattan East*, April 20, 1971; and "Pleasantly Plastered," by John Gruen, *New York Magazine*, April-May 1971, respectively.) Or, as another critic put it, "It is as

though bloodless souls returned from beyond to reenact for us the shallowness of our own tasks and roles.... What Segal provides with devastating insight is an unflattering replica of ourselves, as is." ("Segal Sculpture," by Michael Lenson, Newark *Sunday News*, May 9, 1971.)

In an essay in the catalogue for the "White on White" exhibition at the Chicago Museum of Modern Art, Robert Pincus-Witten implicates Segal in his discussion of "the utopian monochromism of our own age." Pincus-Witten considers monochromism a phenomenon of the "annihilation of art ... the rejection of sensibility and idiosyncratic personality" in favor of an experience of unity with an impersonal and absolute order.

In his article on Robert Whitman's Happenings, Segal speaks of his work and attitudes: "...everybody asks 'Whatever happened to Happenings?' I think it's never been noted that the basic impulse lies in a whole generation of artists who make physical encounter a built-in part of aesthetic response, encountering things. I've been doing that in my work from the beginning...." ("On Whitman and Things," by George Segal, *Arts Magazine*, Nov. 1971, pp. 53-55.)

1972

Joseph Masheck establishes the influence of Segal on younger sculptors: "Both Hanson and De Andrea... have more in common with the poetic clarity of Segal himself than with the vaguer — and often grimmer — human junk of Surrealist tableaux and those of Kienholz. Segal's rigorous, concise poeticism is their real starting point; the smooth, 'buffed' skin of their figures is simply a stylistic variation on Segal's white but painterly surface." ("Verist Sculpture: Hanson and De Andrea," Joseph Masheck, *Art in America*, Vol. LX, No. 6 Nov.-Dec. 1972, p. 95.)

John De Andea talks about Segal in an interview with Duncan Pollock:

"In what ways would you say your figures relate to Segal's figures?"

"I suppose my work is an extension of his, though I don't think it's intended to be. We're both using a real person instead of making up a figure. Segal is after the gesture of a figure. That very subtle thing, the feeling there's a human presence about. Segal has that strong gestural advantage that not even a sculptor like Rodin had. Segal's figures demand space.

Well, I have the advantages he had, the humanness, but I take it a step forward, so that you almost believe a human being is actually there."

"How real do you want your figures to be?"

"I want them to breathe." ("The Verist Sculptors: 2 Interviews," by Duncan Pollock, *Art in America*, Vol. LX, No. 6 (Nov.-Dec. 1972), p. 98.)

"Interview with George Segal," Phyllis Tuchman, *Art in America*, Vol. LX, No. 3 (May-June 1972), pp. 74-81. This relaxed, expansive interview returns to familiar topics, but adds some new observations. Segal dwells on the tension between illusionism and real space in his work, and discusses both his sources in twentieth-century French European painting and the critics who never tire of finding new sources of inspiration for him.

Times Square at Night (Cat. 97)

"Spatial Dialectics in the Sculpture of George Segal," Jan van der Marck, *artscanada*, Vol. XXXIX, No. 2 (Spring 1972), pp. 35-38. Van der Marck brings valuable insight to a problem Segal has often discussed: the relationship between illusionistic and real space in his sculpture. The critic argues convincingly that Segal has found one solution in *Times Square at Night*, in which frontality and illusionistic depth coexist with three-dimensional sculpture. But because he dwells on the illusion of depth to the exclusion of other spatial and compositional relationships, van der Marck is less persuasive when he turns to other works, such as the fragmentary anatomical parts and the figural reliefs.

1973

An *Art News* review of Segal's January show at the Janis Gallery speaks of his combination of "the theatrical sense of Bernini with a sociologist's grasp of *anomie*...." (by Gerrit Henry, Feb. 1973, p. 80.)

A review of John De Andrea's show at O.K. Harris criticizes his inert figures, which pale in comparison to Segal's, whose plaster figures are "at once physical and spiritual" and "hauntingly stolid." ("Utterly Lifelike, Yes, But Is It Anything More?," by Peter Schjeldahl, *New York Times*, Dec. 23, 1973.)

James R. Mellow considers Segal's turn from full to fragmentary casts the rejection of a stagnating pattern in exchange for a new and exciting development. ("Segal Sculptures on Display at Janis," *New York Times*, Jan. 20, 1973.)

Segal on his fragmentary casts: "Now I've raised this question to myself: 'Can a fragment or a glimpse of the way a person's head turns, or arms cross, be as telling as a whole scene?' When you ask a question like that, you open up new, fertile territory. There's an awful lot to explore along the way." "George Segal: A Sculptor of Suburbia," by Piri Halasz, *New York Times*, Jan. 28, 1973).

Barbara Rose considers Segal's work of 1973 to be evidence of his durability as an artist. His plaster reliefs are more technically masterful, refined, and sensitive in their execution than were his earlier figures. These casts work at a deeper level than the shock inducements of Pop Art; they evoke a "mood of reverie and meditation totally at odds with the spirit of the sixties." ("Passing the Endurance Test," *New York Magazine*.

* "The Private World of George Segal," José L. Barrio-Garay, *The Private World of George Segal*, exhibition catalogue, Art History Galleries, The University of Wisconsin-Milwaukee, March 14-April 10, 1973, unpaginated. Inspired by the theories of José Ortega y Gasset, Barrio-Garay offers a literary interpretation linking Segal's work to a variety of sources from James Bond films to William Shakespeare, the

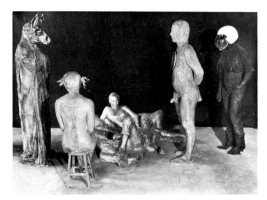
The Costume Party (Final Version) (Cat. 118)

Hegelian master-slave relationship, and Nietzsche's eternal recurrence. Some comparisons are more apt than others, but Barrio-Garay's entire argument is weakened by the work he chooses to discuss — the 1965 *Costume Party* — which is better viewed as Segal's laboratory for experimentation with color than as a complete and definitive aesthetic statement. More interesting is the examination of Segal's series of pastels on the "Lot and his Daughters" story; John Lloyd Taylor's introduction also suggestively broaches the themes of intimacy and the "private world" in Segal's work.

1974

* "Pop" by Phyllis Tuchman, *Art News*, Vol. LXXIII, No. 5 (May 1974), pp. 24-29. The portion of this article devoted to an interview of George Segal reveals the artist's ambivalence about Abstract Expressionism, his desire to see the most universal and spiritual themes expressed in material terms, and the process of abstraction with which he intensifies his everyday experience and creates an aesthetic one.

George Segal on his status as a Pop artist: "If we are talking about environments, facts and objects — this is an entire territory that I inhabit. Of course, if Pop has to mean witty, ironic detachment, count me out. I make no bones about the fact that I am involved in the whole human situation. But Pop is not as narrow as all that." ("On the Nature of Pop," by Carl R. Baldwin, *Artforum*, June 1974, p. 37.)

Segal speaks of his fragmentary nudes, with their new technique of "inside casting," as having a "different necessity" from his earlier environmental work: "Lots of twentieth-century cerebral play, but more about what each girl is about and all the qualities she radiates."

In the same article, he discusses his attitudes towards the political commitment of art in the "Rock/Leary era": "There I was in a tribal society, fighting like hell to keep my independence. Yet everything is all tangled together. Everybody's got this responsibility for society. Is there a value or a place for free play of the mind in art? How useful do you want to be? Or are you useful letting your minds and hands go? It's not settled. We're in the middle of that." ("George Segal: Plastered People," by John Perreault, The Village *Voice*, Oct. 24, 1974.)

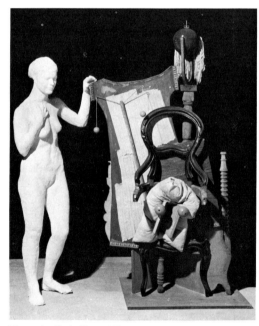
Picasso's Chair (Cat. 127)

In a review of the 1974 Janis show, John Russell praises the bas-reliefs as a successful adaptation of nineteenth-century arthistorical tradition. Earlier references to the past (*Picasso's Chair*) had been less convincing than their originals; the bas-reliefs, reminiscent of Matisse's *Backs*, are great original art, and provide an alternative to the diminishing possibilities of his set pieces. "But the real advantage of the relief from Mr. Segal's point of view," writes Russell, "is that it allows him to fragment the body without cruelty and to protect it without mawkishness... This show offers us the specific pleasure of seeing a good man get himself out of a corner." ("Art: George Segal Uses Past in a Jolt to Present," *New York Times*, Oct. 5, 1974.)

"George Segal" by Joanna Rees, The Soho *Weekly News* (June 20, 1974). This cover story on Segal offers little new insight, but contains a valuable discussion of the changing role of space in Segal's work. In Segal's earlier sculpture, the space was "too real to be real"; in his bas-reliefs, the explicitly manipulated and "aesthetic" surface shapes a space we must regard as physically actual.

1975

* "Ten Portraitists: Interviews/Statements" by Gerrit Henry, *Art in America* (Jan.-Feb. 1975), p. 36. In this brief and illuminating interview, Segal talks about the different aims in his environmental work and the bas-reliefs (portrayed gestures vs. depicted surfaces), his reason for attempting portraiture, and the conflict of humanistic and formal concerns in his œuvre.

* Robert Pincus-Witten writes that Segal, once the new Hopper, has become, with his nudes and reliefs, the new Rodin. The nude form becomes, in his hands, the basis for abstract, formal composition, thus marking a turning from his earlier, content-heavy works. Pincus-Witten attempts to identify a "Jewish historical sculpture" in Segal's work, expressed in his "tragic or elegiac" themes and "the new opulence, the voluptuous warmth and fructification incarnated by his more recent female figures... If Matisse's metaphor is the easy chair, then Segal's is the home-cooked meal." ("Reviews," *Artforum,* Jan. 1975, pp. 58, 59.)

* *George Segal,* Jan van der Marck (New York: Harry N. Abrams, 1975). This substantial and carefully pondered treatment of Segal's œuvre has much to recommend it: lengthy discussions of each major work and an incisive and refreshing formalist approach make this more than a litany of familiar critical perspectives. Singlemindedness, however, can transform virtue into a shortcoming. By limiting his commentary to discussions of formal relationships, van der Marck peremptorily excludes consideration of much of the literary, allusive, and humanistic aspects of Segal's work, as well as the artist's lifelong fascination with color, light, emotion and eroticism. The illustrations are numerous and generously proportioned; the bibliography is rather limited for a work of this scope.

1976

Segal's first outdoor bronze sculpture — *Restaurant,* in Buffalo — was well received initially by the local press. Nancy Tobin Willig, a

The Restaurant (Cat. 144)

critic for the Buffalo *Courier Express,* writes enthusiastically: "Not like monumental outdoor sculpture, this invites a close look, a touch... More importantly, it will stimulate interest not only in itself as an artwork, but in others walking by. Unlike the frozen bronze people, viewers will be challenged to notice one another. The Segal piece points up the infinite importance of public artworks that touch the human spirit." ("Segal Sculpture Installed at Fed. Bldg.," *Courier Express,* May 28, 1976.) Grace Glueck writes that the work was commissioned by Don Thalacker, of the G.S.A. The agency, she says, demanded only "permanence and safety" from Segal. He added: "They gave me complete freedom. I'm delighted I didn't have to do anything heroic or pretentious." ("Art People," *New York Times,* May 14, 1976.)

In a long and general article, critic Elisabeth Stevens makes a few interesting points. She considers Segal's three 1975 pieces with doors — *The Yellow Door; The Gray Door; The Corridor* — meditations on "the far-from-secure demarcations between the viewer's world and the artist's province of mystery and metaphor." She compares his work, and especially the bas-reliefs, to the incisive painting of Thomas Eakins and the probing fiction of Henry James. Finally, she attempts a typology of Segal's work, and produces three categories: "real people" and real objects; personal mood and viewer confrontation; and form. ("The real world and real people of George Segal," Trenton, New Jersey, *Times Advertiser,* March 21, 1976.

In an enlightening comparison, the critic Benjamin Forgey distinguishes the separate, elevated, aesthetic space of a sculpture in the realist tradition at the beginning of the twentieth century (i.e., the sculpture of Rodin's pu-

The Corridor (Cat. 142)

pil Bourdelle) from Segal's work, which invades and inhabits "real space" ("Sculptures That Can Portray the Real World," by Benjamin Forgey, Washington *Star,* June 23, 1976.)

* In a few short paragraphs of a much broader article, Brian O'Doherty makes several perceptive and well-stated observations. He describes the relationship between tableaux, pictures, and galleries — "the gallery 'impersonates' other spaces" — and describes the spectator of a Segal work as a trespasser. ("Inside the White Cube; Part II: The Eye and the Spectator," *Artforum,* Vol. XIV, No. 8, April 1976, pp. 31-33.)

Segal responds to the charge that his white casts suggest death: "That's strange. White is life. I deal with thoughts of death, thoughts of love. I think that's part of life." (p. 16) On his difference from the "metaphysical" abstract expressionists: "I could only do what I could feel strongly myself. And the only thing I was sure of was the space immediately around me, the few people that I knew extremely well, and those ordinary objects in my own space.

Everything else was pretending for me." ("Fragments," by Marshall Ledger, *The Pennsylvania Gazette,* Vol. 74, No. 7, May 1976, pp. 14-20.)

The Red Light (Cat. 119)

* "The Red Light by George Segal," Edward Henning, *The Bulletin of the Cleveland Museum of Art,* Vol. LXIII, No. 5 (May 1976), pp. 146-50. Edward Henning makes several useful distinctions. Segal uses real objects from the material world while Pop artists use representations of that world (comic strips, billboards, advertising); Pop artists are cool, ironic, detached, while Segal is thoughtful and sympathetic. Against the flurry of Hopper comparisons, Henning points out that Hopper was truly uncomfortable, alienated and lonely in the modern industrial world; he was suspicious and made few friends. Segal, on the other hand, is sympathetic to the human situation in all its forms, as his many depictions of work and effort evince. Finally, the Abstract Expressionists created their abstract images as tokens of subjective experience. Although Segal wants to express a similar subjectivity, he refuses to do so at the expense of figuration and realistic depiction of the external world. His subjective impressions are inseparable from external experience.

Segal on humanism: "I guess my thinking is a schizophrenic mix of elitist art and populist ideas. I have an intuition that my container for elitist ideas lies in everybody's body — that there's an infinite universe within an ordinary person and his everyday acts. I still think we are riding the last wave of the Renaissance. When Leonardo painted Mona Lisa, that twenty-mile vista behind her was the infinity of the external physical universe, with all its mystery and unknowability. Her face expresses some secret wisdom. Then, centuries later, Freud started charting a road map of that interior infinity — the infinity within each person." Segal says that he has taken the abstract expressionist's gestural art one step back, to depicting the body in the act of gesturing; he is still dealing with Pollock's interest in gestures, "the extension of that inspired human body that expressively recapitulated the universe... The human condition is what is eternal — not any ideal form. ...the American art that is valued all over the world is incredibly immaterial and metaphysical. That is what I like about this country." Also, in a suggestive aside, Segal acknowledges his own debt to Futurism. ("Psychological Sculpture," by Barbara Rose, *Vogue,* Sept. 1976, pp. 348 ff.)

* "George Segal: Environments," José Barrio-Garay, *George Segal: Environments,* exhibition catalogue, The Baltimore Museum of Art, Baltimore, Maryland, June 15-Aug. 8, 1976, pp. 8-35. Barrio-Garay's catalogue essay, couched in the argot of semiotics, offers few critical revelations. The purely literary elucidations of the iconography in Segal's tableaux are a novel, if one-sided, addition to the literature. In her brief foreword, Susan Delehanty touches on a valuable concept in her discussion of the role of paradox in Segal's work.

1977
* "'Mind bending' with George Segal," by Albert Elsen, *Art News,* Vol. LXXVI, No. 2 (Feb. 1977), pp. 34-37. An illuminating and serious discussion that focuses on Segal's fragments and reliefs, and their relation to Rodin's exploration of form, feeling, and "mutuality."

Grace Glueck found the use of flat, bright primary colors in Segal's recent work to have some "shock value," but, on balance, "gimmicky" and "gratuitous, even jarring the emotional presence of the plaster figures. ...More interesting is another Segal device — the use of the flat planes of doors and jambs to cut into the rounded contours of figures." ("Art: A New Cast in Plaster by Segal," *New York Times,* Jan. 28, 1977.)

Segal on color: "Obviously I'm entranced with white, especially white in three-dimensional form, the way white catches light... I seem to bounce back and forth from white and its subtleties to those saturated intensities. I can't begin to give any theories or reasons other than temperamental. Obviously, this use of white and/or color is linked in my head with feelings, passions, and states of mind." ("White in Art is White?," *The Print Collector's Newsletter,* Vol. III, No. 1, March-April 1977, p. 3.)

Lovers' Hands (Cat. 265)

* "George Segal: On the Verge of Tragic Vision," by Donald B. Kuspit, *Art in America,* Vol. LXV, No. 3 (May-June 1977), pp. 84-85. Kuspit's critique is more applicable to the early alienated Segal than his recent, erotic and life-affirming manifestations. Kuspit sees color as a way for Segal to punctuate the moment when the individual awakens to the meaning of the world and his place in it. Like Kandinsky, Segal combines realism with "the power of abstraction — without which the articulation of reality does not succeed... His consistent aim is to convert fact to symbol by charging it abstractly."

* "On George Segal's Reliefs," by Leo Rubinfein, *Artforum,* Vol. XV, No. 9 (May 1977), pp. 44, 45. Rubinfein criticizes Segal's tableaux for their "awkward straddle of art and life." His discussion of the erotic reliefs is more persuasive: eroticism depends on the alternation between concealment and exposure. Segal's reliefs, with their super-real details and abstract forms and grounds, evince this same alternation, heightened by the use of saturated colors.

Segal mentions works and artists that have influenced him: Matisse, Cézanne, Michelangelo's *Slave,* Egyptian sculpture that combines massive abstract form with fine detail (Nefertiti's lips); but especially Rembrandt's *A Girl with a Broom* — "a few mysterious details of a figure looming out of the darkness." ("The Genetics of Art; Part II," by Margaret Staats and Lucas Matthiessen, *Quest/77,* July-August 1977, p. 43.)

* "George Segal — Links Between Early and Recent Work," by Louise Lewis, *Artweek* (Oct. 29, 1977). This review of Segal's show at the art galleries of California State University at Long Beach focuses, as does the exhibition, on the relation of Segal's early pastels (1957-65) to his recent sculpture. Lewis links the expressionist handling of color in the pastels, and their articulation of space and the body, to recent sculpture; she also makes convincing comparisions between Segal and Degas.

* "A Conversation with George Segal," by Christopher B. Crosman and Nancy E. Miller, *Gallery Studies 1* (Buffalo: Buffalo Fine Arts Academy, 1977), pp. 11-17. These important interviews deal primarily with Segal's outdoor sculpture, and, in particular, the *Restaurant* piece at the Buffalo Federal Building. Segal discusses his aim to make public sculpture that does not compete with the architecture, but speaks on its own terms about the local environment and universal values. Segal also talks lucidly about some of his recurring themes: the attempt to materialize the spiritual ambitions of Abstract Expressionism, and to convey gesture and feeling through objects; his debt to Duchamp; the adoption of an "American, pragmatic" attitude; his reluctance to discuss metaphorical implications; the exploration of repeated motifs (restaurants and beds, for example); the analogy between his composition and a musical score; and his formal economy and emphasis on spatial relationships.

Untitled (Cat. 341)

* "A Conversation with the Artist," Constance W. Glenn, *George Segal: Pastels 1957-1965,* exhibition catalogue, The Art Galleries, California State University, Long Beach, Oct. 17-Nov. 6, 1977, pp. 5-14. This important exhibition explores the relationship between Segal's pastels and his sculpture, and the diffusion of color from one medium to the other. Glenn's interview confirms this view of the artist's intention. Segal talks about his love for color, nuance, and light, and his "unabashed heterosexuality," the rich, joyous eroticism in so much of his work; in the course of the conversation, the man emerges. The catalogue is of further importance for its forty-four fine plates of pastels and sculptures, and the short critical essay "Why Meyer Schapiro?" by curator Maudette Ball, which discusses the "life affirming properties" of Segal's work, and its relation to Camus' *Sisyphus.*

1978

Segal's *Blue Jean Series,* on exhibit at the Staten Island Museum, continued the tension between reality and pure formalism at work in his casts, at once particular and generalized. In the aquatints, "Segal fully exploits the hesitancy of anticipation that comprises the basic element of the erotically suggestive moment." But no sooner has he depicted bulging buttocks and gaps of skin, than the forms dissolve into abstract volumes and variations of

The Bus Station (Cat. 42)

bright colors on the black-ground. ("S. I. Museum's Segal exhibit bridges realism and abstract art," by Paul Master-Karnik, Staten Island *Advance,* Feb. 16, 1978.)

In the catalogue for the Staten Island exhibition of the *Blue Jean Series,* curator Diane Kelder notes the "spatial tension" in the etchings, an effect of Segal's colors:"... acrid red-purples and oranges animate the advancing, slightly sinister forms, while the generous and resonant blacks envelop, qualify or obscure them, insinuating a dense and limitless ambience that may cause the viewer to speculate about that which is unseen but uneasily felt." ("George Segal," essay for the catalogue of the exhibition at the Staten Island Museum, Feb. 5 to March 5, 1978.)

By 1978 George Segal's work had become so familiar that an essay in the *New York Times Magazine* on discoveries at Pompeii termed the Pompeiian death-casts "George Segal-like" — a somewhat anomalous allusion, especially in light of the fact that only a few years earlier the point of reference had been reversed. ("Out of the Ashes: Glowing Treasures of Pompeii," by Blanche R. Brown, *New York Times,* April 23, 1978.) Similarly, the review of the traveling museum exhibition "Pompeii — A.D. '79" in *Time* magazine mentions "Segal-like" plaster corpses. ("The Coming of the Pompeians," by Robert Hughes, *Time,* April 24, 1978, p. 87.)

Segal became an increasingly attractive artist for outdoor sculpture commissions in 1978, receiving commissions for the proposed Franklin D. Roosevelt memorial in Washington ("Roosevelt Memorial: Finally, a Plan is Set," by Grace Glueck, *New York Times,* July 18, 1978) and the Kent State Memorial.

In Memory of May 4, 1970: Kent State - Abraham and Isaac (Plaster) (Cat. 158)

Although a private foundation (Cleveland's Mildred Andrews Foundation) had commissioned *Abraham and Isaac* for Kent State, the university rejected the work on the grounds that it might incite more violence. Segal responded: "I don't ever remember seeing a work of art that inspired violence." He explained: "Basically, the piece calls on older people who have the power of life and death over their children to exercise love, compassion, and restraint." Kent officials suggested Segal depict a nude woman employing her feminine wiles to entice a soldier to put down his gun and leave the battlefield. "We merely proposed the idea as one that would not show any violence," said Dr. Robert McCoy, executive assistant to the president of Kent State. "But the use of sex probably also would have in-

vited controversy." Segal was reportedly "surprised" at the alternative proposal. ("Kent State rejects Segal sculpture," by Annemarie E. Cooke, *Home News,* Sept. 2, 1978.) The rejection of the sculpture became a national media event. *Newsweek* reported Kent State's objection: "An apparent act of violence (is) inappropriate to commemorate an act of violence." Robert Mc-Coy added: "There's always the potential (for protest activities) here. We're trying to do what we can to establish a tranquil atmosphere." *Newsweek* agreed that the sculpture might be objectionable: "Some may not find the Old Testament story especially relevant to the Kent State shootings, except in a superficial way. The sculpture may strike others as portentous and self-important. The arguments made by the administration for rejecting the work, however, do not seem very respectable." *Newsweek* argued that the Kent killings were an act of violence, and to skirt this would be willfully sentimental and intentionally blind to the facts. Moreover, educational institutions in particular should never shy away from issues for fear of debate and controversy. The article concludes: "The artist deserved better." ("Kent State Memorial," by Mark Stevens with Cathleen McGuigan, *Newsweek,* Vol. XCII, No. 11, Sept. 11, 1978, p. 99.)

The rejected *Abraham and Isaac,* still financed by the Mildred Andrews Foundation, eventually found a home at Princeton University. The administration of Princeton and the artist were both reportedly happy with the gift of the work. Dr. Fred Licht, then director of the Princeton University Art Museum, told the *New York Times* that the work marks a return to "the monumental origins of sculpture, to the possibility it gives us to express our culture and our society. We have a good deal of first-rate twentieth-century sculpture on our campus, but none has a specific relationship to the crises that contemporary students and contemporary teachers have lived with. This sculpture has a living presence that goes beyond the appeal of our other works and has a direct meaning which can hold the attention of all our students, even those who are not interested in art as such." Meanwhile, Kent State stood by its decision. A spokesman in their art department admitted: "The people around here are very conservative. Many of them believe that the kids who were shot got what they deserved. They don't like what they consider radicalism." ("Princeton to Get Sculpture Rejected by Kent State," by Grace Glueck,

New York Times, Nov. 18, 1978.) The *Princeton Weekly Bulletin* noted that the sculpture transcends the specific historical event by referring to a Biblical story with profound implications, which the philosopher Soren Kierkegaard, among others, contemplated. ("Princeton acquires Kent State commemorative sculpture," *Princeton Weekly Bulletin,* Vol. LXVIII, No. 9 Nov. 27, 1978.)

In a footnote to Kent State's reason for turning down Abraham and Isaac, Segal observed: "It's possible that the potential for violence exists because there has not been a just resolution of that event." ("Is Story of Abraham Too Violent for Kent State?" by Richard K. Rein, *New Jersey Monthly,* Dec. 1978, p. 11.)

* "Try again in twenty years," *Art News* (Nov. 1978), p. 6. A clear and succinct summary that fills in some details on the events at Kent State and after.

One critic talks about Segal's voyeurism, and dubs his retrospective at the Walker Art Center in Minneapolis a "peep show": "Most of the tableaux were designed for voyeurism, and space is even provided for viewers' participation in some instances. And most of the sculptured personages need all the company and comfort they can get." ("Segal exhibit in peep show," by Margherita Mazzola Glendenning, St. Paul *Dispatch,* Dec. 14, 1978.)

Segal on the Kent State fiasco: "The people in power there seem to be extremely right-wing. They were still furious at the radical-hippie disregard for patriotism. Those people were behaving as if the Vietnam War hadn't ended, as if Nixon and Agnew had never been chastised for Watergate and everything else. I was apparently interfering with the real exercise of power on the campus. Why I was considered a threat, I don't know... I refused to modify my work to make it acceptable to their standards, because I don't believe in them." ("Segal's sculpture forms own reality," by Marshall Fine, Sioux Falls, South Dakota, *Argus-Leader,* Nov. 10, 1978.)

Segal: "We go to school, we learn history and somehow we never seem to connect our history lessons. It's why I do (my work)... It helps me connect." Segal also feels that objects, as historical memoirs, carry the "message" of their creators' moods and intentions. ("Ghostly Presences: Sculptor 'mummifies' subjects in wet plaster," by Carole Nelson, Baltimore *Sun,* Nov. 28, 1978.)

* "George Segal," by Ron Blitz, *Arts Exchange,* Vol. II, No. 2 (March-April 1978), pp. 30, 1. Segal's *Blue Jean Series* aquatints are of a piece with the rest of his work, and attempt to convey sculptural insights into musculature and movement in an apparently hostile medium. As in the fragments, so here, individual features (heads, limbs) are reduced, and concentration on specific gesture creates universal import. This gestural interest recalls Segal's Abstract Expressionist background, as does his use of color in the aquatints. The reviewer suggests the limited expressive repertoire of these prints — which may be manipulated only in their color arrangement — is a "measuring post" for Segal, but not the starting point for future development in the medium — a prediction borne out by events.

Street Meeting (Cat. 154)

Hilton Kramer received Segal's use of color in his 1978 Janis show enthusiastically. In the combination of figural realism and color-field abstraction, as in *Street Meeting* and *Black Girl, Blue Wall, Red Door,* Segal "has achieved something quite remarkable." The blue figures emphasize Segal's normal "sheer eeriness" and "dreamlike quality" — more effectively, Kramer judges, in anonymous figures than in portraits. "One thing seems certain, however. In future discussions of color in sculpture, Mr. Segal will have to be taken into serious consideration, for his new work makes the most interesting use of color since Claes

Oldenburg painted his plaster sundaes and sandwiches nearly twenty years ago." ("Art: Segal Casts New Role for Color," by Hilton Kramer, *New York Times,* Dec. 8, 1978.)

* *George Segal: Sculptures,* Martin Friedman and Graham W.J. Beal (Minneapolis, Minnesota: Walker Art Center, 1978). Issued in conjunction with the retrospective exhibition that traveled from the Walker Art Center to San Francisco's Museum of Modern Art and finally the Whitney, this indispensable volume is properly synthetic and comprehensive. Friedman's essay "George Segal: Proletarian Mythmaker," is an accomplished survey of Segal's work and his critical reception, while Beal's "Realism at a Distance" focuses on Segal's much-discussed relationship to past and contemporary artists and movements. The illustrations are profuse; the bibliography is adequate, if not exhaustive. Perhaps the most original essays are a commentary by the sculptor on six of his works, and a narrative by Friedman, recounting the tribulations of undergoing Segal's casting process.

The Butcher Shop (Cat. 43)

* "George Segal Takes World of Plaster to Whitney," by John Russell, *New York Times,* June 1, 1978. Describing *The Butcher Shop* in Segal's Whitney retrospective, Russell notes that the objects in the work gain their necessity and emotional power from Segal's own past, "an upbringing in which nothing could

be taken for granted. Yet it is also a piece of make-believe in which the pure music of the eye is mated with what Segal calls 'the convention of the Western cowboy set, the false-front town.'" Russell observes that the continuing challenge for Segal is making his plaster figures interesting once the initial shock has worn off, and finding stage settings with the emotional impact of *The Butcher Shop.*

1979
* "George Segal," *Inside New York's Art World,* Barbaralee Diamonstein (New York: Rizzoli International Publications, 1979), pp. 354-366. This interview, the transcript of a conversation in a class at the New School For Social Research, returns to some of Segal's perennial themes: his handling of space, his sources and influences, the possibilities for public sculpture, and the origins of his casting process. Segal is less forthcoming in this interview than he has been in others originating in private conversations; nevertheless, his closing remarks about his faith in American art and democratic forms are revealing and original.

In Memory of May 4, 1970: Kent State - Abraham and Isaac (Bronze) (Cat. 157)

Abraham and Isaac was finally officially dedicated at Princeton on October 5, 1979 — a year after Kent State University had rejected it. Segal was pleased with the site, between Firestone Library and the University Chapel:

"A library is a repository of history; the chapel, a repository of religious and ethical values. I think we would be poverty-stricken without those two elements in our civilization." Segal hoped that the work would stir reflection in these larger contexts, beyond the event at Kent State that was its inspiration: *"I'm interested in whether it's an effective image in a long-term point of view. Art work is seldom sensational; good art lasts."* ("Once-controversial art awaits unveiling," by Hank Hersch, *Home News,* Oct. 4, 1979.) The audience of more than one hundred people at the dedication included six of the students wounded in the protest and the parents of three of the four who were killed. Segal remarked: "I chose the image of Abraham and Isaac, despite its sexual sado-masochism, and in spite of the conflict of the generations, because it deals with mercy and compassion and has a happy ending." Alan Canfora, one of those injured, said: "it's an insult to the families and the memories of the students that Kent State refused to accept the sculpture. Kent State is being insensitive by not recognizing the significance of the events." ("Princeton Ceremony Dedicates a Memorial to Kent State Victims," *New York Times,* Oct. 7, 1979.)

The Steelmakers (Cat. 167)

* "Segal's World," by Paula L. Cizmar, *Books and Arts,* Nov. 23, 1979. Despite the controversy surrounding the Kent State piece, Segal has remained popular as a creator of public sculpture. In late 1979, the city of Youngstown asked him to design a sculpture for the center of the city as part of a revitalization project, and in commemoration of the dying steel mill industry. The year before the piece was built, five thousand workers lost their jobs when Youngstown Sheet and Tube shut down

one of its plants. While Segal was discussing the project with Youngstown officials, U.S. Steel was considering closing down another plant and putting thousands more out of work. In a lyrically written article, Paula Cizmar discusses Segal's reaction to the mills, his enthusiasm and respect for the workers, the impression the blast furnaces made on him, and his attempt to combine an abstract theme — "steel working" — with visceral emotions in his sculpture.

Woman Brushing Her Hair (Cat. 36)

To All Gates (Cat. 108)

* "George Segal's old friends," by William R. Hegeman, *Art News* (Jan. 1979). In an *Art News* review of the Segal retrospective (which traveled from the Walker Art Center in Minneapolis to the San Francisco Museum of Mo-

The Curtain (Cat. 138)

dern Art and to the Whitney), the critic notices repeated motifs in Segal's work: *Woman Brushing Her Hair* (1965) reappears in the reliefs of women at their toilettes; the old woman of *Bus Station* is seen in *To All Gates;* and the image of a figure staring out of a window, constructed in Segal's first cast, is repeated in *The Curtain* (1974). Also, the critic discerns a shift from the crowded and localized tableaux of the sixties, "rich in the associative evidence provided the spectator" to the bleaker, generalized environments of the seventies: "the continual attenuation of the dramatic situation..."

One critic writes: "Segal's work invites recognition of the cutting edge of the aesthetic: concentration upon them drives you into yourself, away from the moment you cannot touch, even as it stands tangible before you." Segal on his work: "The hunt is not for verisimilitude, not for naturalistic reproduction — it's a hunt for the spirit." On color: "Color is like forms. They're exactly like words. It's the language artists use to talk about feelings or qualities. Like all the notes in the piano are sound." On Kent State: "And my attitude was that the real way to get peace was to draw the pus from the wound, to face, somehow, a situation that has not been resolved for eight years." On art criticism: "...all of us are subjected to very ruthless, professional art criticism. Any of us can be sliced up by a verbal or written scalpel if we do something *dumb.* Literally. There is a very cruel, art critical world, and all of us with any history of exhibiting have jumped those hurdles. And we're never immune, so that pure, total freedom is not really the case." ("Hunting for the spirit," by Lawrence Sutin, *Minnesota Monthly,* Jan. 1979, p. 16 ff.)

April Kingsley, reviewing the Whitney retrospective for *Newsweek,* writes of Segal's "home ly humanism." Kingsley suggests that Segal's shift in the seventies away from genre and towards greater generality has been accelerated by the use of saturated, non-descriptive color, and the "inside-casting" technique, which, when used in fragments and classical motifs, paradoxically abstracts from the individual while heightening detail. The critic also makes two insightful art-historical comparisons: like Hopper, Segal has "a deep formal understanding of the role architecture can play in the composition of figurative work." Also, Segal's emulation of Cézanne goes beyond the handling of space: Cézanne's *Still Life with Plaster Cast* prefigures the components in the standard Segal tableau. ("The Great Body Snatcher," by April Kingsley, *Newsweek,* July 9, 1979, pp. 66-67).

A critic asks: "Is it possible that the reason for the relative blandness of Segal's figures is to facilitate our greater identification with the subject sketched in by him but not quite finished? If he had particularized them more; given them more of the illusion of life, would we have felt so impelled to identify with these anonymous figures?" ("Doing double takes at Segal's sculpture," by Theodore F. Wolff, *Christian Science Monitor,* Aug. 16, 1979.)

Critic Vicki Goldberg draws several incisive parallels: between Segal's uninflected color backdrops and Ellsworth Kelley's field painting; the grid in Segal's bus stops, butcher shops, scaffolds and movie marquees — and most explicitly, in the ceiling of the *Hot dog stand* — and Mondrian; Segal's frozen tableaux and the non-narrative, allusive and disconnected sense of time in Happenings. Goldberg also sees the reliefs, with their sculptural figures emerging from flat grounds, as a continued chapter in Segal's struggle between two-and three-dimensional form. ("Segal's Plaster of Reality," by Vicki Goldberg, *Saturday Review,* Vol. VI, No. 16, Aug. 4, 1979, pp. 48, 9.)

Hot Dog Stand (Cat. 162)

Robert Hughes praises Segal's sense of space and arrangement: "His sense of the abstract underpinning of sculpture cuts down on what might otherwise have been a tough-but-tender street sentimentality." ("Invasion of the Plaster People," by Robert Hughes, *Time,* Aug. 27, 1979, p. 68.)

Segal on his two sources of inspiration: "One thing is as valid as the other: the hedonism of the mental life, and the puritanical industrial northeastern spirit." ("Poetry in Plaster," by Jane Petroff, in "Time Off" supplement to the Princeton *Packet,* May 16-22, 1979, pp. 6-8.)

A rather Marxist interpretation praises Segal's work as a critique of "reification, passivity, (and) vacuity." The white casts risked complacency with the alienation of life, and reduced criticism to "stoicism," "godly indifference" and "serenity." On the other hand, Segal's color, which the critic calls "putrid, awful, arbitrary," refuses any rapprochement with the forces of capitalism that reduce people to the thinghood of commodities. The color of Segal's nudes is opaque, arbitrary, cloying: it represents the white-wash of conventional attitudes that vitiates men's relationships with women. The empty gestures of Segal's figures demonstrate the vacuity of all human expression. They are not even conscious of their alienation; their curves and human forms are "no more sensuous or emphatic than a panel of the wall." (review by Hal Foster, *Artforum,* Feb. 1979, pp. 67, 68.)

Segal refuses to be pushed into abstraction by the expectations of his contemporaries: "I never pretended to be cool," Segal says. ("South Brunswick Sculptor Featured on Public Television," by Ann Ledesma, *Home News,* May 13, 1979.)

Alfred Frankenstein compares Segal to Oldenburg, Manuel Neri, and Edward Kienholz. (The omission of reference to Kienholz from van der Marck's book was a source of critical complaint when it was published.) ("Innovative Sculptor of the Life Cast," by Alfred Frankenstein, San Francisco *Sunday Examiner and Chronicle,* Feb. 25, 1979.)

Segal has referred to his work as "a soap-opera world." ("Segal: new forms for everyman," by Cathy Curtis, University of California, Berkeley, *Friday Magazine,* Vol. 9, No. 34 Feb. 23, 1979, pp. 7, 8.)

An *Art News* critic, reviewing the 1979 Janis show, identifies Segal's shift from matte, unmodulated color (reminiscent of both polychromed ancient sculpture and post-painterly abstractionists, like Ellsworth Kelly) to a succession of layers of transparent glazes, often suggesting flesh (as in *Street Meeting*), but less effective in individual portraits (i.e., the Meyer Schapiro bust, which is judged to be too similar to a death mask.) The glazes make the object more lifelike, while simultaneously mummifying the cast figure. ("George Segal," Ellen Schwartz, *Art News,* Vol. LXXVIII, No. 2, Feb. 1979.)

Gay Liberation (Cat. 165)

In the summer of 1979, Segal agreed to execute a homosexual-liberation monument for Sheridan Square. Reportedly, the idea was first proposed by Dr. Bruce Voeller, former co-executive director of the National Gay Task Force. Peter Putnam, a physicist and philanthropist, and son of Mildred Andrews — whose fund supported Segal's Kent State piece — took up the idea and presented it to Segal. Segal was at first reluctant to execute the work, "since I'm an unregenerate heterosexual, and my first reaction was that a gay artist should do it. But I've lived in the art world for many years, and I'm extremely sympathetic to the problems that gay people have. They are human beings first. I couldn't refuse to do it." At the time, Segal was searching for a way to present the subject in a park where he saw "young mothers pushing strollers." The work would also have to overcome the obstacles of approval by the Department of Parks, the local Community Planning Board, and the city's Art Commission. ("Homosexual-Liberation Statue Is Planned for Sheridan Square," by Grace Glueck, *New York Times,* July 21, 1979.)

George Segal on his recent experiments with cast paper (as in *Hand on Buttocks,* 1979): "...paper manages to be itself instead of plaster or metal. It is extremely fragile, with extreme delicacy of detail. ...It's fragile, ephemeral, very beautiful. That appeals to me — plaster and metal are implacable and hard. ...I'll do further pieces in paper, if they fit with an idea." ("George Segal" in "Paper in Transition," Gerrit Henry, *The Print Collector's Newsletter,* Vol. X, No. 3, July-Aug. 1979, p. 84.)

Primarily distinguished for its agreeable enthusiasm, John Perreault's review of Segal's Whitney retrospective makes the interesting point that Segal's progeny — Duane Hanson and John De Andrea — have taught us to appreciate the finest modulations of surface detail. Turning from Hanson and De Andrea to Segal, the rough and splattered plaster of his figures manifests their expressionism and romanticism. ("A Caste of Plaster People," by John Perreault, *Soho Weekly News,* May 31, 1979.)

1980

* "Sculpture Planned for 'Village' Brings Objections," by Edith Evans Asbury, *New York Times,* August 28, 1980. The homosexual-liberation piece ran into objections in the neighborhood of its proposed site. Despite the approval of Greenwich Village political leaders, including Reps. Theodore Weiss and Bella Abzug, and of Joseph Brenan, Director of Historic Parks for the city's Parks and Recreation Department, protests from residents threatened the proposed monument. Bruce Voeller,

president of the Mariposa Foundation that commissioned the work, condemned the protests: "the basic opposition is homophobic." Voeller also argued that the choice of a gay sculptor would have depended on the sort of discrimination the liberation movement is protesting. "The Friends of Christopher Park" circulated a petition against the sculpture, which they called "wildly inappropriate to the architecture of the neighborhood." Residents questioned the use of the communal property as a center of propaganda for a special interest group. Voeller responded that Christopher Park — the site of the riots of June 28, 1969, that followed a police raid of the nearby, predominantly homosexual "Stonewall Inn" — is a landmark of the gay movement: "The blacks have their Selma, the Jews their wailing wall, the Arabs their Mecca or Medina. For millions and millions of gay people throughout the world Christopher Park on Christopher Street opposite Stonewall Inn is the logical place to put a sculpture commemorating the contributions and lives of gay people." But even some members of the gay community were "incensed," and circulated petitions protesting that the figures in the sculpture were 'grotesque stereotypes' offensive to all in our community." Segal said that he was simply asked to make the work. The location of the sculpture, which was the source of the controversy, was the Park Department's concern.

The gay liberation piece gained the approval of the City Arts Commission, and of the Parks Commissioner. After a stormy debate, Community Board 2 of Greenwich Village overturned a recommendation by the Board's Park Committee and approved the work by a vote of twenty-four to nine. The final obstacle was the Landmarks Preservation Commission, which held an open meeting in November before deciding the issue. Kent Barwick, chairman of the Landmarks Commission, observed that the content of the work was "beside the point. Our concern is the relationship of the work to the protected space and whether or not the work belongs there at all. It's not an issue for us how many people are for or against it." Meanwhile, protests continued from the gay community. Robert Rygor complained: "The content of the piece is overly sexual. Gay people are in every walk of life, not just cruising." He was afraid the work might attract the sort of people who would "want to see the fag sculpture and beat up on gays." ("Landmarks Comm. Holds Hearing on George Segal's 'Gay' Sculpture," *ArtWorkers News,* Dec. 1980.)

Segal protested that the sculpture presented homosexuals in a good light: "The sculpture concentrates on tenderness, gentleness, and sensitivity as expressed in gesture. It makes the delicate point that gay people are as feeling as anyone else." Some local residents feared the work would bring "prostitution to the neighborhood" through its advocacy of "a certain type of sex." Homosexuals, including Craig Rodwell, proprietor of the Oscar Wilde Memorial bookshop, argued that the work was not representative enough: its figures were all white, and none of them elderly. He further protested that gay artists had not been consulted. ("Greenwich Village is Not Amused," by Richard Goldstein, Village *Voice,* Sept. 10-16, 1980). The *Voice* editorialized in favor of the statue. ("Provoke, Don't Placate," Village *Voice,* Sept. 10-16, 1980.)

* "Sculpture," *The New Yorker* (Oct. 27, 1980), pp. 42-45. This article consists of rabid quotations from the Community Board Hearings and a more reasoned discussion at the New York University Institute for the Humanities, with George Segal, Carl Schorske, and others.

* "A tale of a park, a sculpture, and a Village," by Sherryl Connelly, *Daily News,* Oct. 7, 1980. A concise summary of opposing factions and positions in the homosexual sculpture controversy, including the alternative plan for "Quaint touches and Victorian urns" designed by one of the work's critics.

The Hustle: The Four-Hand Pass (Cat. 173)

* "When George Segal Goes Public," by Hilton Kramer, *New York Times,* Oct. 19, 1980. A critique of Segal's outdoor sculpture, which Kramer considers a "sentimental, condescending and mawkish" contradiction in its elevation of the banal. Kramer touches on interesting issues, however — must public monuments differ from museum works? does accessibility come at the cost of aesthetics? — but offers no solutions. He further suggests that Segal's exploration of expressive colorism in 1978 was a progressive moment forgotten in most of his recent work, such as *The Hustle* — the target of particularly scathing comment.

Harry Rand, writing in *Arts Magazine,* argues that George Segal's work can be seen as the counterpart of Jackson Pollock's last paintings: both artists do not represent reality but present objectivities, and as such express a new art-historical mode of myth and imagery. Rand's argument fails to address the political implications and the humanist's insight so important to Segal's art. Most importantly, Rand's system cannot account for the manipulation of figure and gesture that Segal himself has so often identified as his means of representing multiple levels of meaning. ("The Modes and Recent Art", by Harry Rand, *Arts Magazine,* Dec. 1980, pp. 76-92.)

George Segal observes that he does not share his wife's enthusiasm for television soap operas: "I've heard those stories. We all deal with the same things. I'm interested in the very subtle ways the body implies those stresses." Theatricality is present in Segal's tableaux as well as his figures. The idea for the tableaux came from Robert Frank's use of Segal's farm as the set for an early avant-garde movie. ("George Segal's Body Language," by Howard Pousner, Atlanta *Constitution,* Oct. 3, 1980).

* "Readers' Views on the Gay Pride Statues," letters to the editor in the *Villager,* Sept. 11, 1980. More community response on Segal's homosexual-liberation monument. In the same issue, the *Villager* editorialized in favor of the work.

* "A Segal Comes to Youngstown," by Louis Zona, a privately printed and detailed account of the steps in the artist's decisions behind the creation of *The Steelmakers,* written by a member of the panel that selected Segal. A passage from Segal's letter of acceptance, revealing his emotional response to the city and the mills, is especially significant.

Segal on his theory of sculpture: "I decided to break several rules. I made up a new definition of sculpture for myself, to the effect that it was a place I could enter, instead of it being something carved out of a rock and placed on a pedestal to be admired from a psychological and physical distance. I made a new definition — but kept old truths — that the shape of the solids and the shape of the air between them had a lot to do with what sculpture would say." Segal on his medium: 'Plaster — I love the color — carves delicately, it holds a knife blade mark, it has a pristine freshness." Segal on other super-realist sculptors: "I've been frank about the casting, never tried to hide the fact I do it. Many artists picked it up and became very interested in verisimilitude, in making as close to nature as possible. I have a 'let it be' attitude about that. I've discovered that every artist who picks up a method is going to practice that method according to his nature and temperament and isn't going to make the same statement I'm going to make." Segal on the theatrical aspect of his work: "There is theater in my work, but not in the same definition of when you see a play. ...Mine is a different kind of theater, there is no proscenium, there is no plot and you make up your own story and wander through this labyrinth seeing things from ever changing viewpoints." ("Sculptor George Segal Breaks the Rules, Casts the Real Things in Life," by W. C. Burnett, Atlanta *Journal,* April 16, 1980.)

The Commuters (Cat. 170)

Segal received another important public sculpture commission in 1980: a group of three bronze commuters for the Port Authority Bus Terminal. Segal was pleased with the site: "A lot of my mental life has been spent in that bus terminal. For thirty years I have regularly commuted an hour each way to the New York art world." For Segal, the terminal is "an emotionally moving place, with particularly interesting people." ("3 Commuters, Waiting," *New York Times,* April 23, 1980.) Segal received the commission by winning an invitational competition. He is concerned that public art be truly accessible to the public: "I feel strongly that public art should concern itself with what means a great deal to people who pass by." ("'Commuters' sculpture to be given place of honor in N.Y. Port Authority terminal," *Home News,* April 27, 1980.)

Woman on a Bench II (Cat. 174)

Segal took part — and was honored — in New Brunswick's tercentennial celebration. He cast the bronze figure of a woman, *Woman on a Bench II,* from a plaster mold of Rosie Donato, owner of New Brunswick Housewreckers and Salvage Co., Inc., which was the source of many of the objects in Segal's tableaux. *Woman on a Bench II* was his "artistic tribute" to the city; it was exhibited in a New Brunswick storefront along with two other works, and premiered at a reception attended by Mrs. Joan Mondale. Said Segal: "Historically, New Brunswick has been a working man's town with an ethnic mix. I'm attracted to its strength and to the simplicity of much of its architecture.'' ("Segal characterizes New Brunswick in Tercentennial sculpture," by Barbara Frankel, *Home News,* April 27, 1980.)

Appalachian Farm Couple-1936 (Cat. 161)

In a demonstration of his popular appeal and the expressiveness of his work, Segal's *The Appalachian Farm Couple — 1936* was selected by popular ballot as part of a permanent collection. The Neuberger Museum at the State University of New York at Purchase organized a show of forty-four important works of the sixties. Called "Hidden Desires," the exhibition gave visitors to the museum the opportunity to vote on which work was to be purchased as part of the permanent collection. Segal's work was "the overwhelming choice" of the 2300 ballots cast. The *Appalachian Farm Couple — 1936* was originally destined for the Franklin D. Roosevelt Memorial, which has been postponed since Congress failed to approve funding in 1977. The reporter suggests that the Segal commanded popular appeal because of its resemblance to Grant Wood's familiar *American Gothic.* ("Public Helps Museum in Purchase Decide on a Sculpture," by Charlotte Evan, *New York Times,* May 20, 1980.) Suzanne Delehanty, the Director of the Neuberger Museum, thinks Segal won for other reasons: "He lifts what Coleridge called the 'film of familiarity' which dulls our senses, and by so doing, Segal uncovers

the essential qualities of the human spirit hidden beneath the surface of routine and habit.'' Segal's sculpture competed against artists representing "major movements in American art in the sixties," including Motherwell, Warhol, Louis, Christo, and Oldenburg. ("Neuberger's *Hidden Desires:* The Whys and Wherefores," by Suzanne Delehanty, *Westchester Illustrated,* Vol. V, No. 1, June 1980, p. 15 ff.)

Art Historian Sam Hunter includes Segal's recent outdoor work in an article on public sculpture. Hunter identifies the inevitable conflict that Segal faces between private sensibility and public expectations; Segal makes important comments about his desire to create monumental works on a human scale. ("Public Sculpture," Sam Hunter, *National Arts Guide,* Vol. II, No. 3, May-June 1980, pp. 10, 11.)

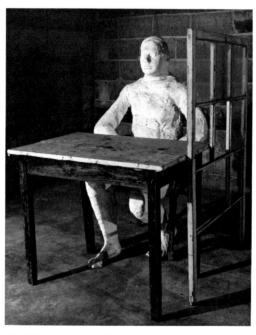

Man Sitting at a Table (Cat. 5)

The widespread adoption of Segal's work by popular magazines and advertising firms attests to its ability to speak to the general public. In its issue devoted to the exile of Andrei Sakharov, *The Sciences* pictured Segal's *Man Sitting at a Table* on the cover. The magazine explained: "It serves as a bleak image of the physical and psychological isolations of exile." *(The Sciences,* Vol. XX, No 8, Oct. 1980, cover and p. 1.)

Kent State University's own radical publication recounted the university's rejection of Se-

gal's *Abraham and Isaac,* and the university president's alternative suggestion for a young, nude woman enticing a soldier, as one among many examples of the university's attitude toward the events of May 4, 1970. Robert Dyal, an Associate Professor of Philosophy, writes: "Once again, KSU made national news, as President Golding's arrogant insensitivity and historical and Biblical ignorance was derided in numerous editorials. One of the tragic ironies is that, while the KSU Administration has, throughout the decade, been primarily concerned with protecting its public image as opposed to seeking justice and displaying the truth, it has by so many of its actions presented the worst possible image of KSU to the public. How might the faculty and administration have responded? They might have exercised academic responsibility, mobilized scholarly energy, and converted this horrible event into an unparalleled educational opportunity for successive generations of KSU students ...making KSU the foremost locus in the world for the study of nonviolent means of change... The KSU Administration, sadly, failed to measure up to the political calling." ("Aftermath and Legacy," Robert A. Dyal, *Left Review,* Vol. IV, No. 2, Spring 1980, p. 36.)

Writing on *The Hustle: Four Hand Pass* in *Artforum,* Jeanne Silverthorne characterizes Segal as a purveyor of "art bathos," "heir apparent to Hopper's alienation and despair, purveyor of the elegiac and the tragic in the Judeo-Christian tradition." Silverthorne considers *The Hustle* a work of conscious self-parody: by making its figures ridiculous and unheroic, and by "belaboring the obvious," it mocks the "preachy interpretations to which his own accomplishments are open." Humor enters in the juxtaposition of the title with the particular figure cast — Segal's hustling dealer, Sidney Janis. Silverthorne's questionable interpretation depends on her limited grasp of her subject; she believes that Segal duplicates reality "with little or no authorial intrusions," and that the only message in his work is "an affecting picture of anomie." ("George Segal," Jeanne Silverthorne, *Artforum,* Vol. XIX, No. 4, Dec. 1980, pp. 78, 79).

* "Testimony of George Segal, Sculptor," United States Senate Committee on Governmental Affairs, Subcommittee on Civil Service and General Services, Hearings on Art in Architecture, 96th Congress, first session, Sept. 25, 1979, pp. 6-8. Segal attests to the cooperation of the General Services Administration, and praises it for its enlightened patronage. The testimony is especially significant in view of the extent of Segal's work on G.S.A. projects and similar government commissions.

Introduction by Ellen Schwartz, *Sculpture in the 70's: The Figure,* exhibition catalogue, Department of Exhibitions, Pratt Institute, New York, Nov. 3-25, 1980, unpaginated. This catalogue is interesting for its attention to the succession of generations and the inheritance of influence: just as Segal was moved by Matisse and Rodin, so Arlene Toonkel has launched her career on the trail Segal blazed.

1981

Segal remains a popular source of public art. In early 1981, he received a commission from the Wisconsin Art Board to execute a sculpture for the General Executive Facility Plaza in Madison. ("George Segal selected for sculpture, *Wisconsin State Journal, Economic Report,* Feb. 1, 1981.)

The controversy surrounding *Gay Liberation* even made "The Year in Sex" wrap-up in the February issue of *Playboy,* showing that George Segal is not without appeal to a more heterosexual audience. (*Playboy,* Vol. 28, No. 2, Feb. 1981, p. 148.)

* "A Sculpture without a Community," James M. Saslow, *Christopher Street,* Vol. V, No. 4 (February 1981), pp. 23-32. This is the definitive article on the controversy surrounding Segal's *Gay Liberation.* Writing in a magazine directed to the gay community, Saslow sorts out the facts and personalities with such painstaking detail that informative *verité* at times threatens to give way to minutiae confusing to anyone not deeply engaged in the issues

and confrontations. Saslow faithfully chronicles the divisiveness in the gay community itself, which would have been quelled only by "a sculpture requiring 8,763 separate figures... right down to a single black lesbian grandmother in a wheelchair." On balance, he supports the work, although his unfortunate ignorance of Segal's work — an ignorance unexpected in a Columbia University art historian — leads him to criticize *Gay Liberation* for its "narrow emotional range" and "banal naturalism."

An *Art News* critic, reviewing Segal's 1981 show at Sidney Janis, suggests that *Gay Liberation* will work as an effective monument *in situ* because it invites passersby to sit on the benches and thus enter and enhance the work itself. The critic is less enthusiastic about the projects for Cleveland's Justice Center and the New York Port Authority Bus Terminal. The sculptures will be totally lost in their vast settings. Moreover, the figures in these works "appear isolated and dejected," and even where this might be appropriate in the bus terminal, the power of the monument will be "too painful" for its viewers. ("George Segal," Ruth Bass, *Art News,* Vol. LXXX, No. 2, Feb, 1981, p. 211.)

John Beardsley discusses Segal's attitude towards *The Steelworkers* in an article on the problems posed by public sculture. Segal recognizes the need to make public sculpture accessible, to tailor it to its community. He offers his tribute to Youngstown as an instance of accessible art that maintains "the density of [the] subject matter." ("Personal Sensibilities in Public Places," John Beardsley, *Artforum,* Vol. XIX, No. 10 (Summer 1981), pp. 44, 45).

* "George Segal," Malcolm N. Carter, *Saturday Review,* Vol. VIII, No. 5 (May 1981), pp. 26-30. The unsophisticated questions posed in this interview often get unexpectedly profound answers. Segal answers naive questions with important revelations about his life and work, and the intersections between the two.

Blue Girl on Park Bench (Cat. 169)

In a brief meditation on Segal's *Blue Girl on Park Bench,* a recent painted plaster figure, Sam Hunter bridges the gap between the sociological and psychological in Segal's oeuvre. Hunter iterates the observation that Segal's figures reveal the anomie of the modern American landscape; *Blue Girl,* however, goes beyond social comment to speak of psychological truths and mythic verities that resonate in the spectator. ("George Segal's *Blue Girl on Park Bench:* Transforming the Wasteland into the Space of Dreams," Sam Hunter, *Art News,* Vol. LXXX, No. 6, June 1981, pp. 136, 137.)

SELECTED BIBLIOGRAPHICAL LISTINGS

I. Artist's Statements and Interviews

Carter, Malcolm N. "George Segal," *Saturday Review*, VIII, No. 5 (May 1981), pp. 26-30. Segal answers rather unsophisticated questions with important revelations about his life, his work, and the intersections between the two.

"Testimony of George Segal, Sculptor," United States, Senate Committee on Governmental Affairs, Subcommittee on Civil Service and General Services, Hearings on Art in Architecture, 96th Congress, first session, Sept. 25, 1979. Segal praises the GSA for its cooperation.

Coplans, John. "George Segal: An Interview," *Dialogue, Ohio Art Journal*, Akron, Ohio (N. D.)

Henry, Gerrit. "Paper in Transition," *The Print Collector's Newsletter*, X, No. 3 (July-August 1979), p. 84. Segal talks about his recent experiments with cast paper.

Diamonstein, Barbaralee. "George Segal," in *Inside New York's Art World*. New York: Rizzoli International Publications, 1979, pp. 354-366. Transcription of a conversation in a class at the New School for Social Research.

"Commentaries" in *George Segal: Sculptures*, ed. Martin Friedman. Minneapolis: Walker Art Center, 1978, pp. 33-55. Discussions of six sculptures.

Glenn, Constance W. "A Conversation with the Artist," in *George Segal: Pastels 1957-1965*. Long Beach: The Art Galleries, California State University, 1977, pp. 5-14.

Crosman, Christopher B., and Nancy E. Miller. "A Conversation with George Segal," in *Gallery Studies I*. Buffalo: Buffalo Fine Arts Academy, 1977, pp. 11-17. An excellent interview, focussing on *The Restaurant* at the Buffalo Federal Building.

Staats, Margaret, and Lucas Matthiessen. "The Genetics of Art; Part II," *Quest/77* (July-August 1977), p. 43. Segal discusses his influences.

"White in Art is White?," *The Print Collector's Newsletter*, III, No 1 (March-April 1977), p. 3. Segal on color.

Geelhaar, C. "Marriage Between Matter and Spirit, Interview with George Segal," *Pantheon*, XXXIV (July 1976), pp. 231-37.

Henry, Gerrit. "Ten Portraitists: Interviews/Statements," *Art in America*, LXIII, No. 1 (January-February 1975), p. 36. A brief, illuminating discussion of the bas-reliefs.

Baldwin, Carl R. "On the Nature of Pop," *Artforum*, XII, No. 10 (June 1974), p. 37. Segal on his status as a pop artist.

Tuchman, Phyllis. "Pop," *Art News*, LXXIII, No. 5 (May 1974), pp. 24-29.

"Interview with George Segal," *Art in America*, LX, No. 3 (May-June 1972), pp. 74-81. In this relaxed, expansive interview, Segal talks about the tension in his work between illusionism and real space.

"On Whitman and Things," *Arts Magazine*, LXVI, No. 2 (November 1971), pp. 53-55. Segal discusses Whitman's work and the influence of Happenings on his own.

Cyr, Don. "A Conversation with George Segal," *School Arts*, LXVII, No. 30 (November 1967), pp. 30-31.

"The Sense of 'Why not?': George Segal on his art," *Studio International*, CLXXIV, No. 893 (October 1967), pp. 147-149. Segal explains his reservations about abstract expressionism.

"Jackson Pollock: An Artists' Symposium - Part II," *Art News*, LXVI, No. 3 (May 1967), pp. 29, 69-70.

"Everyone Shares a Huge Stew of Ideas," in "Sensibility of the Sixties," *Art in America*, LV, No. 1 (January-February 1967), p. 55.

"George Segal on the New York School," *Gallery Notes*, XXIX, Albright-Knox Art Gallery, Buffalo, New York (Autumn 1966), p. 2.

Molnar, Katherine and Elizabeth Palin. "An interview with George Segal," *Argomag* (Winter 1965), pp. 9-14. Published by Rutgers Preparatory School, Somerset, New Jersey. The sophistication of this interview belies its context.

Geldzahler, Henry. "An Interview with George Segal," *Artforum*, III, No. 2 (November 1964), pp. 30-33, 65.

Statement in *The Artist's Reality: An International Sculpture Exhibition*. New York: New School Art Center, 1964. Unpaginated.

Tillim, Sidney. "Pop Art: A Dialogue," *Eastern Arts Quarterly*, II, No. 1 (September-October 1963), pp. 6-19. Segal on his transition from painting to sculpture.

"Sculpture, Paintings, Pastels: A Discussion of My Recent Work," Master of Fine Arts thesis, Rutgers University, New Brunswick, New Jersey, May, 1963.

II. Books

Amaya, Mario. *Pop Art... And After*. New York: The Viking Press, 1965.

Beardsley, John. *Art in Public Places*. Washington: Partners for Livable Places, 1981, pp. 71, 72. Detailed information on the installation of the *Steelmakers* in Youngstown.

Calas, Nicolas, and Elena. *Icons and Images of the Sixties*. New York: E.P. Dutton, 1971.

Compton, Michael. *Pop Art*. London: Hamlyn, 1970.

Hunter, Sam. *American Art of the Twentieth Century*. New York: Harry N. Abrams, 1972.

Kreytenberg, Gert. *George Segal: Ruth in Her Kitchen*. Stuttgart: Philipp Reclam Jun., 1970.

Lützeler, Heinrich. "Kunst und Literatur um 1960. Drei Stücke aus der Sammlung Ludwig: George Segal, Das Restaurant Fenster, 1967," *Festschrift für Gert von der Osten*. Cologne: DuMont Schauberg, 1970.

Marck, Jan van der. *George Segal*. New York: Harry N. Abrams, 1975. This substantial treatment of Segal's oeuvre features lengthy discussions of many major works and generously proportioned illustrations. Van der Marck's emphasis on formal analysis and art historical categorization provide important and original insights, but at the expense of a balanced account of the literary, allusive, and humanistic aspects of the artist's work.

Seitz, William C. *Segal.* New York: Harry N. Abrams, 1972. This early, heavily biographical monograph has been largely superannuated by more recent publications.

Thalacker, Donald. *The Place of Art in the World of Architecture.* New York: Chelsea House Publishers, 1980. Includes a thorough account of the commission and execution of *The Restaurant,* Segal's first public sculpture.

III.   Catalogues

Backlin-Landman, Hedy. *George Segal.* Princeton, New Jersey: The Art Museum, Princeton University. 1969.

Barrio-Garay, José. *George Segal: Environments.* Baltimore: The Baltimore Museum of Art, 1976. Some interesting literary elucidations of the iconography in Segal's tableaux, couched in the argot of semiotics.

The Private World of George Segal. Milwaukee: Art History Galleries, The University of Wisconsin-Milwaukee, 1973. Sometimes extravagant, often enlightening, literary interpretations of Segal's oeuvre.

Carey, Martin. The New American Realism. Worcester: Worcester Art Museum, 1965.

Courtois, Michel, and Allan Kaprow. *Segal.* Paris: Galerie Ileana Sonnabend, 1963.

Friedman, Martin. *Figures/Environments.* Minneapolis: Walker Art Center, 1970.

George Segal. Paris: Galerie Darthea Speyer, 1969.

Friedman, Martin and Graham W. J. Beal. *George Segal: Sculptures.* Minneapolis: Walker Art Center, 1978. Issued in conjunction with Segal's retrospective exhibition, this volume is properly synthetic and comprehensive. Includes a survey of the artist's career by Friedman, a discussion of influences and relationships to other artists by Beal, and commentaries on six works by the artist.

Geldzahler, Henry. "George Segal," in *Recent American Sculpture.* New York: The Jewish Museum, 1964. A brief elucidation of Segal's early career, elegantly phrased.

Glenn, Constance W. *George Segal: Pastels 1957-1965.* Long Beach: The Art Galleries, California State University, Long Beach, 1977. An enlightening examination of Segal's undeservedly neglected pastels, including forty-four fine plates.

Kelder, Diane. *George Segal/Blue Jean Series.* New York: Staten Island Museum, 1978. The only exhibition devoted to Segal's experiments in etching.

Marck, Jan van der. *George Segal.* Zurich: Kunsthaus, 1971.

"George Segal," *Eight Sculptors: The Ambiguous Image.* Minneapolis: Walker Art Center, 1966.

George Segal: 12 Human Situations. Chicago: Museum of Contemporary Art, 1968. Includes documentation of all Segal's sculpture to date.

Pincus-Witten, Robert. "George Segal," in *Dine Oldenburg Segal: Painting/Sculpture.* Toronto: Art Gallery of Ontario, 1967.

White on White. Chicago: Chicago Museum of Modern Art, 1971. The author includes Segal, rather unconvincingly, in a discussion of the "utopian monochromism of our age."

Rauh, Emily S. *7 for 67: Works by Contemporary American Sculptors.* Saint Louis: City Art Museum of Saint Louis, 1967.

Schwartz, Ellen. *Sculpture in the 70's: The Figure.* New York: Pratt Institute, 1980.

IV.   Magazines, Newspapers, and Miscellaneous

Alloway, Lawrence. "Art," *The Nation* (June 8, 1970), p. 702. A good discussion of the pictorial composition of Segal's sculpture.

"Art as Likeness," *Arts,* XLI, No. 7 (May 1967), pp. 34-39. Alloway compares the desolation of Segal's figures to "the mood of human isolation" in Hopper's paintings.

"Hi-Way Culture: Man at the Wheel," *Arts,* XLI, No. 4 (February 1967), pp. 28-33.

Anonymous. "'George Has Hands Like a Surgeon'," *Art News,* LXXIX, No. 6 (Summer 1980), p. 7.

"Princeton Ceremony Dedicates a Memorial to Kent State Victims," *New York Times,* October 7, 1979.

"Sculpture," *The New Yorker* (October 27, 1980), pp. 42-45. Quotes from discussions of *Gay Liberation* at a Community Board hearing and a seminar at New York University.

"3 Commuters, Waiting," *New York Times,* April 23, 1980. Details on the commission for the Port Authority Bus Terminal.

"Try again in twenty years," *Arts News,* LXXVII, No. 9 (November 1978), p. 6. Good summary of the events surrounding Kent State's rejection of *Abraham and Isaac.*

Asbury, Edith Evans. "Sculpture Planned for 'Village' Brings Objections," *New York Times,* August 28, 1980. Information on the *Gay Liberation* controversy.

A(shbery), J(ohn). "George Segal," *Art News,* LVI, No. 10 (February 1958), p. 11. Review of Segal's third show at the Hansa.

Ashton, Dore. "Unconventional Techniques in Sculpture: New York Commentary," Studio International, CLXIX, No. 861 (January 1965), p. 23.

Baker, Elizabeth C. "Larry Rivers and George Segal: Back in the USSR," *Art in America,* LXV (November 1977), pp. 104-112.

Bannard, Darby. "Present-Day and Ready-Made Styles", *Artforum,* V, No. 4 (December 1966), pp. 30-35.

Barrio-Garay, José. "La escultura de George Segal: imágenes de amor y muerte," *Goya*, CVIII (May-June 1972), pp. 370-377.

Bass, Ruth. "George Segal," *Art News*, LXXX, No. 2 (February 1981), p. 211. Review of the 1981 Janis show.

Beardsley, John. "Personal Sensibilities in Public Places," *Artforum*, XIX, No. 10 (Summer 1981), pp. 44, 45. *The Steelmakers* is discussed as an example of successful public sculpture.

B(eck), J(ames) H. "George Segal," *Art News*, LIX, No. 7 (November 1960), p. 14. Review of Segal's Green Gallery show.

Blitz, Ron. "George Segal," *Arts Exchange*, II, No. 2 (March-April 1978), pp. 30, 31. Discussion of the *Blue Jean Series*.

Canady, John. "Odd Thing to Worry About, Ethics," *New York Times*, June 7, 1970. Canady approves of the "ethics" of Segal's casting technique.

"Plaster People and Plastic Cuties," *New York Times*, April 25, 1971.

D(ash), R(obert) W. "George Segal," *Arts*, XXXII, No. 5 (February 1958), pp. 57-58. Review of third Hansa show.

Eland, Ursula N. "George Segal", *Gallery Notes*, The Buffalo Fine Arts Academy and the Albright-Knox Art Gallery, XXVII, No. 2 (Spring 1964), unpaginated. A flawed interpretation of Segal as a pop artist.

Elsen, Albert. "'Mind bending' with George Segal," *Art News*, LXXVI, No. 2 (February 1977), pp. 34-37. An illuminating discussion, centering on Segal's fragments and reliefs.

Foster, Hal. "George Segal," *Artforum*, XVII, No. 6 (February 1979), pp. 67, 68. A rather forced Marxist interpretation of Segal's work.

Friedman, Martin. "Mallary, Segal, Agostini: The Exaltation of the Prosaic," *Art International*, VII, No. 8 (November 10, 1963), pp. 70-71. A perceptive article distinguishing Segal's humanistic values from the attitudes of other pop artists.

Gablik, Suzi. "Meta-trompe-l'oeil," *Art News*, LXIV, No. 1 (March 1965), pp. 46-49.

Glueck, Grace. "Art: A New Cast in Plaster by Segal," *New York Times*, January 28, 1977.

"Art People," *New York Times*, May 14, 1976. Details of the G.S.A. commission for *The Restaurant*.

"Homosexual-Liberation Statue is Planned for Sheridan Square, *New York Times*, July 21, 1979.

"'No.' Says Yes Art," *New York Times*, October 24, 1965. Review of the 1965 Janis show.

"Princeton to Get Sculpture Rejected by Kent State," *New York Times*, November 18, 1978.

Goldberg, Vicki. "Segal's Plaster Reality," *Saturday Review*, pp. 48-49.

Goldstein, Richard. "Greenwich Village is Not Amused," The Village *Voice*, September 10-16, 1980. Review of the *Gay Liberation* controversy.

Halasz, Piri. "George Segal: A Sculptor of Suburbia," *New York Times*, January 28, 1973.

Hegeman, William R. "George Segal's old friends," *Art News*, LXXVIII, No. 1 (January 1979), pp. 80-82. A review of Segal's retrospective, with interesting observations on his favorite motifs.

Henning, Edward, "The Red Light by George Segal," *The Bulletin of the Cleveland Museum of Art*, LXIII, No. 5 (May 1976), pp. 146-150. A sympathetic interpretation that draws fine distinctions between Segal and pop artists, Abstract Expressionists, and Hopper epigones.

Henry, Gerrit. "George Segal," *Art News*, LXXII, No. 2 (February 1973), p. 80. Review of a show at the Janis Gallery.

Hughes, Robert. "Invasion of the Plaster People," *Time* (August 27, 1979), p. 68.

Hunter, Sam. "George Segal's Blue Girl on Park Bench: Transforming the Wasteland into the Space of Dreams," *Art News*, LXXX, No. 6 (June 1981), pp. 136, 137.

"Public Sculpture," *National Arts Guide*, II, No. 3 (May-June 1980), pp. 10, 11. Segal's outdoor sculpture considered in the context of the issues confronting contemporary public sculpture.

Irwin, David. "Pop Art and Surrealism," *Studio International*, CLXXI, No. 877 (May 1966), pp. 187-191.

Johnson, Ellen H. "The Sculpture of George Segal," *Art International*, VIII, No. 2 (March 20, 1964), pp. 46-49. (Reprinted in Ellen H. Johnson. *Modern Art and the Object*. New York: Harper and Row, Publishers, 1976, pp. 165-170.)

Johnston, Jill. "The Artist in a Coca-Cola World," The Village *Voice*, January 31, 1963.

Kaprow, Allan. "Segal's Vital Mummies," *Art News*, LXII, No. 10 (February 1964), p. 30. Kaprow discusses the relation between figures and objects in Segal's tableaux.

Kenedy, R. C. "George Segal at the Galerie Darthea Speyer," *Art and Artists*, IV, No. 3 (June 1969), pp. 20-21.

Kingsley, April. "The Great Body Snatcher," *Newsweek,* XCIV, No. 2 (July 9, 1979), pp. 66, 67. A perceptive review of the retrospective exhibition.

Kozloff, Max. "American Sculpture in Transition," *Arts Magazine*, XXXVIII, No. 9 (May-June 1964), pp. 19-25.

Kramer, Hilton. "Art: A Surrounding of 'Environments'," *New York Times*, August 27, 1966.

"Art: Segal Casts New Role for Color," *New York Times*, December 8, 1978. Kramer praises the use of color in Segal's 1978 show at the Janis Gallery.

"Plebeian Figures, Banal Anecdotes: The Tableaux of George Segal, *New York Times*, December 15, 1968.

"When George Segal Goes Public," *New York Times*, October 19, 1980. A virulent and unjustified critique of Segal's outdoor sculpture.

Kuspit, Donald B. "George Segal: On the Verge of Tragic Vision," *Art in America* LXV, No. 3 (May-June 1977), pp. 84-85. Interesting comments on Segal's use of color.

Marck, Jan van der. "George Segal: Love's Labors Cast," *Playboy*, XVIII, No. 12 (December 1971), pp. 195-200, 259-260.

"Spatial Dialectics in the Sculpture of George Segal," *artscanada*, XXXIX, No.2 (Spring 1972), pp. 35-38. A valuable discussion of the relationship between illusionistic and real space in Segal's sculpture.

Mazanec, Douglas. "Inside George Segal," Northern *Ohio Live*, I, No. 18 (June 1-14, 1981), pp. 28-30, 39. A sympathetic and perceptive discussion of Segal's public sculpture.

Mellow, James R. "Segal Sculptures on Display at Janis," *New York Times*, January 20, 1973. This review concentrates on the new fragmentary casts.

O'Doherty, Brian. "A New Union of Art and Life," *New York Times*, Sunday, March 22, 1964.

"Art: Avant-Garde Revolt," *New York Times*, October 31, 1962. Segal is mentioned in a review of the "New Realists" show at the Janis Gallery.

"Inside the White Cube; Part II: The Eye and the Spectator," *Artforum*, XIV, No. 8 (April 1976), pp. 31-33.

"Urogenital Plumbing," *Art and Artists*, I, No. 8 (November 1966), pp. 14-19.

Perreault, John. "George Segal: Plastered People," The Village *Voice*, October 24, 1974. Some valuable insights to Segal's political commitment.

"Plaster Caste," *Art News*, LXVII, No. 7 (November 1968), pp. 54-55, 75-76.

Pincus-Witten, Robert. "George Segal," *Artforum*, XIII, No. 5 (January 1975), pp. 58, 59. This perceptive review brings fresh insight and elegant expression to the investigation of Segal's "Jewish historical sculpture."

"George Segal as Realist," *Artforum*, V, No. 10 (Summer 1967), pp. 84-87. A thorough survey of criticism to date, original for its emphasis on the humanistic ethic in Segal's work.

Rand, Harry. "The Modes and Recent Art," *Arts*, LV, No. 4 (December 1980), pp. 76-92. A flawed attempt to adapt Segal's work to a structural model of art history.

Reid, Richard K. "Is Story of Abraham Too Violent for Kent State?," *New Jersey Monthly* (December 1978), p. 11.

Rose, Barbara. "Dada, Then and Now," *Art International*, VII, No. 1 (January 25, 1963), pp. 23-28.

"Psychological Sculpture," *Vogue*, CLXVI, No. 9 (September 1976), pp. 348 ff. Several valuable quotes from the artist.

"The Second Generation: Academy and Breakthrough," *Artforum*, IV, No. 1 (September 1965), p. 61.

Rosenberg, Harold. "The Art Galleries: Passage of Time," *The New Yorker*, January 18, 1964.

"The Art World: The Art of Bad Conscience," *The New Yorker*, December 6, 1967.

"The Game of Illusion," *The New Yorker* (November 24, 1962), pp. 161-167. Review of the 1962 "New Realists" show at the Sidney Janis Gallery.

Rubinfein, Leo. "On George Segal's Reliefs," *Artforum*, XV, No. 9 (May 1977), pp. 44, 45. Insightful discussion of the erotic reliefs, less perceptive analysis of the art-life dialectic in Segal's tableaux.

Rudikoff, Sonya. "New Realists in New York," *Art International*, VII, No. 1 (January 25, 1963), pp. 39-41.

Russell, John. "Art: George Segal Uses Past in a Jolt to Present," *New York Times*, October 5, 1974. In a review of the 1974 Janis show, Russell praises the bas-reliefs as a successful adaptation of nineteenth century art-historical tradition, and an important innovation in Segal's art.

"George Segal Takes World of Plaster to Whitney," *New York Times*, June 1, 1978. Review of the retrospective exhibition.

Sandler, Irving. "In the Art Galleries," New York *Post*, March 22, 1964. Review of 1964 Green Gallery show.

"In the Art Galleries," New York *Post*, November 18, 1962. Review of the "New Realist" show at the Janis Gallery.

Saslow, James M. "A Sculpture without a Community," *Christopher Street*, V, No. 4 (February 1981), pp. 23-32. The definitive article on the controversy surrounding *Gay Liberation*.

Schjeldahl, Peter. "Utterly Lifelike, Yes, But Is It Anything More?," *New York Times*, December 23, 1973. Segal's sculpture is compared favorably to John De Andrea's "inert" figures.

S(chuyler), J(ames). "George Segal," *Art News*, LVII, No. 10 (February 1959), p. 16. Review of the Hansa show with Segal's first sculpture.

Schwartz, Ellen, "George Segal," *Art News*, LXXVIII, No. 2 (February 1979), p. 168. Review of the 1979 Janis Gallery show.

Silverthorne, Jeanne. "George Segal," *Artforum*, XIX, No. 4 (December 1980), pp. 78, 79. This unperceptive and rather flippant review of *The Hustle: Four Hand Pass* criticizes Segal as a purveyor of "art bathos."

Solomon, Alan. "The New American Art," *Art International*, VIII, No. 2 (March 20, 1964), pp. 50-55.

Sottsass, Ettore, Jr. "Dada, New Dada, New Realists," *Domus*, CCCLXXXIX (February 1963), pp. 27-32.

Stevens, Mark, with Cathleen McGuigan, "Kent State Memorial," *Newsweek*, XCII, No. 11 (September 11, 1978), p. 99. Interviews with Kent State officials and details of the dispute over *Abraham and Isaac*.

Tillim, Sidney. *"George Segal,"* *Arts*, XXXV, No. 3 (December 1960), p. 54. Review of the 1960 Green Gallery show.

Tsiaras. ''George Segal,'' *Arts*, Summer Issue, 1982.

Tuchman, Phyllis. ''George Segal,'' *Art International*, XII, No. 7 (September 20, 1968), pp. 51-53. This valuable article combines lucid summary of critical perspectives with original observations about Segal's pictorial composition and relation to contemporary philosophical trends.

T(yler), P(arker). ''George Segal,'' *Arts*, XLIII, No. 2 (November 1968), p. 57. Review of the 1969 exhibition at the Janis Gallery.

''George Segal,'' *Art News*, LVI, No. 3 (May 1957), p. 12. Review of the second show at the Hansa Gallery.

Zeifer, Ellen, ''George Segal: Sculptural Environments,'' *American Artist*, XXXIX (January 1975), pp. 74-79.

CHRONOLOGY

1924
Born, New York City, November 26.

1930-40
Attends P.S. 70 in the Bronx and Stuyvesant High School in Manhattan.

1940
Moves with family to South Brunswick, New Jersey; family begins chicken farming.

1941-42
Studies in the foundation art course at Cooper Union School of Art and Architecture, N.Y.C.

1942
Returns to work on farm when older brother drafted.

1942-46
Studies part time at Rutgers University, North Brunswick, New Jersey, attending courses in psychology, literature, history, and philosophy.

1946
Marries Helen Steinberg, April 7.

1947-48
Studies at Pratt Institute of Design, Brooklyn, New York.

1948-49
Studies at New York University; graduates with B.S. in Art Education; teachers include William Baziotes and Tony Smith; frequents the Eighth Street Club.

1949-58
Operates a chicken farm on Davidson's Mill Road in Middlesex County, New Jersey, across the road from his parents' farm.

1950
His son, Jeff, born.

1953
Befriends Allan Kaprow; daughter Rena born.

1956-59
Spends several weeks each summer at artists' community in Provincetown, Massachusetts; meets Hans Hofmann.

1956
First one-man show, at the Hansa Gallery, New York City.

1957
Second one-man show at the Hansa; also participates in a group show, "The New York School, Second Generation," at the Jewish Museum; Kaprow stages his first Happening at the farm.

1957-58
Teaches English at Jamesburg High School to avoid bankruptcy.

1958
Stops chicken farming; begins to experiment in sculpture; one-man show at Hansa.

1958-61
Teaches industrial arts at Piscataway High School.

1959
One-man show at Hansa in February includes first plaster figures; serves as acting director during closing of Hansa; moves to Reuben Gallery, New York City; participates in group show at Reuben and in Whitney Museum's Annual Exhibition of Contemporary Art.

1960
Participates in group show at Reuben; moves to Richard Bellamy's Green Gallery, New York City; one-man show at Green includes first plaster figures with environments; Robert Frank films *The Sin of Jesus* at the farm.

1961-63
Enrolled in MFA program at Rutgers University; earns degree with a thesis on his own work and exhibition of his sculptures at Douglass College.

1961-64
Teaches art at Roosevelt Junior High School.

1962
One-man show at Green Gallery includes first life casts; participates in "New Realists" show at Sidney Janis Gallery, New York City, and Pace Gallery, Boston.

1963
One-man shows at Green Gallery, in Paris, and in Dusseldorf.

1964
Last one-man show at Green Gallery; begins to devote himself entirely to art.

1965-82
Begins to exhibit regularly with Sidney Janis Gallery, New York City.

1966
Executes first bas-relief.

1968-69
Lecturer in sculpture, Creative Arts Department, Princeton University, Princeton, New Jersey.

1969
Executes first fragments.

1970
Receives honorary doctorate from Rutgers University.

1976
Sent by State Department on a cultural exchange program to Soviet Union; executes first public sculpture, *The Restaurant*, in Buffalo, New York.

1978
Shown in major retrospective exhibition: Walker Art Center, Minneapolis, Minnesota, San Francisco Museum of Modern Art, and Whitney Museum of American Art.

1979
Begins two important public commissions: *In Memory of May 4, 1970, Kent State: Abraham and Isaac*, later rejected by Kent State University after much public controversy; and *Next Departure* for The Port Authority of New Jersey and New York.

1980

One-man show at Sidney Janis Gallery.

The Steelmakers commissioned by the Youngstown Area Arts Council and installed in urban renewal district of Youngstown, Ohio.

Kent State Memorial, commissioned by the Mildred Andrews Fund, is accepted by Princeton University and installed on the campus.

1982

One-man show at the Sidney Janis Gallery.

Large retrospective exhibition at the Seibu Museum of Modern Art, Tokyo, Japan.

The Commuters installed at the Port Authority bus terminal, New York.

1983

The *Holocaust* commissioned and installed in San Francisco under the auspices of the Committee for a Memorial to the Six Million Victims of the Holocaust.

Gay Liberation monument, commissioned by the Mildred Andrews Fund, is installed in Sheridan Square, Manhattan, after lengthy public dispute.

Retrospective exhibition at The Israel Museum, Jerusalem, Israel.

Continues to live and work in South Brunswick, New Jersey.

LIST OF EXHIBITIONS

Exhibitions held in New York unless indicated otherwise.

1956
One-Man: Hansa Gallery.

1957
One-Man: Hansa Gallery
Group: "The New York School, Second Generation," Jewish Museum.

1958
One-Man: Hansa Gallery.

1959
One-Man: Hansa Gallery.
Group: "Below Zero," Reuben Gallery; 1959 Annual Exhibition of Contemporary Art, Whitney Museum of American Art.

1960
One-Man: Green Gallery.
Group: Reuben Gallery; "Figurative Painting in the United States," American Federation of Arts traveling exhibition (1960-61.)

1961
Group: "Work by New Jersey Artists," Newark Museum.

1962
One-Man: Green Gallery.
Group: "New Realists," Sidney Janis Gallery; Pace Gallery, Boston.

1963
One-Man: Douglass College Art Gallery, New Brunswick, N. J.; Green Gallery; Galerie Ileana Sonnabend, Paris; Galerie Schmela, Dusseldorf.
Group: Sixty-sixth Annual American Exhibition, Art Institute of Chicago; "New Work, Part I," "New Work, Part II," and "Morris, Segal and Others," Green Gallery; "Ten American Sculptors," VII São Paulo Bienal, Brazil.

1964
One-Man: Green Gallery.
Group: "Ten American Sculptors," Walker Art Center (Minneapolis), San Francisco Museum of Art, City Art Museum of St. Louis, The Dayton Art Institute; "Ten from São Paulo," Howard Wise Gallery; "New Work, Part III," Green Gallery; "Amerikansk Pop Konst," Moderna Museet, Stockholm; "American Pop Art," Stedelijk Museum, Amsterdam; "Nieuwe Realisten," Gemeentemuseum, The Hague; "Pop, etc., etc.," Museum des 20. Jahrhunderts, Vienna; "Neue Realisten," Akademie der Bildenden Kunste, Berlin; "The Atmosphere of '64," Institute of Contemporary Art, University of Pennsylvania, Philadelphia; "4 Environments by 4 New Realists" and "3 Generations," Sidney Janis Gallery; "The Artist's Reality," New School Art Center; The 1964 Pittsburgh International Exhibition of Contemporary Painting and Sculpture, Carnegie Institute; "Recent American Sculpture," Jewish Museum; 1964 Annual Exhibition of Contemporary Art, Whitney Museum of American Art.

1965
One-Man: Sidney Janis Gallery.
Group: "In Focus: A Look at Realism in Art," The Memorial Art Gallery, University of Rochester; "The New American Realism," Worcester Art Museum; "Pop Art and the American Tradition," Milwaukee Art Center; "Nouveau Realisme et Pop Art," Palais des Beaux-Arts, Brussels; "Recent Work by Arman, Dine, Fahlstrom, Marisol, Oldenburg, Segal" and "Pop and Op," Sidney Janis Gallery; Corcoran Biennial, Washington, D.C.; "Etats-Unis: Sculpture du XXe Siècle," Musée Rodin, Paris; "Art of the '50s and '60s," The Aldrich, Museum of Contemporary Art, Ridgefield, Conn.; "Portraits from the American Art World," New School Art Center; "Eleven from the Reuben Gallery," The Solomon R. Guggenheim Museum; "New Jersey and the Artist," New Jersey State Museum, Trenton; "Selected Work by Contemporary New Jersey Artists," Newark Museum; "Sculpture 20th Century," Dallas Museum of Fine Arts; "Ten from Rutgers Univesity," Bianchini Gallery.

1966
Group: Sixty-eighth Annual American Exhibition, Art Institute of Chicago; "Erotic Art '66," Sidney Janis Gallery; "Eight sculptors: The Ambiguous Image," Walker Art Center, Minneapolis; "Art of the United States 1670-1966," Whitney Museum of American Art; "Environmental Paintings and Constructions," Jewish Museum; "The Found Object: Can It Be Art?" Institute of Contemporary Art, Boston; 1966 Annual Exhibition of Contemporary Art, Whitney Museum of American Art.

1967
One-Man: Sidney Janis Gallery.
Group: "Dine-Oldenburgh-Segal," Art Gallery of Ontario, Toronto, and Albright-Knox Art Gallery, Buffalo; "American Sculpture of the Sixties," Los Angeles County Museum and Philadelphia Museum of Art; "7 for '67," City Art Museum of St. Louis; "Focus on Light," New Jersey State Museum, Trenton; "Environment U.S.A.: 1957-67," IX São Paulo Bienal, Brazil; The 1967 Pittsburgh International Exhibition of Contemporary Painting and Sculpture, Carnegie Institute; "Protest and Hope: An Exhibition on Civil Rights and Vietnam," New School Art Center; "Homage to Marilyn Monroe," Sidney Janis Gallery; Guggenheim International, The Solomon R. Guggenheim Museum; "Original Pop Art," Stadtische Kunstausstellung, Gelsenkirchen.

1968
One-Man: Museum of Contemporary Art, Chicago; The Art Museum, Princeton University; Sidney Janis Gallery.
Group: "The Sidney and Harriet Janis Collection," The Museum of Modern Art; "Environment U.S.A.: 1957-67," Rose Art Museum, Brandeis University, Waltham, Mass.; 4. Dokumenta, Kassel; "In Honor of Dr. Martin Luther King, Jr.," The Museum of Modern Art; 1968 Annual Exhibition of Contemporary Art, Whitney Museum of American Art; "Menschenbilder," Kunsthalle, Darmstadt; "3," Galerie Rudolf Zwirner, Cologne; "Art from New Jersey," New Jersey State Museum, Trenton; "3 Environmental Happenings," Newark Museum.

1969
One-Man: Galerie Darthea Speyer, Paris.
Group: "The Obsessive Image," Institute of Contemporary Arts, London; "7 Artists," Sidney Janis Gallery; "Ars '69," The Art Gallery of Atenaeum, Helsinki; "Neue Figuration USA," Museum des 20. Jahrhunderts, Vienna; "American Sculpture of the Sixties," The Grand Rapids Art Museum; "Pop Art," Hayward Gallery London, "New York 13," Vancouver Art Gallery, Norman MacKenzie Art Gal-

lery (Regina), Musée d'Art Contemporain (Montreal); "New York Painting and Sculpture: 1940-1970," Metropolitan Museum of Art.

1970
One-Man: Sidney Janis Gallery.
Group: "String and Rope," Sidney Janis Gallery; "Art from New Jersey," New Jersey State Museum, Trenton; "Expo 70," Expo Museum of Fine Arts, Osaka; "American Artists of the Nineteen Sixties," Boston University School of Fine and Applied Arts Centennial Exhibition; "Figures Environments," Walker Art Center, Minneapolis; The 1970 Pittsburgh International Exhibition of Contemporary Painting and Sculpture, Carnegie Institute; "7 Artists," Sidney Janis Gallery; 1970 Annual Exhibition of Contemporary Art, Whitney Museum of American Art.

1971
One-Man: Sidney Janis Gallery; Galerie Darthea Speyer, Paris; Onnasch Galerie, Cologne; Kunsthaus, Zurich; Hessisches Landesmuseum in Darmstadt.
Group: IVe Exposition Internationale de Sculpture Contemporaine, Musée Rodin, Paris; "La Metamorphose de l'Objet. Art et Anti-Art 1910-1970," Palais des Beaux-Arts (Brussels), Museum Boymans van Beuningen (Rotterdam), Nationalgalerie (Berlin), Palazzo Reale (Milan); Third Triennial New Jersey Artists, Newark Museum; "White on White," Museum of Contemporary Art, Chicago.

1972
One-Man: Museum Boymans van Beuningen, Rotterdam; Stadtisches Museum, Leverkusen; Centre National d'Art Contemporain, Paris; Tubingen Museum; Stadtische Galerie, Munich; Palais des Beaux-Arts, Brussels.
Group: "La Metamorphose de l'Objet. Art et Anti-Art 1910-1970," Kunsthalle (Basel); Musée des Arts Decoratifs (Paris); "Recent Painting and Sculpture," Munson-Williams-Proctor Institute, Utica, N.Y.; "Abstract Expressionism and Pop Art," Sidney Janis Gallery; "Green Gallery Revisited," Emily Lowe Gallery, Hofstra University, N. Y.; "Recent Figure Sculpture," Fogg Art Museum, Harvard University, Cambridge, Mass.

1973
One-Man: Sidney Janis Gallery; University of Wisconsin, Milwaukee, traveling to the Indianapolis Museum of Art.
Group: "Kurt Schwitters and Related Developments," La Jolla Museum of Contemporary Art; "The Emerging Real," Storm King Art Center, Mountainville, N.Y.; "Art in Space," Detroit Institute of Art; "Contemporary American Artists," Cleveland Museum of Art; "Works from 15 New York Galleries," New York Cultural Center.

1974
One-Man: Sidney Janis Gallery; Onnasch Galerie, Basel Art Fair.
Group: Merriewold West, Inc., Far Hills, N.J.; "71st American Exhibition," Art Institute of Chicago.

1975
One-Man: André Emmerich Gallery, Zurich; Hopkins Center Art Galleries, Dartmouth College, Hanover, N.H.
Group: "Realism and Reality," Kunsthalle Darmstadt, Germany; "The Nude in American Art," New York Cultural Center; "Sculpture: American Directions 1974-75," National Collection of Fine Arts, Washington, D.C.

1976
One-Man: Institute of Contemporary Art, Philadelphia, traveling to the Baltimore Museum; Nina Freudenheim Gallery, Buffalo; The Art Association of Newport; Suzette Schochet Gallery, Newport; Santa Barbara Museum of Art.
Group: "25 Stills," Whitney Museum of American Art, Downtown Branch; "72nd American Exhibition," Art Institute of Chicago; "Artist's Sketchbooks," Philadelphia College of Art; "Private Images: Photographs by Sculptors," Los Angeles County Museum.

1977
One-Man: Sidney Janis Gallery; Greenwich Arts Council, Greenwich, Conn.; "George Segal's Pastels, 1957-65," The Art Galleries, California State University at Long Beach, traveling to the Fine Arts Gallery of San Diego; Modern Art Pavilion, Seattle Art Museum; The Boise Gallery of Art, Boise, Idaho; William Rockhill Nelson Gallery and Atkins Museum of Fine Arts, Kansas City, Missouri; Walker Art Center, Minneapolis.
Group: "Nothing but Nudes," Whitney Museum of American Art, Downtown Branch; "Still-Life Exhibition," Joslyn Art Museum, Omaha. "Contemporary Figuration," New Gallery of Contemporary Art, Cleveland; Ohio State University, Columbus; "Dokumenta," Kassel, Germany; "Cooper Union Alumni Exhibition," The Cooper Union; "New York, the State of Art," New York State Museum, Albany; "Drawings for Outdoor Sculpture 1946-47," John Weber Gallery, traveling to Amherst College, Amherst, Mass.; University of California at Santa Barbara; Laguna Gloria Art Museum, Austin, Texas; Massachusetts Institute of Technology, Cambridge, Mass.

1978
One-Man: Sidney Janis Gallery; Trisolini Gallery, Ohio University College of Fine Arts; Walker Art Center, Minneapolis, traveling to the San Francisco Museum of Modern Art.
Group: "Art About Art," Whitney Museum of American Art.

1979
One-Man: Whitney Museum of American Art; Hope Makler Gallery, Philadelphia, Pa.; Serge DeBloe, Brussels, Belgium.
Group: "Christo, Di Suvero, Irwin, Segal," Neuberger Museum, Purchase, New York; "American Portraits of the 60's and 70's," Aspen Center for the Visual Arts, Colorado.

1980
One-Man: Gloria Luria Gallery, Bal Harbour, Florida; Akron Art Institute, Akron, Ohio; New Brunswick Tercentennial Committee, New Brunswick, New Jersey; Gatodo Gallery, Tokyo, Japan; Fay Gold Gallery, Atlanta, Georgia; Sidney Janis Gallery.
Group: "Reflections of Realism," Museum of Albuquerque, N.M.; "Hidden Desires," Neuberger Museum, Purchase, New York; "Sculpture on the Wall: Relief Sculpture of the Seventies," University of Massachusetts, Amherst; "Pop Art: Evolution of a Generation," Palazzo Grassi, Venice, Italy; "Seven Decades of 20th Century Art from the Sidney Janis Collection," La Jolla Museum of Contemporary Art, Cal.; Santa Barbara Museum, Cal.; "Mysterious and Magical Realism," The Aldrich Museum of Contemporary Art, Conn.

1981
Group: 11th International Sculpture Conference, Washington, D.C.; "Inside Out: Self Beyond Likeness," Newport Harbor Art Museum, Cal.

1982
One-Man: Sidney Janis Gallery, New York; Seibu Museum of Art, Tokyo, Takanawa Museum, Karuizawa; Toyama Prefectural Museum of Modern Art, Toyama, The National Museum of Art, Osaka.
Group: ''Real, Really Real & Super Real,'' San Antonio Museum, Texas; ''Exhibition of Work by Newly Elected Members and Recipients of Honors and Awards,'' American Academy of Arts and Letters, New York; ''Contemporary Realism since 1960,'' Pennsylvania Academy of Fine Arts, Virginia Museum, Oakland Museum; ''Flat and Figurative: 20th Century Wall Sculpture,'' Zabriskie Gallery, New York.

1983
One-Man: Israel Museum, Jerusalem.

1984
One-Man: Sidney Janis Gallery.

PUBLIC COLLECTIONS:

The Museum of Modern Art, New York City
The Whitney Museum of American Art, New York City
National Collection of Fine Arts, Smithsonian Institution, Washington, DC
Moderna Museet, Stockholm
Albright-Knox Art Gallery, Buffalo, NY
Stedelijk Museum, Amsterdam
Museum of Modern Art, Teheran, Iran
The Solomon R. Guggenheim Museum, New York City
Philadelphia Museum of Art, PA
Musée National d'Art Moderne, Beaubourg, Paris
Birmingham Museum of Fine Art, AL
Cleveland Museum of Art, OH
Art Institute of Chicago, and Collection, Mr. & Mrs. Frank G. Logan, Chicago, IL
Art Gallery of Ontario, Toronto, Canada
Walker Art Center, Minneapolis, MN
The National Gallery of Canada, Ottawa
Mint Museum, NC
Newark Museum, NJ
Milwaukee Art Center, WI
San Francisco Museum of Art, CA
Museum Boymans van Beuningen, Rotterdam, The Netherlands
Von Der-Heydt Museum, Wuppertal, Turmhof, Germany
Wallraf-Richartz Museum, Cologne, Germany
Hessisches Landesmuseum, Darmstadt, Germany
Weatherspoon Gallery, University of North Carolina
Kaiser Wilhelm Museum, Krefeld, Germany
Vancouver Art Gallery, Canada
New Jersey State Museum, Trenton
City Art Museum of St. Louis, MI
Detroit Institute of Art, MI
Staatsgalerie Stuttgart, Germany
Kunsthaus Zurich, Switzerland
Akron Art Institute, OH
Wadsworth Atheneum, Hartford, CT
Indiana University Museum of Art, Bloomington, IN
Art Museum of Atenaeum, Helsinki, Finland
Joslyn Art Museum, Omaha, NB
Stadtische Galerie im Lenbachhaus, Munich, Germany
Des Moines Art Center, IA
The Pennsylvania Academy of the Fine Arts, Philadelphia

Tel Aviv Foundation for Literature & Art, Mann Auditorium, Israel
Carnegie Institute, Museum of Art, Pittsburgh
Neue Galerie der Stadt Aachen, Germany
Dartmouth College, Museum of Art, NH
San Francisco Museum of Modern Art, CA
Neuberger Museum, Purchase, NY
Metropolitan Museum of Art, New York City
The Museum of Modern Art, Seibu Takanawa, Karuizawa, Japan
Hirshhorn Museum & Sculpture Garden, Smithsonian Institution, Washington, DC
Centre National d'Art Contemporain, Paris
Hudson River Museum, Yonkers, NY
Tamayo Museum, Mexico City, Mexico
Huntington Art Gallery, University of Texas at Austin, TX
Westdeutsche Spielbanken, Munich, Germany
White Memorial Museum, San Antonio, TX
Israel Museum, Jerusalem
Columbus Museum of Art, OH
Portland Museum of Art, OR
Suermondt Museum, Aachen, Germany
Seattle Museum of Art, WA
John B. Putnam, Jr. Memorial Collection, Princeton, Princeton University, NJ
Staatsgalerie Moderner Kunst, Munich, Germany
Gatodo Gallery, Tokyo, Japan
Tokyo Central Museum, Japan
Shiga Museum of Art, Japan
The National Gallery of Art, Washington, DC
Cuyahoga County Justice Center, Cleveland, OH
Youngstown Area Arts Council, OH
Port Authority of New York and New Jersey
Seventh and Chestnut Associates, Philadelphia, PA
Virlane Foundation, New Orleans, LA
Des Moines Register & Tribune, IA
Bayerische Staatsgemaldesammlungen, Munich, Germany
Musée d'Arte Contemporain, Montreal, Canada
City of Greenwich, CT
PEPSICO Sculpture Garden, Purchase, NY
Museo de Arte Contemporáneo, Caracas, Venezuela
Fukuoka Municipal Museum of Art, Japan
Stadtische Kunsthalle Mannheim, Germany
Gewebesammlung der Stadt Krefeld, Germany

CATALOGUE

A chronological listing, by categories, of all works that appear in the text and illustrations section. Figure numbers indicate location in the book.

ENVIRONMENTAL SCULPTURE

1
Legend of Lot. 1958. (Fig. 21)
Oil on canvas, plaster, wood and chicken wire, 72 × 96 in.
Collection of the artist.

2
Woman in Red Jacket. 1958. (Fig. 127)
Plaster, 71 × 30 × 24 in.
Collection of the artist.

3
Man on a Bicycle I. 1958-1959. (Fig. 17)
Plaster, wood and chicken wire, 65 × 58 × 24 in.
Collection of the artist.

4
Woman on a Chair. 1961. (Fig. 128)
Plaster, modeled by hand.
Collection of the artist.

5
Man Sitting at a Table. 1961. (Fig. 26)
Plaster, wood and glass, 53 × 48 × 48 in.
Städtische Kunsthalle Mannheim, Germany.

6
Woman in a Restaurant Booth. 1961. (Fig. 30)
Plaster, wood, metal, vinyl and Formica (curtain and radiator are not part of the work), 51½ × 65 × 43¼ in.
Collection Wolfgang Hahn, Cologne.

7
Man on a Bicycle (Version III). 1962. (Fig. 22)
Plaster and bicycle parts, 63 × 29 × 61 in.
Moderna Museet, Stockholm.

8
The Bus Driver. 1962. (Fig. 31)
Plaster, wood and metal, 75 × 52 × 76 in.
The Museum of Modern Art, New York
(Philip C. Johnson Fund).

9
The Dinner Table. 1962. (Fig. 71)
Plaster, wood, metal and mirror, 72 × 120 × 120 in.
Schweber Electronics, Westbury, N.Y.

10
Lovers on a Bench. 1962. (Fig. 129)
Plaster, wood and metal, 48 × 60 × 36 in.
Collection Dr. and Mrs. Hubert Peeters, Bruges, Belgium.

11
Woman Painting Her Fingernails. 1962. (Fig. 130)
Plaster, wood, glass, mirror, cloth and nail polish, 55 × 35 × 25 in.
Collection Mrs. Fann Schniewind, Neviges, Germany.

12
The Bus Riders. 1962. (Fig. 131)
Plaster, metal and vinyl, 74 × 48 × 108 in.
Hirshhorn Museum and Sculpture Garden,
Smithsonian Institution, Washington, D.C.

13
Lovers on a Bed I. 1962. (Figs. 103 and 132)
Plaster, wood, metal, mattress and cloth, 48 × 54 × 70 in.
Collection Mrs. Robert B. Mayer, Chicago.

14
Woman Shaving Her Leg. 1963. (Fig. 35)
Plaster, metal, porcelain and Masonite, 63 × 65 × 30 in.
Collection Mrs. Robert B. Mayer, Chicago.

15
Cinema. 1963. (Fig. 37)
Plaster, metal, Plexiglas and fluorescent light, 118 × 96 × 39 in.
Albright-Knox Art Gallery, Buffalo (Gift of Seymour H. Knox).

16
Woman Leaning Against a Chimney. 1963. (Fig. 133)
Plaster and cinder block, 96 × 28 × 16 in.
Collection Mr. and Mrs. R. Matthys, Ghent.

17
Gottlieb's Wishing Well. 1963. (Fig. 134)
Plaster and pinball machine, 65 × 25 × 76 in.
Private collection, Brussels.

18
Woman Fastening Her Bra. 1963. (Fig. 135)
Plaster, wood and mirror, 72 × 18 × 30 in.
Collection Mr. and Mrs. Morton G. Neumann, Chicago.

19
The Artist's Studio. 1963. (Fig. 136)
Plaster, wood, metal, paint and mixed media, 96 × 72 × 108 in.
Harry N. Abrams Family Collection, New York.

20
The Farm Worker. 1963. (Figs. 80 and 137)
Plaster, wood, glass and imitation brick, 96 × 96 × 42 in.
Collection Reinhard Onnasch, Berlin.

21
Man Leaning on a Car Door. 1963. (Fig. 138)
Plaster, wood and metal, 96 × 48 × 30 in.
Staatsgalerie Stuttgart, Stuttgart.

22
Woman on a Bed. 1963. (Fig. 139)
Plaster, canvas and wood, 50½ × 77 × 56¼ in.
Seattle Museum of Art, Seattle, Wash.
Gift of Mr. and Mrs. Bagley Wright.

23
The Gas Station. 1963-1964. (Fig. 40)
Plaster, metal, glass, stone and rubber, 96 × 264 × 60 in.
The National Gallery of Canada, Ottawa.

24
Man in a Phone Booth. 1964. (Fig. 32)
Plaster, metal, glass and plastic, 86 × 30 × 30 in.
Collection Mrs. Robert B. Mayer, Chicago.

25
The Dry Cleaning Store. 1964. (Fig. 38)
Plaster, wood, metal, aluminum paint and neon tubing,
96 × 108 × 86 in.
Moderna Museet, Stockholm.

26
Rock and Roll Combo. 1964. (Fig. 39)
Plaster, wood, tiling and musical instruments, 84 × 84 × 69 in.
Hessisches Landesmuseum, Darmstadt, Germany
(Collection Karl Stroher).

27
Woman on a Church Pew. 1964. (Fig. 140)
Plaster, wood and paper, 42 × 60 × 24 in.
Collection Mr. and Mrs. Leonard J. Horwich, Chicago.

28
Woman in a Doorway I. 1964. (Fig. 141)
Plaster, wood, glass and aluminum paint, 113 × 63¼ × 18 in.
Whitney Museum of American Art, New York.

29
Richard Bellamy Seated. 1964. (Fig. 142)
Plaster and metal, 54 × 48 × 48 in.
Collection Mr. and Mrs. Adam Aronson, Saint Louis.

30
Girl on a Green Kitchen Chair. 1964. (Fig. 143)
Plaster and wood, 50 × 32 × 24 in.
Collection Frederick R. Weisman, Beverly Hills.

31
The Tar Roofer. 1964. (Fig. 145)
Plaster, wood, metal and tar paper, 84 × 96 × 79 in.
Gewebesammlung der Stadt Krefeld, Germany.

32
Woman in a Red Wicker Chair. 1964. (Fig. 144)
Plaster and wicker, 48 × 32 × 42 in.
Collection Vivian Tyson, New York.

33
Couple at the Stairs. 1964. (Fig. 146)
Plaster, wood and metal, 120 × 104 × 96 in.
Museum Boymans-van Beuningen, Rotterdam.

34
Woman in a Doorway II. 1965. (Fig. 147)
Plaster and wood, 96 × 72 × 96 in.
Stedelijk Museum, Amsterdam.

35
Woman Washing Her Foot in a Sink. 1965. (Fig. 148)
Plaster, wood, metal and porcelain, 60 × 48 × 36 in.
Wallraf-Richartz-Museum, Cologne (Ludwig Collection).

36
Woman Brushing Her Hair. 1965. (Fig. 149)
Plaster, wood and plastic, 40 × 24 × 46 in.
Walker Art Center Minneapolis, Minn. (Gift of Mrs. Julius Davis).

37
The Actress. 1965. (Fig. 150)
Plaster and wood, 72 × 36 × 48 in.
Hirshhorn Museum and Sculpture Garden,
Smithsonian Institution, Washington, D.C.

38
Robert and Ethel Scull. 1965. (Fig. 151)
Plaster, wood, canvas and cloth, 96 × 72 × 72 in.
Collection Mr. and Mrs. Robert C. Scull, New York.

39
Couple on a Bed. 1965. (Fig. 152)
Plaster and metal, 47 × 81 × 50 in.
Art Institute of Chicago (Mrs. Robert B. Mayer Collection).

40
Old Woman at a Window. 1965. (Fig. 153)
Plaster, wood, glass, chrome and board, 96 × 36 × 48 in.
Collection Mr. and Mrs. Melvin Hirsh, Beverly Hills.

41
Vera List. 1965. (Fig. 154)
Plaster and metal, 52 × 27 × 40 in.
The Albert A. List Family Collection, New York.

42
The Bus Station. 1965. (Fig. 155)
Plaster, wood and plastic, 96 × 48 × 24 in.
Collection Howard and Jean Lipman, New York.

43
The Butcher Shop. 1965. (Figs. 156 and 157)
Plaster, metal, wood, vinyl, Plexiglas and other objects,
94 × 99¼ × 48 in.
Art Gallery of Ontario, Toronto
(Gift from the Women's Committee Fund, 1966).

44
Woman Listening to Music I. 1965. (Fig. 158)
Plaster, wood and hi-fi set, 72 × 96 × 72 in.
Collection Spencer Samuels and Co., Ltd., New York.

45
Ruth in Her Kitchen (First Version). 1964-1966. (Fig. 36)
Plaster and wood, 50 × 72 × 60 in.
Von der Heydt Museum, Wuppertal, Germany.

46
Ruth in Her Kitchen (Final Version). 1964-1966. (Fig. 160)
Plaster and wood, 50 × 72 × 60 in.
Von der Heydt Museum, Wuppertal, Germany.

47
The Diner. 1964-1966. (Figs. 92 and 161)
Plaster, wood, metal, Formica, Masonite and fluorescent light,
102 × 108 × 87 in.
Walker Art Center, Minneapolis.

48
The Shower Curtain. 1966. (Fig. 162)
Plaster, 69 × 47 × 16 in.
Private collection.

49
Pregnant Woman. 1966. (Fig. 163)
Plaster, wood and canvas, 46 × 23½ × 32 in.
Collection *Playboy* Magazine, Chicago.

50
Walking Man. 1966. (Fig. 165)
Plaster, wood and painted metal, 85 × 58 × 34 in.
Collection Mrs. Norman B. Champ, Jr., Saint Louis.

51
The Billboard. 1966. (Figs. 108 and 166)
Plaster, wood, metal and rope, 189 × 117 × 20 in.
South Mall Project, Albany.

52
The Truck. 1966. (Fig. 167)
Plaster, wood, metal, glass, vinyl and film projector,
66 × 60 × 53 in.
Art Institute of Chicago (Mr. and Mrs. Frank G. Logan Fund).

53
Legend of Lot. 1966. (Fig. 168)
Plaster, 72 × 96 × 108 in.
Kaiser Wilhelm Museum, Krefeld, Germany (Lauffs Collection).

54
The Photobooth. 1966. (Fig. 170)
Plaster, wood, metal, glass, fluorescent and
incandescent light, 72 × 73 × 29 in.
Collection Martin Z. Margulies, Bay Harbour, Fla.

55
Sunbathers on a Rooftop. 1963-1967. (Fig. 159)
Plaster, wood, metal, glass and tar, 30 × 144 × 78 in.
Collection Dr. Giuseppe Panza di Biumo, Milan, Italy.

56
John Chamberlain Working. 1965-1967. (Fig. 185)
Plaster, metal, plastic and aluminum paint, 69 × 66 × 56 in.
The Museum of Modern Art, New York (Promised gift of Carroll
Janis and Conrad Janis).

57
The Moviehouse. 1966-1967. (Fig. 174)
Plaster, wood, plastic and incandescent lights,
102 × 148 × 153 in.
Musée National d'Art Moderne, Paris (on loan from Centre
National d'Art Contemporain, Paris).

58
The Laundromat II. (Original Version). 1966-1967. (Fig. 175)
Plaster, metal and plastic, 47 × 97 × 43 in.
Collection Reinhard Onnasch, Berlin.

59
The Motel Room. 1967. (Fig. 169)
Plaster and wood, 72 × 78 × 72 in.
Collection P. Janlet, Brussels.

60
The Movie Poster. 1967. (Fig. 171)
Plaster, wood and photograph, 74 × 28 × 36 in.
Collection Kimiko and John Powers, Aspen, Colorado.

61
Girl Washing Her Foot on a Chair. 1967. (Fig. 172)
Plaster and wood, 48 × 24 × 46 in.
Collection Mr. and Mrs. E. A. Bergman, Chicago.

62
Girl on Chair, Finger to Mouth. 1967. (Fig. 173)
Plaster and wood, 52 × 42 × 16 in.
Collection Mr. and Mrs. Morton G. Neumann, Chicago.

63
Seated Girl. 1967. (Fig. 177)
Plaster, wood and metal, 52 × 42 × 16 in.
Private collection.

64
Girl Putting on an Earring. 1967. (Fig. 178)
Plaster and wood, 50 × 40 × 40 in.
Collection Joan Avnet, New York.

65
Girl Undressing. 1967. (Fig. 179)
Plaster and wood, 63 × 34 × 22 in.
New Jersey State Museum, Trenton
(The Governor of New Jersey Purchase Award).

66
Girl Putting Up Her Hair. 1967. (Fig. 180)
Plaster and wood, 53 × 24 × 26 in.
Neue Galerie, Aachen (Ludwig Collection).

67
Circus Girl. 1967. (Fig. 181)
Plaster, wood and plastic, 51 × 32 × 35 in.
Collection Mrs. Miriam Keller, Stuttgart.

68
Sidney Janis with Mondrian's "Composition" of 1933, on an Easel. 1967. (Fig. 182)
Plaster, wood, metal and canvas, 67 × 50 × 33 in.
The Museum of Modern Art, New York.

69
Man Leaving a Bus. 1967. (Fig. 183)
Plaster, painted metal, glass, chrome and
rubber, 88½ × 39 × 33½ in.
Harry N. Abrams Family Collection, New York (Sidney and Harriet Janis Collection).

70
Restaurant Window I. 1967. (Figs. 94, 96, 97 and 184)
Plaster, wood, metal and plastic, 96 × 138 × 69 in.
Wallraf-Richartz-Museum, Cologne (Ludwig Collection).

71
The Execution. 1967. (Figs. 126 and 186)
Plaster, wood, metal and rope, 96 × 132 × 96 in.
Vancouver Art Gallery.

72
Man Leaning Against a Wall of Doors. 1968. (Fig. 187)
Plaster, wood and paper, 120 × 80 × 36 in.
The Hudson River Museum, Yonkers, New York
(Gift of Geigy Pharmaceuticals, Division of
Geigy Chemical Corporation).

73
Man Leaning Against a Wall of Doors. 1968. (Fig. 188)
(Back of doors, with billboards.)
Plaster, wood and paper, 120 × 80 × 36 in.
The Hudson River Museum, Yonkers, New York
(Gift of Geigy Pharmaceuticals, Division of
Geigy Chemical Corporation).

74
Girl Putting on Her Shoe. 1968. (Fig. 189)
Plaster, wood and plastic, 37 × 24 × 48 in.
Collection Mr. and Mrs. William S. Paley, New York.

75
Man in a Chair. 1968. (Fig. 190)
Plaster, aluminum, plastic and glass, 42 × 24 × 42 in.
Collection Thomas Benenson, New York.

76
The Shower Stall. 1968. (Fig. 191)
Plaster and metal, 78 × 34 × 43 in.
Private collection, Italy.

77
Self-Portrait with Head and Body. 1968. (Fig. 192)
Plaster and wood, 66 × 32 × 42 in.
Collection Carter Burden, New York.

78
Artist in His Studio. 1968. (Fig. 193)
Plaster, wood, paper and pastel, 96 × 120 × 108 in.
Collection Reinhard Onnasch, Berlin.

79
The Subway. 1968. (Fig. 194)
Plaster, metal, glass, rattan, incandescent light and electrical
parts, 90 × 115 × 53 in.
Collection Mrs. Robert B. Mayer, Chicago.

80
Girl Holding a Cat. 1968. (Fig. 195)
Plaster and wood, 48 × 17 × 32 in.
Collection Mrs. Helen Segal, New Brunswick, N.J.

81
Girl Sitting Against a Wall I. 1968. (Fig. 196)
Plaster, wood and glass, 84 × 96 × 37 in.
Staatsgalerie, Stuttgart.

82
The Parking Garage. 1968. (Fig. 197)
Plaster, wood, metal, electrical parts and light bulbs,
120 × 152 × 48 in.
Newark Museum, New Jersey.

83
Girl on a Chaise Lounge. 1968. (Fig. 198)
Plaster and metal, 36 × 24 × 72 in.
Collection Irma and Norman Braman, Miami, Florida.

84
Construction Tunnel. 1968. (Fig. 199)
Plaster, wood and metal, 168 × 60 × 93 in.
The Detroit Institute of Arts (Founders Society Purchase).

85
The Girl Friends. 1969. (Fig. 104)
Plaster, 41 × 72 × 42 in.
Sidney Janis Gallery, New York.

86
The Artist in His Loft. 1969. (Fig. 200)
Plaster, wood, metal, glass and porcelain, 90 × 69 × 60 in.
Collection Reinhard Onnasch, Berlin.

87
Girl Putting on Mascara. 1969. (Fig. 201)
Plaster, wood and plastic, 52 × 36 × 21 in.
Suermondt Museum, Aachen (Ludwig Collection).

88
Seated Girl, Hands Clasped. 1969. (Fig. 202)
Plaster and wood, 52 × 36 × 21 in.
Private collection, Paris.

89
The Girl on the Flying Trapeze. 1969. (Fig. 203)
Plaster, metal and rope, 96 × 60 × 24 in.
Collection Mrs. Robert B. Mayer, Chicago.

90
Man in a Chair (Helmut von Erffa). 1969. (Fig. 204)
Plaster and wood, 50 × 29 × 36 in.
Collection Dr. Giuseppe Panza di Biumo, Milan, Italy.

91
The Tightrope Walker. 1969. (Fig. 205)
Plaster, metal and rope, 78 × 204 × 60 in.
Museum of Art, Carnegie Institute, Pittsburgh.

92
Sleeping Girl. 1969. (Fig. 206)
Plaster and metal, 22 × 73 × 33 in.
Private collection, Cologne.

93
The Store Window. 1969. (Fig. 208)
Plaster, wood, plastic and aluminum, 96 × 104 × 36 in.
Milwaukee Art Center (Gift of Friends of Art, 1970).

94
The Laundromat II (Late Version). 1966-1970. (Fig. 176)
Plaster, metal and plastic, 72 × 72 × 30 in.
Collection Reinhard Onnasch, Berlin.

95
The Dentist. 1966-1970. (Fig. 216)
Plaster, metal, glass, plastic, aluminum paint, rubber and dental
cement, 81 × 53 × 53 in.
Sidney Janis Gallery, New York.

96
The Bowery. 1970. (Fig. 41)
Plaster, wood and metal, 96 × 96 × 72 in.
Kunsthaus, Zurich.

97
Times Square at Night. 1970. (Fig. 47)
Plaster, wood, plastic, incandescent and fluorescent light,
108 × 96 × 60 in.
Joslyn Art Museum, Omaha, Nebraska.

98
Man on a Scaffold (First Version). 1970. (Fig. 109)
(Whereabouts unknown).

99
Girl Looking into Mirror. 1970. (Fig. 207)
Plaster, wood and mirror, 72 × 28 × 27 in.
Collection Frederick R. Weisman, Beverly Hills.

100
Girl Sitting Against a Wall II. 1970. (Fig. 209)
Plaster, wood and glass, 91 × 60 × 40 in.
Collection Akron Art Institute, Akron, Ohio.

101
Man on a Scaffold. 1970. (Fig. 210)
Plaster, metal and wood, 144 × 96 × 60 in.
Whereabouts unknown.

102
Man on a Ladder. 1970. (Figs. 110 and 211)
Plaster, wood, metal, plastic and fluorescent light,
108 × 108 × 57 in.
Neue Galerie, Aachen (Ludwig Collection).

103
Lovers on a Bed II. 1970. (Fig. 212)
Plaster and metal, 48 × 72 × 60 in.
Collection Phillip Johnson, New York.

104
Girl Walking Out of the Ocean. 1970. (Fig. 213)
Plaster and wood, 84 × 60 × 28½ in.
Private collection, Brussels.

105
Alice Listening to Her Poetry and Music. 1970. (Fig. 214)
Plaster, wood, glass and tape recorder, 96 × 96 × 33 in.
Staatsgalerie Moderner Kunst, Munich.

106
The Brick Wall. 1970. (Fig. 215)
Plaster, wood and plastic, 96 × 152 × 42 in.
Gatodo Gallery, Tokyo, Japan.

107
The Aerial View. 1970. (Fig. 218)
Plaster, wood, plastic, incandescent and fluorescent light,
96 × 105 × 48 in.
The Art Museum of the Atenaeum, Helsinki (Collection Sara
Hilden).

108
To All Gates. 1971. (Fig. 48)
Plaster, wood, metal, plastic and fluorescent light,
96 × 144 × 96 in.
Des Moines Art Center (Coffin Fine Arts Trust Fund).

109
Restaurant Window III. 1971. (Fig. 95)
Plaster, wood, metal, plastic and incandescent light,
72 × 48 × 60 in.
Collection Attilio Codegnato, Venice, Italy.

110
Man on the Flying Trapeze. 1971. (Fig. 119)
Plaster, wood, metal and rope, 72 × 36 in.
Wadsworth Atheneum, Hartford.

111
The Dancers. 1971. (Fig. 121)
Bronze, 72 × 144 × 96 in.
1/5: Collection Seymour Schwebber, King's Point, New York.
2/5: National Gallery of Art, Washington, D.C.
3/5: Collection Mr. and Mrs. Perry R. Bass, Fort Worth, Texas.

112
Girl Washing Her Hair at a Sink. 1971. (Fig. 217)
Plaster, wood, metal and porcelain, 62 × 60 × 30 in.
Indiana University Art Museum, Bloomington (Gift of Mr. and Mrs.
Henry R. Hope and Dr. Richard D. Youngman and purchased
with the aid of funds from the National Endowment for the Arts).

113
The Bar. 1971. (Figs. 93 and 219)
Plaster, wood, metal, glass, plastic, neon light and television,
96 × 102 × 36 in.
Collection Martin Z. Margulies, Grove Isle, Florida.

114
Girl Leaning Against a Doorway. 1971. (Fig. 220)
Plaster, wood, plastic and incandescent light, 108 × 56 × 48 in.
Tokyo Central Museum, Japan.

115
Man Standing on a Printing Press. 1971. (Figs. 111 and 221)
Plaster, wood and metal, 96 × 96 × 24 in.
Des Moines Register and Tribune Company, Des Moines, Iowa.

116
Restaurant Table Still Life. 1971. (Fig. 227)
Plaster, wood, metal, 35 in. high × 36 in. diameter.
Courtesy Sidney Janis Gallery, New York.

117
The Costume Party (First Version). 1965-1972. (Fig. 79)
Acrylic on plaster, metal, wood and mixed media,
72 × 144 × 108 in.
Sidney Janis Gallery, New York.

118
The Costume Party (Final Version). 1965-1972. (Fig. 164)
Acrylic on plaster, metal, wood and mixed media,
72 × 144 × 108 in.
Sidney Janis Gallery, New York.

119
The Red Light. 1972. (Fig. 50)
Plaster and mixed media, 114 × 96 × 36 in.
Cleveland Museum of Art (Andrew R. and Martha Holden
Jennings Fund).

120
Girl on Swing. 1972. (Fig. 120)
Plaster, metal and rope, 42 × 18 × 68 in. (variable heights).
Galerie Onnasch, Cologne.

121
Man Installing Pepsi Sign. 1972. (Fig. 222)
Plaster, wood, plastic, metal and fluorescent light, 112 × 96 × 54 in.
Collection Reinhard Onnasch, Berlin.

122
Man in Green Doorway. 1972. (Fig. 223)
Plaster, wood and porcelain, 85 × 38 × 29 in.
Collection Gilbert B. Silverman, Southfield, Michigan.

123
Woman Listening to Music II. 1972. (Fig. 224)
Plaster, wood, hi-fi set and record, 72 × 96 × 72 in.
Courtesy Sidney Janis Gallery, New York.

124
Gertrude: Double Portrait. 1972. (Fig. 225)
Plaster, wood, plastic and super-8 film, 96 × 144 × 72 in.
Collection of the artist.

125
Girl with Arm on a Chair. 1972. (Fig. 226)
Plaster, 33 × 18 × 14 in.
Collection M. Riklis, New York.

126
Girl Looking Through Window. 1972. (Figs. 112 and 228)
Plaster and mixed media, 96 × 36 × 24 in.
Museum Boymans-van Beuningen, Rotterdam.

127
Picasso's Chair. 1973. (Fig. 70)
Plaster and mixed media, 78 × 60 in.
Guggenheim Museum, New York.

128
Abraham's Sacrifice of Isaac. 1973. (Fig. 102)
Plaster, 7 × 9 × 8½ in.
Donated by Tel Aviv Foundation for Literature and Art to the city
Tel Aviv-Yato.

129
Girl Drying Her Knee. 1973. (Fig. 229)
Plaster, aluminum and cloth, 59 × 24 × 44 in.
Collection Ercole Lauro, Naples.

130
Girl on Red Wicker Couch. 1973. (Fig. 230)
Plaster and mixed media, 35 × 80 × 58 in.
Hopkins Center Art Gallery, Dartmouth College, Hanover,
New Hampshire.

131
Girl on Bed III. 1973. (Figs. 231 and 232)
Plaster and metal, 50½ × 79½ × 35¾ in.
Courtesy Sidney Janis Gallery, New York.

132
Girl on Bed. 1973. (Fig. 240)
Plaster and metal, 50½ × 79½ × 35¾ in.
Collection Harry Torczyner, New York.

133
Corice in Shower. 1973. (Fig. 233)
Plaster, ceramic tile and wood, 67 × 22½ × 24 in.
Collection Arman, New York.

134
Waitress Pouring Coffee. 1973. (Fig. 234)
Plaster, wood, metal and porcelain, 96 × 42 × 34 in.
Shiga Museum of Art, Japan.

135
The Rock. 1974. (Fig. 99)
Plaster prototype, 114 × 120 × 36 in.
Courtesy Sidney Janis Gallery, New York.

136
Girl on Red Chair with Blue Robe. 1974. (Fig. 235)
Plaster, wood and acrylic, 96½ × 48 × 45 in
Collection Leonard and Gloria Luria, Miami, Florida.

137
Girl Next to Bathroom Column. 1974. (Fig. 236)
Plastic and ceramic tile, 64¼ × 29¼ × 16½ in.
Courtesy Sidney Janis Gallery, New York.

138
The Curtain. 1974. (Figs. 113 and 237)
Plaster and mixed media, 84 × 39 × 32 in.
National Collection Fine Arts, Smithsonian Institution,
Washington, D.C.

139
The Rock. 1974. (Fig. 238)
Plaster prototype, 114 × 120 × 36 in.
Courtesy Sidney Janis Gallery, New York.

140
Exit. 1975. (Fig. 239)
Plaster, wood, plastic and electric light, 84 × 72 × 36 in.
Philadelphia Museum of Art (Gift of the Friends of the
Philadelphia of Art Museum).

141
Girl Putting on Scarab Necklace. 1975. (Fig. 241)
Plaster, wood, metal and glass, 84 × 45 × 45 in.
Collection Mission of Iran.

142
The Corridor. 1975. (Fig. 242)
Plaster and wood, 84 × 84 × 48 in.
Tamayo Museum, Mexico City, Mexico.

143
Walk, Don't Walk. 1976. (Fig. 49)
Plaster, cement, metal, painted wood and electric light,
104 × 72 × 72 in.
Whitney Museum of American Art, New York.

144
The Restaurant. 1976. (Fig. 91)
Bronze, brick, cement, steel, aluminum, tempered glass,
and fluorescent light, 120 × 192 × 96 in.
Federal Office Building, Buffalo.

145
Girl Standing in Nature. 1976. (Fig. 98)
Bronze, 67 in. high.
Collection City of Greenwich, Conn.

146
Man on Wood Scaffold. 1976. (Fig. 243)
Plaster, wood and metal, 144 × 60 × 120 in.
Courtesy Sidney Janis Gallery, New York.

147
Claire Entering Doorway. 1976. (Fig. 244)
Plaster and painted wood, 92 × 38 × 33 in.
Private collection, Brussels.

148
Black Girl Behind Red Door. 1976. (Fig. 245)
Painted plaster and wood, 82 × 38 × 24 in.
Collection Madame Landau, Paris.

149
Post No Bills. 1976. (Fig. 246)
Work destroyed.

150
Couple on Black Bed. 1976. (Fig. 247)
Painted plaster and wood, 44 × 82 × 60 in.
Collection Sydney and Frances Lewis Foundation, Virginia.

151
Red Girl Behind Red Door. 1976. (Fig. 248)
Painted plaster and wood, 91 × 50 × 25 in.
Collection Irma and Norman Braman, Miami, Florida.

152
Blue Girl on Black Bench. 1977. (Fig. 249)
Plaster, wood and paint, 42 × 72 × 36 in.
Collection Martin Z. Margulies, Grove Isle, Florida.

153
Couple in Open Doorway. 1977. (Fig. 252)
Painted plaster, wood and metal, 96 × 69 × 52 in.
Courtesy Sidney Janis Gallery, New York.

154
Street Meeting. 1977. (Fig. 251)
Painted plaster and painted wood, 96 × 95 × 52 in.
Collection Bruce and Judith Eissner, Marblehead, Mass.

155
Blue Girl in Front of Black Doorway. 1977. (Fig. 254)
Painted plaster, painted wood and metal, 98 × 39 × 32 in.
Collection Leonard and Gloria Luria, Miami, Florida.

156
Blue Girl Behind Blue Door. 1977. (Fig. 255)
Painted plaster, painted wood and metal, 96 × 53 × 23 in.
Courtesy Sidney Janis Gallery, New York.

157
In Memory of May 4, 1970: Kent State - Abraham and Isaac.
1978. (Fig. 100)
Bronze, 84 × 120 × 50 in.
John B. Putnam, Jr. Memorial Collection, Princeton University.

158
In Memory of May 4, 1970: Kent State - Abraham and Isaac.
1978. (Fig. 101)
Plaster, rope and metal, 84 × 120 × 50 in.
Collection of the artist.

159
Flesh Nude Behind Brown Door. 1978. (Fig. 253)
Painted plaster, painted wood and metal, 96 × 60 × 40 in.
Courtesy Sidney Janis Gallery, New York.

160
Go-Go Dancer. 1978. (Fig. 250)
Plaster, wood, mirror, electric lights and vinyl, 108 × 59 × 48 in.
Collection Irma and Norman Braman, Miami, Florida.

161
Appalachian Farm Couple-1936. 1978. (Fig. 256)
Plaster, wood, metal and glass, 108 × 90 × 36 in.
Neuberger Museum, Purchase, New York.

162
Hot Dog Stand. 1978. (Fig. 260)
Painted plaster, painted wood, plastic, metal and electric lights,
108 × 72 × 84 in.
San Francisco Museum of Modern Art, San Francisco, Ca.

163
Man in Toll Booth. 1979. (Fig. 115)
Bronze: 108 × 43 × 43 in.; figure: 74 in. high.
Newark Museum, Newark, New Jersey.

164
Three People on Four Benches. 1979. (Figs. 116 and 257)
Plaster, wood and metal, 52 × 144 × 58 in.
Sidney Janis Gallery, New York.
A.P.: Pepsico Sculpture Gardens, Purchase, New York.
1/3: Cuyahoga County Justice Center, Cleveland, Ohio.
2/3: Martin Z. Margulies, Grove Isle, Fla.
3/3: Sidney Besthoff, New Orleans, La.

165
Gay Liberation. 1980. (Fig. 105)
Plaster and metal, 71 × 192 × 80 in.
The Museum of Modern Art, Seibu Takanawa, Karuizawa, Japan.

166
The Steelmakers. 1980. (Fig. 106)
Plaster, wood, plastic and metal, 120 × 120 × 60 in.
Courtesy Sidney Janis Gallery, New York.

167
The Steelmakers. 1980. (Fig. 107)
Bronze, painted plastic and steel, 216 × 240 × 180 in.
Commission Youngstown Area Arts Council, Youngstown, Ohio.

168
Girl in Kimono Looking Through Window. 1980. (Fig. 114)
Bronze, glass and plastic, 96 × 43 × 30 in.
Collection Mr. and Mrs. Norman Wolgin, Philadelpia, Pa.

169
Blue Girl on Park Bench. 1980. (Fig. 117)
Painted plaster and painted aluminum, 51 × 78 × 44 in.
Collection Melvin Golder, Melrose Park, Pa.

170
The Commuters. 1980. (Fig. 122)
White Bronze, 84 × 72 × 96 in.
Installation at Port Authority Bus Terminal, New York.

171
Man Looking Through Window. 1980. (Fig. 258)
Plaster, plastic, wood and glass, 96 × 37 × 28 in.
Courtesy Sidney Janis Gallery, New York.

172
Girl in White Wicker Chair. 1980. (Fig. 259)
Plaster and wicker chair, 40 × 40 × 69 in.
Collection Eli Broad, Los Angeles, Ca.

173
The Hustle: The Four-Hand Pass. 1980. (Fig. 261)
Plaster, wood, plastic, video-tape and sound/studio,
96 × 144 × 192 in.; figures 68 × 38 × 38 in.
Courtesy Sidney Janis Gallery, New York.

174
Woman on a Bench II. 1980. (Fig. 262)
Painted plaster and painted wood, 47 × 47 × 40 in.
Collection Dr. and Mrs. Paul Todd Makler, Philadelphia, Pa.

175
Woman in Front of Corrugated Wall. 1980. (Fig. 271)
Plastic, wood and painted plaster, 106 × 76 × 24 in.
Courtesy Sidney Janis Gallery, New York.

176
Cézanne Still Life No. 1. 1981. (Fig. 269)
Painted plaster, wood and metal, 27 × 30 × 14 in.
Courtesy Sidney Janis Gallery, New York.

177
Cézanne Still Life No. 2. 1981. (Fig. 74)
Painted plaster, wood and metal, 32 × 40 × 18½ in.
Courtesy Sidney Janis Gallery, New York.

178
Cézanne Still Life No. 3. 1981. (Fig. 75)
Painted plaster, wood and metal, 24 × 40 × 27½ in.
Courtesy Sidney Janis Gallery, New York.

179
Cézanne Still Life No. 4. 1981. (Fig. 76)
Painted plaster, wood and metal, 57 × 48 × 24 in.
Courtesy Sidney Janis Gallery, New York.

180
Cézanne Still Life No. 5. 1982. (Fig. 270)
Painted plaster, wood and metal, 37 × 36 × 29 in.
Collection Sydney and Frances Lewis Foundation, Richmond, Va.

181
The Circus Flyers. 1981. (Fig. 118)
Plaster, wire and rope, 72 × 144 × 20 in.
Collection James H. Binger, Minneapolis, Minn. for Butler Square.

182
Helen with Apples II. 1981. (Fig. 263)
Painted plaster, 96 × 48 × 42 in.
Portland Museum of Art, Portland, Oregon.

183
Earlier Version of **Helen with Apples.** 1981 (No longer extant).
(Fig. 264)
Painted plaster and wood, 96 × 48 × 42 in.

184
Woman Standing in Blue Doorway. 1981. (Fig. 265)
Painted plaster and wood, 82 × 55 × 33 in.
Courtesy Sidney Janis Gallery, New York.

185
Blue Woman in Black Chair. 1981. (Fig. 266)
Painted plaster and metal, 52 × 26 × 44 in.
Huntington Art Gallery, University of Texas at Austin, Texas.

186
Woman in White Wicker Chair. 1982. (Fig. 267)
Plaster and wood, 45 × 37 × 52 in.
Collection Shaindy and Bob Fenton, Ft. Worth, Texas.

187
Seated Woman with Dangling Shoe. 1982. (Figs. 90 and 268)
Plaster and wood, 49 × 17 × 37½ in.
Courtesy Sidney Janis Gallery, New York.

188
Japanese Couple Against Brick Wall. 1982. (Fig. 272)
Painted plaster and wood, 96 × 95 × 27½ in.
Courtesy Sidney Janis Gallery, New York.

189
Restaurant Diner: Still Life. 1983. (Fig. 77)
Painted plaster and wood, 16 × 33 × 17¼ in.
Courtesy Sidney Janis Gallery, New York.

190
The Holocaust. 1983. (Fig. 125)
Plaster and mixed media, 120 × 240 × 120 in.
Courtesy Sidney Janis Gallery, New York.

191
Machine of the Year. 1983. (Fig. 273)
(Time Magazine Cover)
Plaster, wood, plastic and mixed media, 96 × 144 × 96 in.
Collection Time-Life Inc., New York.

192
Nude in Doorway. 1983. (Fig. 274)
Plaster and wood, 37 × 22½ × 12 in.
Courtesy Sidney Janis Gallery, New York.

193
Woman in Coffee Shop. 1983. (Fig. 275)
Painted plaster, wood, metal and plastic, 86 × 62 × 52 in.
Collection Frederich Weisman, Los Angeles, Ca.

194
Saul Steinberg with Rubens Painting. 1983. (Fig. 276)
Plaster and wood, 92 × 36¾ × 26 in.
Courtesy Sidney Janis Gallery, New York.

195
Resting Dancer. 1983. (Fig. 277)
Plaster, wood and flourescent lights, 96 × 82½ × 48 in.
Courtesy Sidney Janis Gallery, New York.

196
Two Bathers. 1983. (Fig. 278)
Plaster and wood, 68½ × 36 × 22 in.
Courtesy Sidney Janis Gallery, New York.

197
Morandi's Still Life. 1983. (Fig. 279)
Plaster, wood and acrylic paint, 16 × 24 × 14 ¼ in.
Courtesy Sidney Janis Gallery, New York.

198
Paint Cans with Barn Wood. 1983. (Fig. 280)
Plaster, wood and acrylic paint, 12¾ × 24 × 11 in.
Courtesy Sidney Janis Gallery, New York.

199
Rush Hour. 1983. (Fig. 281)
Plaster, 96 × 96 × 192 in.
Courtesy Sidney Janis Gallery, New York.

200
Jacob and the Angels (Work in progress). 1984. (Fig. 282)
Plaster, wood, plastic and rock, 132 × 144 × 76 in.
Courtesy Sidney Janis Gallery, New York.

BAS-RELIEFS

201
Nude. 1958. (Fig. 16)
Plaster, 36 × 66 × 3 in.
Collection of the artist.

202
Man in a Bar (Box). 1969. (Fig. 45)
Plaster, wood, metal and cloth, 60 × 24 × 12 in.
Collection Mr. and Mrs. E. A. Bergman, Chicago.

203
Woman Looking Through Window (Box). 1969. (Fig. 46).
Plaster, wood and celotex, 60 × 24 × 12 in.
Collection Serge de Bloe, Brussels.

204
The Coffee Shop (Box). 1969. (Fig. 284)
Plaster, wood, metal, plastic and cloth, 60 × 24 × 12 in.
Collection I. Lechien, Brussels.

205
The Open Door (Box). 1969. (Fig. 285)
Plaster, wood and metal, 60 × 24 × 12 in.
Collection of the artist.

206
Woman on Chair (Box). 1969. (Fig. 286)
Plaster, wood and windowshade, 60 × 24 × 12 in.
Private collection.

207
Girl Buttoning her Raincoat. 1970. (Fig. 283)
Plaster, wood and plastic, 24 × 48 × 15 in.
Collection Kenneth Newberger, Highland Park, Ill.

208
The Embrace. 1971. (Fig. 287)
Plaster, 39 × 36 × 10½ in.
Collection Dalmau, New York.

209
Couple Embracing. 1972. (Fig. 288)
Plaster, 30 × 36 × 10½ in.
Collection Adam Aronson, St. Louis, Missouri.

210
Girl in the Shower. 1972. (Fig. 289)
Plaster, ceramic tile and chrome, 42 × 28 × 10 in.
Galerie Kriwin, Brussels.

211
Artist's Daughter. 1972. (Fig. 290)
Plaster, wood, 28 × 26 × 12 in.
Collection Helen Segal, New Jersey.

212
Girl with Folded Arms. 1972. (Fig. 292)
Plaster, 48 × 36 × 15 in.
Collection Mr. and Mrs. Burton Hoffman, Stamford, Conn.

213
The Clock. 1972. (Fig. 291)
Plaster, wood and electric clock, 33½ × 24½ × 17½ in.
Abrams Family Collection, New York.

214
The Bather. 1972. (Fig. 293)
Plaster, 36½ × 28 × 8 in.
Courtesy Sidney Janis Gallery, New York.

215
Girl on Blanket: Hand on Leg. 1973. (Fig. 52)
Plaster, 50 × 39 × 10 in.
Collection Mr. and Mrs. Robert Kardon, Philadelphia, Pa.

216
Girl on Blanket: Finger to Chin. 1973. (Fig. 53)
Plaster, 56 × 36 × 9 in.
Private collection.

217
Girl in Gray Corner. 1973. (Fig. 294)
Plaster, 48 × 48 × 15 in.
Collection Mr. and Mrs. Fred Greenberg, New Rochelle, NY.

218
Girl with Clasped Hands. 1973. (Fig. 295)
Plaster, 33 ¼ × 17¾ × 18 in.
Courtesy Sidney Janis Gallery, New York.

219
His Hand on Her Back. 1973. (Fig. 296)
Plaster, 42 × 29 × 12 in.
Collection Mission of Iran.

220
Standing Girl Looking Right. 1973. (Fig. 297)
Plaster, 42 × 28 × 13 in.
Galerie HM, Brussels.

221
Girl Against a Post. 1973. (Fig. 298)
Plaster, 60 × 21 × 20 in.
Pennsylvania Academy of the Fine Arts.

222
Still Life with Red Ball. 1973. (Fig. 299)
Plaster, 37 × 16³/₄ × 8½ in.
Courtesy Sidney Janis Gallery, New York.

223
Girl in Doorway. 1973. (Fig. 300)
Plaster, 56 × 29 × 10½ in.
Courtesy Sidney Janis Gallery, New York.

224
Girl in Robe I. 1974. (Fig. 301)
Plaster, 33 × 14½ × 8 in.
Courtesy Sidney Janis Gallery, New York.

225
Girl in Robe II. 1974. (Fig. 302)
Plaster, 29½ × 18 × 9½ in.
Collection Mr. and Mrs. Phil Gersh, Beverly Hills, Ca.

226
Girl in Robe III. 1974. (Fig. 303)
Plaster, 36¼ × 18 × 9 in.
Collection D. Makler Gallery, Philadelphia, Pa.

227
Girl in Robe IV. 1974. (Fig. 304)
Plaster, 32³/₄ × 18¼ × 8½ in.
Collection Westdeutsche Spielbanken, Munich.

228
Girl in Robe V. 1974. (Fig. 305)
Plaster, 34¼ × 18¼ × 12½ in.
Collection Westdeutsche Spielbanken, Munich.

229
Girl in Robe VI. 1974. (Fig. 306)
Plaster, 25³/₄ × 16 × 7 in.
Collection Jonathan Goodson, Los Angeles, Ca.

230
Girl Emerging from Tile Wall. 1974. (Fig. 307)
Plastic and ceramic tile, 39 × 16³/₈ × 10 in.
Collection Barry Boonshaft, Quakertown, Pa.

231
Nude Turning. 1974. (Fig. 308)
Plaster, 37³/₄ × 33¼ × 14 in.
Collection Mr. and Mrs. Albert A. List., New York.

232
Girl Entering Doorway. 1974. (Fig. 309)
Plaster, 33 × 23 × 14½ in.
Collection Montedison U.S.A., New York.

233
Girl Seated on Gray Chair. 1974. (Fig. 310)
Plaster, wood and plastic, 36 × 26¹/₈ × 20³/₄ in.
Courtesy Sidney Janis Gallery, New York.

234
The Blue Robe. 1974. (Fig. 311)
Plaster and cloth, 49 × 36³/₄ × 14½ in.
Courtesy Sidney Janis Gallery, New York.

235
Portrait of Suzy Eban. 1974. (Fig. 313)
Plaster, 36½ × 17¼ × 11½ in.
Collection Mr. and Mrs. Abba Eban.

236
Portrait of Tove-Lin Dalmau. 1974. (Fig. 314)
16 × 18 × 7½ in.
Collection Tove-Lin Dalmau.

237
Girl Leaving Shower. 1974. (Fig. 315)
Plaster and ceramic tile, 73½ × 25½ × 17½ in.
Collection William Paley, New York.

238
The Couple. 1974. (Fig. 316)
Plaster, 42 × 24 × 25 in.
Courtesy Sidney Janis Gallery, New York.

239
Seated Girl: Chin on Wrist. 1974. (Fig. 317)
Plaster, 36¹/₈ × 30¼ × 21¼ in.
Private collection, Tokyo, Japan.

240
Girl Pinning Up Her Hair (Version II). 1973-1975. (Fig. 320)
Plaster and ceramic, 39 × 36½ × 9³/₄ in.
Courtesy Sidney Janis Gallery, New York.

241
Red Girl in Blanket. 1975. (Fig. 69)
Painted plaster, 39 × 49 × 13 in.
Collection Baron H. H. von Thyssen-Bornemisza, Lugano.

242
Crouching Woman. 1975. (Fig. 312)
Plaster, 28 × 22½ × 16 in.
Collection Mrs. J. Bellet, Pompton Lakes, NJ.

243
Her Arm Crossing His. 1975. (Fig. 318)
Plaster, 40¼ × 18¼ × 12 in.
Witte Memorial Museum, San Antonio, Texas.

244
Her Hand on His Thigh. 1975. (Fig. 319)
Plaster, 39 × 17¼ × 15 in.
Collection Mr. Jay Bennett, New York.

245
Girl in Shower with Washcloth. 1975. (Fig. 321)
Plaster, wood and plastic, 36 × 27 × 13 in.
Courtesy Sidney Janis Gallery, New York.

246
Girl with Blue Door and Black Jamb. 1975. (Fig. 322)
Plaster and painted wood, 47 × 20 × 15 in.
Collection Lenore Gold, Atlanta, Georgia.

247
The Orange Door. 1975. (Fig. 323)
Plaster and wood, 46 × 28 × 22 in.
Collection Eileen Rosenau, Bryn Mawr, Pa.

248
The Gray Door. 1975. (Fig. 324)
Plaster and wood, 41 × 26 × 17 in.
Collection David W. Doupe, M.D., Erie, Pa.

249
Blue Girl Behind Black Door. 1975. (Fig. 325)
Painted plaster, painted wood and metal, 42 × 22 × 13 in.
Collection Harry Torczyner, New York.

250
Summer Place: Robin. 1975. (Fig. 326)
Plaster, wood and plastic, 36 × 27 × 13 in.
Collection Mr. and Mrs. Harold Ladas, New York.

251
Blue Girl Next to Green Door Frame. 1975. (Fig. 327)
Painted plaster and wood, 34 × 27 × 12 in.
Courtesy Sidney Janis Gallery, New York.

252
Girl Next to Chimney (Version I). 1975. (Fig. 328)
Plaster, wood and plastic, 32½ × 40 × 11½ in.
Courtesy Sidney Janis Gallery, New York.

253
Girl on Blanket, Arm Over Eyes. 1975. (Fig. 329)
Plaster, 60 × 48 × 18 in.
Courtesy Sidney Janis Gallery, New York.

254
Embracing Couple. 1975. (Fig. 330)
Plaster, 34 × 30¾ × 11½ in.
Martin Friedman, Walker Art Center, Minneapolis, Minn.

255
Seated Woman: Floor Piece. 1975. (Fig. 331)
Plaster, 25 × 23 × 29 in.
Courtesy Sidney Janis Gallery, New York.

256
Two Torsos. 1975. (Fig. 332)
Plaster, 41 × 30 × 9 in.
Collection Robert Weiss, Chicago, Ill.

257
Kissing Her Cheek. 1975. (Fig. 333)
Plaster, 28 × 24 × 11 in.
Birmingham Museum of Art, Birmingham, Ala.

258
Hands on Chair (Revised Version). 1975. (Fig. 334)
Plaster, 29 × 22 × 11½ in.
Courtesy Sidney Janis Gallery, New York.

259
Bus Stop. 1975. (Fig. 335)
Plaster and wood, 25 × 19 × 5 in.
Courtesy Sidney Janis Gallery, New York.

260
Lying Woman: Floor Piece. 1975. (Fig. 336)
Plaster, 14 × 38 × 27 in.
Courtesy Sidney Janis Gallery, New York.

261
Girl Touching Her Waist and Thigh. 1975. (Fig. 337)
Plaster, 31 × 16 × 9 in.
Courtesy Sidney Janis Gallery, New York.

262
Girl Seated Next to Birch Tree. 1975. (Fig. 338)
Plaster and wood, 43 × 33 × 23 in.
Collection Jesse Shanok and Toby Forur, New York.

263
Green Girl Next to Green Wall. 1975. (Fig. 339)
Painted plaster and wood, 26 × 18 × 8 in.
Courtesy Sidney Janis Gallery, New York.

264
Girl Behind Chair and Bedpost. 1975. (Fig. 341)
Painted plaster and wood, 35 × 28 × 16 in.
Courtesy Sidney Janis Gallery, New York.

265
Lovers' Hands. 1976. (Fig. 68)
Plaster, 23 × 12 × 8 in.
Courtesy Sidney Janis Gallery, New York.

266
Portrait of Henry. 1976. (Fig. 340)
Plaster, 18 × 40 × 11 in.
Israel Museum, Jerusalem
(Gift of Henry Geldzahler).

267
Portrait of Meyer Schapiro. 1977. (Fig. 78)
Painted plaster, 38 × 26 × 13 in.
Metropolitan Museum of Art (Gift of Paul Jenkins).

268
Brown Girl. 1977. (Fig. 342)
Painted plaster, 35 × 12 × 10½ In.
Courtesy Sidney Janis Gallery, New York.

269
Magenta Girl, Blue Door Frame. 1977. (Fig. 343)
Painted plaster and wood, 43½ × 22½ × 8 in.
Courtesy Sidney Janis Gallery, New York.

270
Flesh Nude in Blue Field I. 1977. (Fig. 344)
Painted plaster, 33½ × 67½ × 8 in.
Courtesy Sidney Janis Gallery, New York.

271
Flesh Nude in Blue Field II. 1977. (Fig. 345)
Painted plaster and wood, 37¾ × 16½ × 7½ in.
Courtesy Sidney Janis Gallery, New York.

272
Girl Sitting on Bed with Bedpost. 1977. (Fig. 346)
Painted plaster and painted wood, 32 × 29 × 20½ in.
Collection R. Looker, Carpentaria, California.

273
Magenta Girl on Green Door. 1977. (Fig. 347)
Painted plaster and painted wood, 72½ × 23 × 12 in.
Collection Dr. Milton D. Ratner Family Collection.

274
Red Girl Next to Blue Doorway. 1977. (Fig. 348)
Painted plaster, 42¾ × 23 × 8⅛ in.
Courtesy Sidney Janis Gallery, New York.

275
Blue Girl Against Barn Wall. 1977. (Fig. 349)
Plaster and painted wood, 50 × 30 × 15 in.
Collection Mr. and Mrs. Jack Friedland, Gladwine, Pa.

276
Two Girls Next to Tree. 1977. (Fig. 350)
Painted plaster and painted wood, 48 × 35 × 12 in.
Collection Howard Estrin, New Jersey.

277
Black Girl, Black Doorframe. 1978. (Fig. 351)
Painted plaster and painted wood, 35 × 18 × 12½ in.
Collection Mrs. R. D. Murray, Princeton, New Jersey.

278
Girl on Blanket, Full Figure. 1978. (Fig. 353)
Plaster, 76 × 42 × 12 in.
Columbus Museum of Art, Columbus, Ohio.

279
Pregnant Series: Seven Stages. 1978. (Fig. 354)
Plaster, No. 1, 2, 3: 28½ × 18 × 8; No. 4, 5, 6, 7: 28½ × 18 × 10 in.
Courtesy Sidney Janis Gallery, New York.

280
Girl Looking Out of Window. 1979. (Fig. 352)
Painted plaster and painted wood, 51 × 21 × 22 in.
Courtesy Sidney Janis Gallery, New York.

281
Blue Girl in Black Doorway. 1979. (Fig. 355)
Painted plaster and painted wood, 64 × 24 × 20 in.
Collection Dr. and Mrs. Harold Joseph, St. Louis, Missouri.

282
Girl for the Whitney Museum. 1979. (Fig. 356)
Fiberglass edition, 19½ × 9¼ × 7½ in.
Courtesy Sidney Janis Gallery, New York.

283
Three Bathers with Birch Tree. 1980. (Fig. 51)
Plaster and wood, 72 × 64 × 14 in.
Collection Michael Gregory, Wayne, New Jersey.

284
Blue Girl in Front of Blue Doorway. 1980. (Fig. 357)
Painted plaster and painted wood, 52 × 36 × 15 in
Courtesy Sidney Janis Gallery, New York.

285
Diana (Red Column). 1981. (Fig. 358)
Painted plaster and painted wood, 48 × 32 × 12 in.
Courtesy Sidney Janis Gallery, New York.

286
Suzanne. 1981. (Fig. 359)
Painted plaster and wood, 36 × 23 × 15 in.
Courtesy Sidney Janis Gallery, New York.

287
Penny. 1981. (Fig. 361)
Painted plaster and painted wood, 32 × 31½ × 12 in.
Courtesy Sidney Janis Gallery, New York.

288
Seated Woman on Red Chair. 1981. (Fig. 362)
Painted plaster, 36 × 36 × 20 in.
Courtesy Sidney Janis Gallery, New York.

289
Woman Eating Apple. 1981. (Fig. 363)
Painted plaster and wood, 38 × 38 × 8 in.
Courtesy Sidney Janis Gallery, New York.

290
Woman Straddling Orange Chair. 1982. (Fig. 360)
Painted plaster, 36 × 24 × 19½ in.
Courtesy Sidney Janis Gallery, New York.

291
Woman Looking into Mirror. 1982. (Fig. 364)
Painted plaster, wood, plastic and ceramic tile, 48 × 32 × 20 in.
Courtesy Sidney Janis Gallery, New York.

FRAGMENTS

292
Figure VIII. 1969. (Fig. 365)
Plaster, 37 × 20 × 10 in.
Collection Giovanni Agnelli, Torino, Italy.

293
Seated Torso with Arm Between Legs. 1970. (Fig. 366)
Plaster, 16 × 13¼ × 8½ in.
Courtesy Sidney Janis Gallery, New York.

294
Lovers I. 1970. (Fig. 367)
Plaster, 26 × 18 × 6½ in.
Courtesy Sidney Janis Editions.

295
Girl Resting. 1970. (Fig. 368)
Plaster, 15 × 15 × 11 in.; edition of 75.
Courtesy Sidney Janis Editions.

296
Lovers II. 1970. (Fig. 369)
Plaster, 36 × 24 × 24 in.
Collection Ms. Renee Lachonsky, Brussels.

297
Studio Wall. 1970. (Fig. 370)
Plaster.
Studio installation, photo credit Hans Namuth.

298
Nude Stretching (Right) Hands on Thighs (Center) Back III (Left). 1971. (Fig. 371)
Plaster.
Installation view of George Segal exhibition, Sidney Janis Gallery, April-May 1971.

299
Hand Fragment Number 4. 1974. (Fig. 372)
Painted plaster, 16 × 11 in.
Courtesy Sidney Janis Gallery, New York.

300
Breast and Wicker Chair. 1978. (Fig. 64)
Painted plaster, 22 × 10 × 8 in.
Courtesy Sidney Janis Gallery, New York.

301
Girl in Wicker Chair. 1978. (Fig. 65)
Painted plaster, 23 × 19 × 7 in.
Collection Dr. and Mrs. Earl Scott, Rydal, Pa.

302
Two Hands and Dress Buckle. 1978. (Fig. 373)
Painted plaster, 14 × 14 × 5 in.
Collection Mr. and Mrs. Alfonso Albarelli, Philadelphia.

303
Hand on Stomach. 1978. (Fig. 374)
Painted plaster, 16 × 10 × 4½ in.
Courtesy Sidney Janis Gallery, New York.

304
Right Hand Holding Left Wrist. 1978. (Fig. 375)
Painted plaster, 14 × 11 × 6 in.
Collection William J. Hokin, Chicago, Illinois.

305
Hands Entwined on Lap. 1978. (Fig. 376)
Painted plaster, 11 × 16 × 7 in.
Collection Mr. and Mrs. Thomas W. Strauss, New York.

306
Two Hands on Blue Lap. 1978. (Fig. 377)
Painted plaster, 11 × 12 × 4½ in.
Collection Mr. and Mrs. Steven Marcus, Milwaukee, Wis.

307
Two Hands Over Breast. 1978. (Fig. 378)
Painted plaster, 12 × 10 × 4½ in.
Courtesy Sidney Janis Gallery, New York.

308
Blue Girl in Blue Wicker Chair. 1979. (Fig. 380)
Painted plaster, 22 × 17 × 8 in.
Collection Jerome Stone, Chicago, Illinois.

309
Flesh Girl in Blue Wicker Chair. 1979. (Fig. 382)
Painted plaster, 33 × 18 × 15 in.
Courtesy Sidney Janis Gallery, New York.

310
Hand Fragment No. 9. 1980. (Fig. 66)
Painted plaster, 10¼ × 14 in.
Courtesy Sidney Janis Gallery, New York.

311
Girl on Wicker Chair. 1980. (Fig. 379)
Painted plaster, 39 × 24 × 16 in.
Courtesy Sidney Janis Gallery, New York.

312
Body Fragment No. 1. 1980. (Fig. 381)
Painted plaster, 22¼ × 14 in.
Collection Herbert Kohl, Milwaukee, Wis.

OIL ON CANVAS

313
Still Life on Green Table. c. 1955. (Fig. 4)
Oil on canvas, 48 × 48 in.
Collection unknown.

314
Nude in Kitchen. 1956. (Fig. 3)
Oil on canvas, 48 × 48 in.
Collection of the artist.

315
Provincetown Interior I. 1956. (Fig. 5)
Oil on canvas, 48 × 48 in.
Collection of the artist.

316
Provincetown Interior II. 1956. (Fig. 6)
Oil on canvas, 48 × 48 in.
Collection of the artist.

317
Man with Dead Chicken Around His Neck. 1957. (Fig. 7)
Oil on canvas, 68 × 30 in.
Collection of the artist.

318
Dead Chicken. 1957. (Fig. 8)
Oil on canvas, 30 × 24 in.
Collection of the artist.

319
Chicken Man. 1957. (Fig. 384)
Oil on canvas, 72 × 96 in.
Collection of the artist.

320
Lot's Wife. 1958. (Fig. 18)
Oil on canvas, 72 × 48 in.
Collection of the artist.

321
Lot and His Daughters. 1958. (Fig. 20)
Oil and charcoal on canvas, 72 × 96 in.
Collection of the artist.

322
Lot's Daughters. 1958-1959. (Fig. 19)
Oil on canvas, 72 × 96 in.
Collection of the artist.

323
Old Testament Moon. 1958-1959. (Fig. 383)
Oil on canvas, 48 × 96 in.
Collection of the artist.

324
Untitled. 1959. (Fig. 15)
Collage, 36 × 108 in.
Collection of the artist.

325
Red Courbet. 1959. (Fig. 23)
Oil on canvas, 72 × 96 in.
Collection of the artist.

326
Woman in Chair. 1959. (Fig. 385)
Oil on canvas, 48 × 72 in.
Collection of the artist.

327
Red Nude and Interior. 1960. (Fig. 24)
Oil on canvas, 72 × 96 in.
Collection of the artist.

328
Upside Down Man. 1960. (Fig. 25)
Oil on canvas, 72 × 96 in.
Collection of the artist.

329
Turkish Delight. 1960. (Fig. 386)
Oil on canvas, 72 × 96 in.
Collection of the artist.

330
Woman in Restaurant Booth. 1960. (Fig. 387)
Oil on canvas, 72 × 96 in.
Collection of the artist.

331
The Blow. 1960. (Fig. 388)
Oil on canvas, 72 × 96 in.
Collection of the artist.

332
Woman in Phone Booth. 1960-1961. (Fig. 389)
Oil on canvas, 72 × 96 in.
Private collection.

WORK ON PAPER

333
Untitled. 1963. (Fig. 54)
Pastel on construction paper, 18 × 12 in.
Courtesy Sidney Janis Gallery, New York.

334
Untitled. 1963. (Fig. 55)
Pastel on construction paper, 18 × 12 in.
Courtesy Sidney Janis Gallery, New York.

335
Untitled. 1964. (Fig. 56)
Pastel on construction paper, 18 × 12 in.
Courtesy Sidney Janis Gallery, New York.

336
Untitled. 1964. (Fig. 58)
Pastel on construction paper, 18 × 12 in.
Courtesy Sidney Janis Gallery, New York.

337
Untitled. 1964. (Fig. 59)
Pastel on construction paper, 18 × 12 in.
Courtesy Sidney Janis Gallery, New York.

338
Untitled. 1965. (Fig. 57)
Pastel on construction paper, 18 × 12 in.
Courtesy Sidney Janis Gallery, New York.

339
Untitled. 1968-1970. (Fig. 390)
Pastel, 19 × 25 in. each.
Courtesy Sidney Janis Gallery, New York.

340
Untitled Pastels. 1968-1970. (Fig. 391)
Pastel, 19 × 25 in. each.
Courtesy Sidney Janis Gallery, New York.

341
Untitled. 1972. (Fig. 393)
Pastel, 24½ × 18½ in.
Courtesy Sidney Janis Gallery, New York.

342
**Blue Jean Series: Three Figures in Red Shirts: Two Front,
One Back.** 1975. (Fig. 392)
4-color aquatint, 44⅞ × 85¹/₁₆ in. Ed. 35.
Published by 2RC, Rome, Italy, Courtesy Sidney Janis Gallery,
New York.

343
Girl in Robe No. 1-5. 1981. (Fig. 394)
Pastel on paper, 18 × 12 in.
No. 1: Collection Mr. and Mrs. Martin Bucksbaum, Des Moines, Iowa.
No. 2: Collection Bob Wagoner, San Antonio, Texas.
No. 3-5: Courtesy Sidney Janis Gallery, New York.

344
Helen. 1982. (Fig. 395)
Ink on paper, 18 × 12 in.
Collection Mr. and Mrs. Jay Wright, Piermont, New Hampshire.

PHOTOGRAPH CREDITS